GAUSE SCHOOL
1100 - 34th ST.
WASHOUGAL, WASHINGTON

Gateways

William K. Durr
Jean M. LePere
Rita M. Bean
Nicholas A. Glaser
Anne A. McCourt

Consultant:
Hugh Schoephoerster

HOUGHTON MIFFLIN COMPANY   BOSTON

Atlanta   Dallas   Geneva, Illinois   Hopewell, New Jersey   Palo Alto   Toronto

Acknowledgments

Grateful acknowledgment is given for the contributions of Paul McKee.

For each of the selections listed below, grateful acknowledgment is made for permission to adapt and/or reprint original or copyrighted material, as follows:

"... and now Miguel," from *... and Now Miguel*, by Joseph Krumgold. Copyright 1953 by Joseph Krumgold. Used by permission of Thomas Y. Crowell, and Julian Bach Literary Agency, Inc.

"The Angalao and the Three Friends," adapted from *Philippine Folktales*, by Gaudencio V. Aquino, Bonifacio N. Cristobal, and Delfin Fresnosa. Copyright 1969. Used by permission of Alemar-Phoenix Publishing House, Quezon City, Philippines.

"Apple Song," from *Pool in the Meadow*, by Frances Frost. Reprinted by permission of Houghton Mifflin Company.

"Are Your Arms a Hundred Years Old?" from *The Hundred Penny Box*, by Sharon Bell Mathis. Copyright © 1975 by Sharon Bell Mathis. All rights reserved. Used by permission of Viking Penguin Inc., and Curtis Brown, Ltd.

"The Arrival of Paddington," from *Paddington on Stage*, by Michael Bond and Alfred Bradley. Copyright © 1974 by Alfred Bradley and Michael Bond. Reprinted by permission of Houghton Mifflin Company, and Collins Publishers, London.

"Arthur Mitchell: Dancer," adapted text of *Arthur Mitchell*, by Tobi Tobias. Copyright © 1975 by Tobi Tobias. Used by permission of Thomas Y. Crowell.

"Carving in Stone," from *The Stone Menagerie*, by Shay Rieger. Copyright © 1970 by Shay Rieger. Published by Charles Scribner's Sons. Used by permission of the author.

"The Challenge," an adaptation of pages 75–102, text only, from *From Anna*, by Jean Little. Text copyright © 1972 by Jean Little. Used by permission of Harper & Row, Publishers, Inc.

"Cinder Ellie," from *Track Comes to Lonesome Point*, by James Ayars. Copyright © 1972 by James Ayars. Reprinted by permission of the publisher, E. P. Dutton.

"A Different Shape," from *Talk About a Family*, by Eloise Greenfield. Text copyright © 1978 by Eloise Greenfield. Reprinted by permission of J. B. Lippincott Company, and Curtis Brown, Ltd.

"Energy," adapted text of *Energy from the Sun*, by Melvin Berger. Copyright © 1976 by Melvin Berger. Used by permission of Thomas Y. Crowell.

"Eugenie Clark: Shark Lady," from *Shark Lady: True Adventures of Eugenie Clark*, by Ann McGovern. Copyright © 1978 by Ann McGovern. Reprinted by permission of Scholastic Book Services, a Division of Scholastic Magazines, Inc.

"The Fast Sooner Hound," from *The Fast Sooner Hound*, by Arna Bontemps and Jack Conroy. Copyright renewed 1942 by Arna Bontemps and Jack Conroy. Reprinted by permission of Houghton Mifflin Company.

"First Snow," from *First Snow*, by Helen Coutant. Copyright © 1974 by Helen Coutant. Adapted by permission of Alfred A. Knopf, Inc.

Credits

Contents

Gateways

MAGAZINE ONE

Contents

A Funny Feeling

by ANNE-CATHERINA VESTLY

Aurora Tege (tay'yah) lived with Mother, Father, and her little brother Socrates on the tenth floor of an apartment building in Tiriltoppen (tih-rihl-top'ehn), Norway. Mother was a lawyer. Father stayed at home, looking after the children and the apartment while he studied to get a degree from the university.

One of Aurora's friends was a girl named Nusse (noo'suh), who lived in the same building. One day, Nusse's mother came to ask Mr. Tege if he wanted her old vacuum cleaner. She had just gotten a new one and would give the old one to him if he would teach Nusse to play the piano. He accepted the offer.

Today was different from other days. It began when Father said, "Aurora, Nusse's coming for a piano lesson this morning. You remember that, don't you?"

"Yes, I do," said Aurora, "I remember it very well. Nusse has told me every time I've seen her."

"It was a strange way to get a vacuum cleaner," said Father. "But it will be fun if Nusse really wants to learn to play. She's a nice girl, and she may have some talent."

That was the first time that day that Aurora had a funny feeling inside. Father went on talking, and the feeling went away for a little while. "You'll have to help me pay for the vacuum too," he said. "Do you know how?"

"No," said Aurora. "I've four kroner that I got for my birthday."

"You don't have to spend your money," said Father. "You'll help me by taking care of Socrates while Nusse is having her lesson. Can you do that?"

"Yes," said Aurora.

"That's fine," said Father. "You and Socrates go into the bedroom and take your cars or something else to play with."

"Mmmm," said Aurora. She got Little Puff, her stuffed dog, and three cars from her own room. She took the doll, Lille-Rora (lih′luh roh′rah), out of Socrates's bed and sat her on the floor beside Little Puff. Father brought in the red and green and yellow bricks. Everything was ready for Socrates.

The doorbell rang. Socrates, Aurora, and Father went to open it.

It was Nusse. Not Nusse as she usually was, oh no. It was Nusse in her best dress and newly washed hair. She was so well dressed that Aurora stood and stared at her. Father looked at her, too, and said, "You're all dressed up today, Nusse."

"Yes, Mom said to wear my best dress the first time," said Nusse. "This isn't like a plain day when I just come here to play with Aurora."

"Yes, your first piano lesson should be special," said Father. "I think it was a very good idea of your mother's."

Nusse hardly looked at Aurora. She just went and sat down at the piano. Father nodded to Aurora and Socrates and said, "Run along and play in the bedroom."

He didn't say that Aurora was to look after Socrates to

help pay for the vacuum. He just told them to run along and play as though she were the same age as Socrates.

Aurora didn't say anything. She just led her brother out of the room.

At first Socrates was delighted to have Aurora to play with. He hugged Little Puff and then carried him over to Aurora.

"Oh, thank you *so* much," said Aurora, and Socrates was highly amused. Afterward, they played with the cars for a little while. Then he heard the sound of the piano and wanted to play it.

"Daddy says no," said Aurora. "He's teaching Nusse to play, you know."

Aurora lifted Socrates up and hugged him before she put him down again. "Now we'll build a house with your bricks."

Socrates knocked down everything she built. He became very enthusiastic about the game.

Aurora wandered around the room, looked out of the window, and went over to the door. She could hear Daddy and Nusse talking. Daddy's voice sounded happy. Once he burst out laughing. Then Nusse said something, some notes were played, and there was Daddy's voice again.

It seemed so strange. Nusse sat in there and had Daddy all to herself, and she, Aurora, had to be out here in another room. She had that funny feeling inside again. This time it was much stronger than the first time. It didn't exactly hurt like a pain but felt kind of heavy inside. Everything was awful.

Socrates went on playing with his bricks and talking to himself. Usually Aurora liked it when Socrates was busy with something and talking away. But right now she wanted him to be quiet so that she could hear what Daddy and Nusse were saying.

Then she heard Daddy's voice. "That's fine, Nusse," he said. "Teaching's easy when you're so quick to learn."

Surely the half hour must be over by now. She went up to the door and put her head around it.

"Have you finished?" she asked.

"Oh no," said Father. "We've only had five minutes."

"Oh," said Aurora.

"Is Socrates all right?" asked Father.

"Oh, yes," said Aurora.

"Be a good girl, then. Don't disturb us," said Father. "Shut the door, will you?"

"Yes," said Aurora. She went back to the bedroom and sat on the floor in front of the bricks. Socrates looked up and saw that she was with him again, so he felt that everything was all right. Aurora sat and thought — at first for a little while and then for a long while. Then she got up quickly and went to the door. But she didn't open it. She turned around and came back to Socrates.

Perhaps the half hour was up now. No, Daddy was still talking. There were some more notes and Nusse's voice saying, "Oh yes, I see, like that. But I can't make my little finger work right."

"You might as well practice moving it right from the start," said Father.

Surely a half hour had passed now. When Daddy was busy with something, he often forgot what time it was. She'd better go in and tell him. What would she say? "The half hour is up?" No, that would be silly, she wasn't really sure. She *could* say what Daddy often said to Mom, "I think you're forgetting the time." But when Aurora stood in the doorway and looked at Father and Nusse busy together, all she said was, "Are you sure the time isn't up, Daddy?"

"Quite sure," said Father. "There are more than fifteen minutes left. Be a good girl; don't interrupt anymore."

"All right," said Aurora. She went back into the bedroom. This time she lay under the bed, thinking. She had never known a half hour could be so long. What if there were a fire? She would have to go in and tell them. But perhaps even then Daddy would just say, "Don't disturb us. That's a good girl." Imagine Daddy having time to sit there and talk to Nusse and teach her to play the piano. Daddy was always so busy. He always had so much reading and so much housework to do. Aurora had never thought this could happen. What if she too . . . well she didn't have a vacuum cleaner to bring him, so it wouldn't be any use.

Socrates came chasing after her under the bed. He thought it was a new game. He whispered right in her ear. It tickled so much that Aurora crawled out the other side. Socrates followed her. They sat on the floor and looked at each other. Aurora began to talk to Socrates as if he were the same age she was. She told him quietly and seriously about everything she had been thinking of that day.

"I'll do it," said Aurora. "As soon as the piano lesson is over, I'll go out."

"Out," said Socrates, and smiled at her.

Then they sat for a long time and waited. At last Father opened the door and said, "Aurora and Socrates, we've finished now."

Nusse climbed down from the piano stool. "I can't stay, Aurora. I have to go upstairs and practice."

"Mmmm," said Aurora. That was a good thing, because Aurora didn't have time to play either.

When Nusse had gone, Father said, "Nusse seemed to find that lesson easy. I think I'll enjoy teaching her to play. Let's see, what was I going to do next? I think it was the dishes."

"Can I go out, Daddy?" asked Aurora.

"Of course you can," he said. "I'm going to the super-market myself today. I'll take Socrates, so you can play with your sled as long as you like."

Aurora put on her outdoor clothes.

"Have a good time, Aurora," Father said as she left.

"You, too," said Aurora. In her pocket was the four kroner she had been given for her birthday. Daddy hadn't noticed. He was whistling and singing. No doubt he was thinking what fun it was to teach Nusse.

Aurora went straight out of the building. She didn't stop to look up at the window to see Daddy. She usually did. Sometimes he waved to her with the tablecloth.

Aurora walked on, but Father stood at the window. "I wonder where she's going?" he said to himself. "She's in such a hurry that the sled can hardly keep up with her."

Aurora went a long way down the hill to where the stores were. She kept thinking about the piano. They had had it since she was born. She had gone and looked at it every day, and sometimes she had pretended to play a note or two, but it had always seemed to be Daddy's. It was Daddy who could play it, and he did so whenever he had time.

But now that Aurora had seen Nusse sitting there playing, she began to think about the piano in a different way.

Nusse's mother had brought Daddy a vacuum cleaner, and then Nusse had been allowed to play the piano.

What could Aurora bring that Daddy would be so pleased with that he would teach her to play? It should be something for the house. He had been pleased to get the vacuum because it would help him with the housework. Aurora looked in the store window. She saw refrigerators and different kinds of washing machines. Then she heard one woman say to another, "Oh, wouldn't it be great to have a dishwasher like that one! Just think, no more washing dishes!"

"Yes," said the other woman. "But I don't think washing dishes is the worst job."

"I do," said the first woman. "I think it's the very worst. I wonder what it costs — at least a few thousand kroner. . . ."

"Four kroner isn't enough," Aurora said to herself. She stood there for a little while imagining that she was bringing the big white dishwasher home. She would need help to get it out of the store. Then she could carry it on her sled. No, it would be too heavy for the sled. She would have to get the store to send it home in the delivery truck. The two men with the truck would come up in the elevator with her and help her as far as her door. Then she would say, "I can manage by myself now." And she would wait until they had gone. She would ring the bell and Daddy would come and open the door. Then she would say, "Daddy, here is something to help you get through the housework quicker. Now maybe you'll have time to —"

"Look out, little girl!" said a voice. "We've got to fix this window." Aurora looked up. Two workers with ladders and tools were going to repair the top part of the big window.

Oh, well — the dishwasher was too expensive, but maybe she could find something else for Daddy. She went in and walked around, looking at the shelves. She looked at the beautiful red cake pans, the big white and blue breadboxes, and the blue and yellow and red buckets.

There were some brushes for washing dishes hanging on the wall. Aurora remembered that Daddy said their brush at home was a sorry sight. He might like to have a new one.

"Have I enough money for a brush?" she asked a salesperson.

"Yes, you have," said the man. "I'll wrap it up for you."

Aurora put it on her sled and pretended that it was terribly heavy. She had to pull with all her might. No, it was too heavy for her to pull on her own. She pretended that two people from the store would have to pull it all the way home into the elevator and along the hall. Then they could go away. When she was quite sure that the make-believe people had gone, she rang the bell. Daddy opened the door.

"A dishwasher costs too much," said Aurora, "but I've brought a brush for dishes. You can have it. And I'd really like to learn the piano, but I guess it's no use because you're so busy with Nusse — and your studies. But you can have the brush anyway."

Father looked at Aurora. It was as if he was seeing her for the first time that day. He lifted her up and carried her indoors, brush and all.

"Take your coat off," he said. "What does Socrates like doing best?"

"He'd like to empty the sewing box," said Aurora.

"Just a minute. I'll take out the needles and the razor blade," said Father. "Here, Socrates, tidy this up."

Socrates could hardly believe his ears, but he began to empty the sewing box. He looked so thoughtful that it was plain he was taking the job seriously.

"Now you can sit yourself at the piano, Aurora," said Father.

"Yes, but there's something else first," said Aurora. She disappeared into her own room. In a little while she came back wearing one of her best outfits — the red one that Father had made a little apron for, to hide the hole he had burned in it when he was ironing it. She felt that they both had a share in that one.

"Let me feel your fingers," said Father. "Goodness me, how cold they are. Come along. I'll warm them for you."

Then he and Aurora began to play.

"Can you imagine why we didn't think of this before?" said Father.

"Yes, I can," said Aurora. "You've had a lot of things to do."

"That's true," said Father, "but still we could have found time for this."

"Not before you got the dishes brush, you know," said Aurora, as she waggled her little finger up and down.

She had been practicing this all day. Here was a girl who was very eager to learn the piano!

AUTHOR

When the Norwegian author Anne-Catharina Vestly was young, she wanted to be an actor, and she wrote skits that she acted out. After some years of acting for the Norwegian Broadcasting Company and a theater group, she decided she was more interested in writing. She went on to write many books for adults and children, some of which have been published in the United States. When two of her children's books were made into Norwegian movies, she acted the part of a major character. "A Funny Feeling" comes from her book *Aurora and Socrates,* a sequel to *Hello, Aurora.*

Born in Rena, Norway, Anne-Catharina Vestly moved to the capital city of Oslo, Norway, when she was nineteen. She still lives there with her artist-husband, Johan Vestly, who has illustrated all of her books.

Juegos

by RUBEN SANDOVAL

Juegos is the Spanish word for *games*. All around the world, children play games. If you were able to be everywhere at once, you'd see that the games are very much alike.

Here are some games that Chicano children play. How many of them do you know?

This game is called **Maria's Going on a Picnic.**

Any number of people can play. The first one says, "Maria's going on a picnic, and she's taking ——." *(Give the name of something that can be taken on a picnic.)* The second player repeats the sentence, naming what the first player named and adding something else. The next player does the same, adding still another item. A player is out when he or she forgets to name something that has already been named.

This one is called **El Correo (ehl koh-ray'oh) (The Mail).**

One player stands in the middle of a circle. Everyone else marks the spot he or she is on and gives it the name of a city. Then the player in the middle calls out the names of two of those cities. Those cities (players) must try to change places with one another. While this is going on, any other player — including the one in the middle — can try to take over the places of the two cities. When the scramble is over, there will be one player without a place. He or she will go into the middle and call out the names of two more cities.

Elephant, Elephant is a game that looks like a beautiful dance.

> Elephant, elephant, sitting on a bench,
> Trying to make a dollar out of fifty-five cents.
> He missed, she missed, he missed like this. . . .

This rhyme is sung as the players play the game. They start with legs apart. Then each one jumps and twists in this way — right leg in front, legs apart, left leg in front, then legs apart again. The player caught with legs apart at the end of the rhyme is out. The others go on.

Las Ollitas (lahs oh-lee'tahs) (The Pots) is a market game.
One player is a buyer. One is a seller. The others are pots
for sale. Each pot has a secret name and a secret price. One
might be *beans* for nine centavos. Another might be *rice* for
ten centavos. The buyer asks for different foods until he or
she names one the seller has. The seller tells the buyer the
price. As the buyer counts out the money, centavo by centavo, the bought pot runs to a marker and back to his or her
place. If the pot fails to return to the starting place before
the money is counted out, that pot becomes the buyer.

Hitting the Piñata (peen-yah'tah) is a favorite party game.

The piñata is a decorated pot or a papier-mâché figure. For parties, it is filled with candy and everyone has a turn at hitting it to try to break it. Each person is blindfolded and given a bat with which to hit it. When it finally breaks and the candy spills out, everyone runs to grab the candy.

AUTHORS

"Juegos was taken from the book *Games, Games, Games/ Juegos, Juegos, Juegos.* The author, Ruben Sandoval, wanted to write down games that Chicano children play that are bridges between the past and the present and between Latin America and the United States. Mr. Sandoval grew up and went to school in Los Angeles, California, and now teaches there.

The Search

by ROBERTA SILMAN

Ten-year-old Peter and his school bus driver are good friends. Peter calls the driver "Puddin' Paint." Puddin' Paint calls Peter "Smiley." One day Puddin' Paint visits Peter's home. Not knowing that Peter is adopted, Puddin' Paint carelessly says that he wouldn't want to bring up somebody else's child, even though he and his wife are childless. Peter is hurt, but his mother helps him understand that Puddin' Paint didn't mean to hurt him. A few days later, Peter offers to help look for Puddin' Paint's lost dogs — Black and Brown.

I liked being alone with Puddin' Paint. The warm car was like a cocoon that protected us from the cold. The snow that had fallen during the night glared in the bright sunlight. I had to close my eyes to keep them from getting watery while I talked to Puddin' Paint. "Where're we going?" I said.

"There's a spot about fifteen miles away that borders the big state park. I used to take the dogs there fishing. I went there the third day we were looking for the dogs, but it started to rain so we didn't get as far as the lake." Puddin' Paint pulled down the window visor. "There, now you can open your eyes, Smiley," he said.

When I did, I could see that his face was worried. "Every-thing's turned to ice," he said with a frown. "If we don't find the dogs today, they're going to freeze to death." He really loved those dogs. He would do anything for them, I thought.

He seemed able to read my mind.

"Those dogs mean a lot to us, Smiley." He looked down at me. "When you've had ani-mals since they were pups, well, they get into your bones. They become part of you." He stared straight ahead, the way people do when they're afraid they are going to cry.

"The way kids do?" I asked softly.

"I guess. I guess so."

I started to understand what Mom had been trying to tell me the other day about the

love parents have for children. If Puddin' Paint loves his dogs this much, then imagine how much Mom and Dad care about Kate and me. Mom was right. You can't really describe that. I was getting a feeling for what she was talking about, and right then I knew I had to tell Puddin' Paint I was adopted. I'm not sure why it had to be then. It isn't the sort of thing you can lead up to, so I just said, "I think you ought to know I'm adopted."

I thought he would be surprised, but he took off his cap and slowed the car down a little and looked at me. "I kind of suspected that the day I came to your house. You all got very quiet when I said I didn't believe in adoption. And on my way home, I realized that I didn't know any-

thing about it, and I had just blown my mouth off."

"That's okay, Puddin' Paint," I said.

"I felt bad then, Smiley, and I'm sorry now. I want you to know that."

"I do," I said, and for a while there wasn't anything to say.

After about a half hour, we came to a town, well, not really a town, just a clump of houses.

"This must be one of the smallest villages in the state." Puddin' Paint said, "It has a post office and a grocery and a vet. They say he's a good vet too. But I never understood how he could stay in business in this little place." Puddin' Paint shook his head. "Years ago there was more farming around here, before the state bought most of the land for a park."

A few people were walking on the road. An old man in a red hat waved; then soon we were all by ourselves again. More snow had fallen up here. The trees glittered; the woods were so still. Occasionally, a white-tailed rabbit hopped across the road, which was getting bumpier and bumpier.

Suddenly the car lurched to a stop.

"Road ends here," Puddin' Paint said. "We'll have to walk from now on."

I pulled on two pairs of mittens and my hat that looks like a mask. I had thought Mom was crazy when she insisted I take this hat, but now I was glad to have it.

Puddin' Paint pulled down the earflaps on his fur hat and reached for the knapsack. Then he rolled the two blankets together, tied them up, and lashed them to the knapsack with a long rope. He put the whole thing on his back. I knew that the blankets were for the dogs if we found them.

Our feet scrunched the crusted snow as we walked. "It's almost a mile from here," Puddin' Paint said. He kept looking down on the ground for paw prints, he said, so I did too.

"Deer droppings," he said occasionally. Our breath misted across our faces. I could feel my ears stretching toward some sound, any sound really, but mostly the sound of a dog barking. All we could hear was our own feet.

We neared a widening in the path. "Well, here's the lake," Puddin' said. The lake was frozen. He looked at his watch, then walked over to a rock and brushed the snow off it.

"Come on, Smiley, time for some food. We don't want to freeze to death."

The cocoa felt so good going down, and the biscuits were

still warm. Puddin' Paint handed me a sandwich.

"I'm not that hungry after the biscuit," I said.

"Better eat it anyway. When it's this cold, you need a lot of fuel to keep that fire going." Puddin' Paint was right. I felt warmer as soon as I ate the sandwich.

"I don't know whether to turn around or take the path into the woods at the north end of the lake." Puddin' Paint frowned. "I have this nagging feeling that those dogs are somewhere in those woods."

"Let's take the path then."

"It'll be a longer walk back," he warned.

"Oh, don't worry about me," I said.

For safety's sake we walked around the lake instead of across it. "You never know. All we need is to fall in. That would top everything," Puddin' Paint said.

The path from the lake was narrower and rockier than the one we walked on before. It wasn't as silent, though.

"More animals live here. There's a salt lick a few miles away," Puddin' Paint said over his shoulder. We had to walk single file in lots of places.

Suddenly he stopped and walked off the path. "Look," he said, pointing to some drop-pings. "That's not deer; that's a dog." Puddin' Paint dug his hand into his pocket and pulled out a compass. I watched him sight it. Then we started to walk. I was getting used to the cold now, so I rolled back the mask part of my hat. A little later, there were some more droppings.

"I may be crazy, but let's call," Puddin' Paint said.

We began. "Black, Brown, Black, Brown." Then we stopped shouting and walked some more. "Black! Brown! Black! Brown!" we called again. Nothing.

Then I put my hand on Puddin' Paint's arm. "Wait a second," I whispered. I thought I had heard something.

"Did you hear anything?" he said.

"I thought so, something little. Did you?"

Puddin' Paint shook his head. "No, but you have younger ears. Let's walk a little farther and call again."

The next time I was sure I heard it. Puddin' Paint still didn't hear anything. "Which direction, Smiley?"

I pointed. "That's more northwest," Puddin' Paint said as he sighted the compass. "Well, lets give it a try."

We walked for several minutes. There were no more dog droppings; I began to think I had made a mistake. Puddin' Paint stopped. "Let's stand very still and call and see what happens." He cupped his hands around his mouth. I did the same. "Black, Brown, Black, Brown!" we called, and waited. In the distance there was a thin thread of sound.

"Did you hear it?" I said.

"That time I did." Puddin' Paint bent his ear toward the sound. We were almost running. I had to be careful not to slip on the thin sheet of ice that covered the rocks.

We called again, and the same thin thread-like sound answered.

"I'd swear it was miles away from the sound of it. But then they couldn't hear us," Puddin' Paint said, scanning the woods. "They both have such big barks when they want to," he added.

"Even if they're hurt?" I asked.

He nodded. "Let's keep moving." He hunched his shoulders, sighting the compass again.

Suddenly, a low whimpering sound floated toward us. I leaned toward it. "You lead," Puddin' Paint whispered.

We were in a thicker part of the forest. Evergreens surrounded us. I had to push

away the branches to get
through. My eyes were watery
from the cold. I blinked a lot.
It was hard to see. But then I
saw something red.

"Look!"

We ran toward the dogs.
They were caught in two animal traps that had been set side
by side. The snow around
them was stained with blood.

Puddin' Paint's face was
grim as he approached the
dogs. Their legs were tangled
in the traps, and their eyes
were glassy. They scarcely
looked alive. Black was deeper
in his trap than Brown. It was
Brown who had whimpered.

"We've got to work fast,"
Puddin' Paint said. Quickly he
unrolled the blankets and
opened the knapsack. "Here,
hold this." He gave me a cup,

then filled it with cocoa. "Try Black first." But the dog couldn't even drink. He looked at me and seemed to shake his head. I gave the cup to Brown. He lapped it up, but very slowly. Puddin' Paint was unpacking a small wrench.

"Good dog," he said. "Now Smiley, I'm going to try to release these traps, but it's tricky. They're not made to get animals out alive. You stand back."

It seemed like hours while Puddin' Paint worked on the releases. There was a trickle of blood from both dogs the whole time. I was sweating all over. Brown had stopped whimpering.

"Now . . . ." Puddin' Paint's voice was tense. "I think this'll do it. I hope so." You could feel the silence pressing all around us. Then, with a snap, Black was free. But he didn't even move. He just lay there. After a few minutes, Puddin' Paint got Brown out. He couldn't move either.

"We'll have to make a stretcher with the blankets and carry them to the car," said Puddin' Paint. Now I knew why he had taken so much rope. Quickly we wrapped the blankets around the rope. Then Puddin' Paint pulled some diaper pins from his pocket.

"I've been carrying these around with me all week. But I didn't think the dogs would be hurt like this — just cold or very hungry." He pressed his lips together; his mouth was a thin straight line across his face. Then he shook his head as if he couldn't believe all this was happening.

We carried the dogs back to the car on the homemade stretcher. At one point I was sure my shoulders would break. Just then Puddin' Paint said, "Want to rest?" I shook my head. How could we stop when Black was bleeding to death?

Back at the car, Puddin' Paint made a tourniquet out of two old towels for each dog. As he was tying Black's leg up, the dog's eyes rolled back; he was unconscious. I kept watching to see if Black's chest was moving as we rode back to the village.

"I sure hope that vet is there," Puddin' Paint said as we got into the car.

When we got to the village, it looked like a ghost town.

Puddin' Paint frowned. He pulled up at the grocery store and jumped out. The store looked closed. But the door was open. He went in.

He came back quickly. "The grocer's the vet!" he shouted. Behind him was the old man in the red hat. They pulled the stretcher out of the back of the station wagon.

" 'Round the back," the old man said. The blankets were dripping blood. I ran behind them. An old woman was holding the door open.

"Why, you're just a boy!" was all I remembered hearing. Later they told me I had fainted.

When I woke up I was on a funny-shaped couch in a very odd kitchen. It was filled with books and papers and plants, as well as pots and pans and dishes. A door at the far end of the large warm room was open. I could see a table with Brown on it. But it was Black I was worried about.

"Here, son." The old woman blew on a spoon and held it up to my mouth. I swallowed some soup. It was thick and good. I could hear the vet's voice. "The black one will probably have a limp, but he's lucky to be alive. The brown one will walk just fine." I closed my eyes. Both dogs were alive!

When I opened my eyes again, the woman was smiling and handing me another spoonful of soup. I heard the vet's voice again.

"They're lucky you found them when you did. A few more hours and they would have both been dead."

Then I heard Puddin' Paint's voice. "I didn't find them.

The boy did. He heard Brown whimper. It was the tiniest sound you can imagine. I still don't know how he heard it, but he did."

Then I realized that the vet's office was the room attached to the kitchen. When they came into the kitchen, Puddin' Paint rumpled my hair a little. "Well, hello, Smiley. Feeling better?"

"What happened?" I asked.

Puddin' Paint explained, "You were so exhausted that the minute you hit the warm kitchen, you just fell over. Then you opened your eyes and said, 'I'm so sleepy,' and went to sleep."

I smiled, but I felt like going to sleep again right then.

"That was about a one-and-a-half-mile walk back to your car, if you were where I think you were," the vet said.

"And those dogs weigh about thirty pounds apiece," Puddin' Paint added. He smiled at me.

"You should be mighty proud of your son," the woman said. She kept spooning more soup into my mouth. I didn't really want it, but I didn't know how to tell her that.

Puddin' Paint winked at me. "Oh, Smiley's not mine. He has two handsome young parents. But you know, I wish he was ours. With a son like old Smiley here, well, you'd have nothing in the world to worry about." A shiver went down my spine. I leaned back on the pillows. All I wanted to do was sleep. But Puddin' Paint said, "Say now, Smiley, don't go back to sleep. Everyone's already getting worried, I'm sure. We're late right now."

I looked out the window. The sky, the trees and the snow were all kind of purple. The sun was almost down.

"Come on, Smiley, time to go," Puddin' Paint said.

"Not till he finishes his soup," the woman said. I felt

like I was floating as I put on my shoes. I started to tell her how light-headed I felt, but she said, "There now, save your strength, son."

I ate the rest of the soup. Then, while Puddin' Paint and the vet carried the dogs to the car, the woman insisted I eat a piece of her homemade raisin bread with butter. It was good, but I was already full. I felt stuffed when I started to walk.

The vet and his wife stood at the door while we walked to the car. I had to lean on Puddin' Paint because my legs felt so funny.

"By, good-by," they called, and we drove off into the peaceful sunset. Black and Brown were already fast asleep.

AUTHOR

Roberta Silman is a graduate of Cornell University. She has written for both adults and children. The short stories that she writes for grown-ups appear in several magazines. The story "The Search" is from the author's first book for children, *Somebody Else's Child*. This book was the 1977 winner of the Child Study Association Wel-Met Award, given to a distinguished book that deals honestly with young people's problems. Like Peter in the story, one of Ms. Silman's three children is adopted.

Roberta Silman says that when she is not writing or working in her garden, she enjoys vacations with her family, hiking in the Austrian Alps.

ENERGY

by MELVIN BERGER

Everything that grows or moves or changes must have energy. You must have it. All plants and animals must have it. Machines big and small must have it.

Think what the world would be like without energy. Nothing would move. Nothing would grow. There would be no light, no warmth, and no sounds. There would be no people, plants, or animals. It would be a dead, still world.

But our world does have energy — and much of it comes from the sun.

How do plants and animals and people get energy from the sun? The light and heat of the sun help plants to grow. The sun's energy is stored in the plants. People and animals eat food that comes from those plants. People also eat food that comes from animals, which eat plants.

Just think of the many foods you eat in a single day. The peanut butter in your peanut-butter sandwich is made by grinding up the seeds of the peanut plant. The bread is made from flour that is made from wheat, the seed of a plant. Your milk comes from a cow that has eaten grass — a plant. The chicken on your dinner plate comes from chickens that have been fed corn and other grains — plants. You can see how people and animals get energy from the sun every time they eat. But how do machines get energy from the sun?

Some machines — cars, trains, airplanes, for example — burn fuel. Usually they burn oil, gas, or coal. These fuels come from the earth. Wells are dug to get oil or gas. Mines are dug to get coal. How did these fuels get into the earth?

Sun warms water.

Warm Water

Cool Water

Warm Water

Pump

Pump

Storage Tank

All fuels were once living plants and animals. (As you know, they got their energy from the sun.) Over many, many years, the plants and animals died and became pressed down into the earth. As they were pressed farther and farther down, they were changed into fuel by the heat of the earth. And where did the heat of the earth come from? The sun! So the fuel that makes machines go is really energy from the sun.

Now think about this a little bit. Was the sun used directly to give energy? No, what you have been reading about is *indirect* use of the energy from the sun. The *results* of the light and heat of the sun have been used, rather than the sun itself. The sun has been *stored* in the plants, the animals, and the fuels. Now scientists are finding ways to capture the rays of the sun so that they can be used more directly. This will mean that energy will be available more quickly.

One of the ways they have found to use the sun directly is to heat water on the roof of a house and make the house stay warm day and night. The picture on page 46 shows you how this is done. They have also found a way to use light from the sun to make electricity.

Scientists are still working hard to find better ways to use energy from the sun. Perhaps you will become a scientist who will work in this area. It may be your discovery that will help people to live better by using more of the energy from the sun.

AUTHOR

Melvin Berger is the author of over three dozen books on science and music for young people. A school teacher, musician, editor, and antiques collector, he lives in New York State with his two daughters and his wife, Gilda Berger, who is also an author.

SKILL

SQRRR

When you study a history book or some other book for school, you want to understand and remember as much information as you can. Did you know that there is a way to study that will help you to understand what you read and to remember it longer? If you use this way of studying, you will sometimes find that you can also learn more from your book in less study time than you spent before.

There are five steps that you can use to get more out of your study time, and there are five letters that stand for those steps. The five letters are **SQRRR.** This lesson will explain what these five steps are and how you can use them to help you with your school work.

What is Step 1 of SQRRR?

Step 1, **S,** stands for **Survey.** *To survey* means "to look over." Many of the books that you study have headings. They are in special type that sets them apart from the rest of the material that you are reading. The question *What is Step 1 of SQRRR?* is a heading.

When you start to study a book, first survey these headings. Do not just begin at the first page of a chapter and read through to the end of it.

Adaptation of "The SQ3R Method of Studying" in *Effective Study,* 4th Edition, by Francis P. Robinson. Copyright 1941, 1946 by Harper & Row, Publishers, Inc.; Copyright © 1961, 1970 by Francis P. Robinson. Used by permission of Harper & Row, Publishers, Inc.

If you were studying a chapter about pets, there might be a heading in the center of the page like this:

Kinds of Pets

The first heading under it might be located at the left of the page and look like this: **Pets for the home** or **What kinds of pets live in homes?** A later heading, also located at the left of the page, might be **Farm pets** or **What kind of pets live on farms?** There would be information following each of these headings.

Kinds of Pets

Pets for the home
Dogs, cats, birds, and fish are the most common kinds of pets for the home. People who have enough outdoor space for a large dog might have a collie or a boxer. Others might choose a small dog, such as a Scottish terrier or a cocker spaniel. Some favorite pet cats are the striped tabby and the Siamese. Common pet birds include canaries and parakeets. Guppies are easy fish to keep.

Farm pets
People on farms often have horses and ponies as pets as well as cats and dogs. Children on farms often care for such animals as chicks, ducklings, lambs, rabbits, young pigs, or calves. A child who has a calf or another farm ani-

Kinds of Pets

What kinds of pets live in homes?
Dogs, cats, birds, and fish are the most common kinds of pets for the home. People who have enough outdoor space for a large dog might have a collie or a boxer. Others might choose a small dog, such as a Scottish terrier or a cocker spaniel. Some favorite pet cats are the striped tabby and the Siamese. Common pet birds include canaries and parakeets. Guppies are easy fish to keep.

What kinds of pets live on farms?
People on farms often have horses and ponies as pets as well as cats and dogs. Children on farms often care for such animals as chicks, ducklings, lambs, rabbits, young pigs, or calves. A child who has a calf or another farm ani-

Surveying a chapter by first reading the headings is something like looking over a map before you begin a trip to a place that you have never been before. You get an idea of where you are going and the kinds of things you may find there before you start.

Do not take a lot of time to make this survey. You just want to get a general idea of what the chapter is about. If you take much more than one minute to survey the headings in a chapter or lesson, you may be spending more time than you should.

What is Step 2 of SQRRR?

Step 2, **Q,** stands for **Question.** Did you notice that in the second set of headings that might be under **Kinds of Pets,** each was a question? Some authors write headings in a few words. Others write them as questions. In Step 2 of SQRRR, change the heading into a question if it is not already written as one. You are more likely to pick out and remember the important information when you want to find the answer to a particular question. Write your question down on a separate piece of paper so that you will remember it. If the heading is already a question, you are ready to go on to Step 3.

What is Step 3 of SQRRR?

Step 3, the first **R,** stands for **Read.** Read the material under the heading to answer the question you asked in Step 2. Read very carefully, and try to get as complete an answer to the question as you can.

What is Step 4 of SQRRR?

Step 4, the second **R,** stands for **Recite.** *To recite* means "to repeat aloud." When you have finished reading the information under the first heading, recite to yourself in your own words the answer to your question. When you recite the answer in your own words, you are more likely to remember it. Spend up to one half of your total study time doing this step.

Steps 2, 3, and 4 must be repeated for each heading. That is, for the information under each heading, you must have a *question* to ask about it, you must *read* to answer that question, and you must *recite* the answer to yourself.

What is Step 5 of SQRRR?

Step 5, the third **R,** stands for **Review.** *To review* means "to go back over." When you have finished studying all the material under each heading, look back at the headings and tell yourself, once again, the answers to the questions you asked in Step 2.

You will remember more if you review the material again the day after you first studied it. Then, if you are going to have a test on it, review it quickly again and again up to the time that you take the test.

REVIEW

Can you answer these questions?

1. For what five words do the letters *SQRRR* stand?
2. What should you do in the first step? About how much time should you spend doing the first step?
3. What should you do in the second step of SQRRR? Why is this step helpful to you?
4. In the third step, what should you do to help yourself understand and remember the information?
5. What should you do in the fourth step of SQRRR? Why is this step helpful to you? How much time should you spend on this step?
6. What should you do in the last step? How should you do this?
7. How would you change the heading **Pets in school** into a question?

USING SQRRR

Now follow the SQRRR steps with the following article about air. After reading the short paragraph that introduces the material, first, *survey* the headings. Second, think about the *question* the first side heading asks. Third, *read* the material under that first side heading to answer the question. Fourth, *recite* to yourself the answer to the question. Fifth, after repeating Steps 2, 3, and 4 for each side heading in the article, *review* all the material. Be prepared to tell what important information you learned that answers the question in each heading.

Air

As you read this article, you are surrounded by something that has no color, taste, or smell. You cannot see it, but if it were not there, you would die in a very few minutes. This thing that is so important to you is air.

What does air contain?

Air contains several different kinds of gases. If people, plants, and animals do not have these gases to breathe, they will soon die.

Air also contains tiny bits of water. These are so small that you cannot see them. Millions and millions of those bits of water laid side by side will not even measure one inch.

Air contains tiny bits of dust too. These bits are also so small that you usually cannot see them.

How does air help you?

You already know that air helps you breathe, but air helps you in other ways too.

The heat from the sun goes through the air and warms the earth. The air then acts as a blanket. It traps the heat near the earth. This makes the earth warm enough for people and things to live on it.

Air also makes it possible for you to hear sounds. When people talk, you can hear them because the sounds they make are carried through the air. If there were no air, the world would be silent.

You know that when air moves fast, it is called wind. The power of the wind is used to make sailboats sail and windmills turn. Someday scientists will probably find new and better ways to use the wind to get power to run our machines.

A Different Shape

by ELOISE GREENFIELD

As Genny James drifted off to sleep, she could hear
the muffled voices downstairs. She hoped it meant
that her older brother, Larry, who had just come
home from the army, was doing something to stop
their parents from arguing so much. Could he? . . .

Moving slow. Coming slow up from sleep. Leaving her
party dream slow. Moving up from sleep. Slow. Kitchen
dream pancake smell. Kitchen dream pancake smell. Pancake smell. Slow eyes opening. Moving. Moving fast up
from sleep. Fast awake. Morning. It's morning.

It's morning.

Genny got up quickly. She washed up and dressed and
hurried toward the pancake smell. She was the last one up.
Everybody else had just about finished eating.

"I didn't want to wake you up," her mother said. "You
looked so worn out."

"I did?" Genny said. "Well, I feel real good now."

"I guess you do," Mac said. "You tried to sleep for a
week."

"You mean a month!" Kim said. "Hey! That reminds me of a joke. You want to hear it?"

Genny got her plate of pancakes out of the warm oven and took it to the table. She felt so good that it wasn't until she had eaten a few mouthfuls that she realized something was wrong. This breakfast wasn't like old times. Everybody was laughing and talking, but something in their voices wasn't real. Maybe they could fool Kim, her younger sister, but they couldn't fool her. She put her fork down.

"Something's the matter," she told them.

They looked at each other. All except Kim.

"Something's the matter," she said again. "What's the matter?"

"Why don't you finish eating, Genny?" her mother said. "We can talk about it after breakfast."

"Talk about what?" Kim asked.

Genny shoved her plate away. "I don't want my breakfast," she said.

Her mother picked up the plate and set it on top of her own. "There's something we have to tell you," she said. "Your daddy —"

Mr. James was hitting the table softly with his fist, and Genny remembered another time — the time when he had been in bed with a bad pain in his back. Genny could still see the way his fist had looked hitting the blanket over and over in that same soft way.

Something terrible was about to happen. There was only quiet at the table, and trouble.

"I'm getting a room," Mr. James said. "I'm getting a room over on Warren Street."

He said some other things too, about loving them and visiting them and taking care of them, but Genny couldn't listen. She was having a hard time hearing the words he had
already said.

And then she did hear. But she didn't understand.

"You're going to *move?*" she said.

For a moment, nobody said anything. Then Kim stood up,
making her chair scrape loudly as it slid back.

"I'm sorry, Daddy!" She was screaming.

And then her father was up too, hugging her with tears in his eyes. "No, baby, no," he said. "It's not your fault. It's me and your mamma; it's our fault."

But Kim was saying over and over into his chest, "Don't leave us, Daddy; please don't leave us."

Genny turned to her mother, still trying to understand. "But Larry fixed everything last night," she said.

"Genny," her mother said, "Larry couldn't —"

"But I heard him talking," Genny said. "I heard him!"

Larry shook his head slowly. "I don't know how to work magic, Genny," he said. "I wish I could, but I can't." He reached to touch her shoulder, but she leaned away.

Genny saw the hurt in his eyes and was glad. Then she saw that Mac was hurt too, for Larry, and that made her sorry. She was angry and glad and sorry, all at the same time. And mixed up. Most of all, mixed up. She wished Kim would shut up crying so she could think. Then all of a sudden she didn't want to be around any of the people in that house. She couldn't stand being around them any more.

"I'm going outside!" she said.

Standing on the porch with her arms folded on the rail and her head on her arms, she could think. It was Larry shaking his head that had really made her angry. Shaking his head was saying no hope, no hope. But Larry could do anything, fix anything. He always used to fix her toys. And one time, he had even fixed a friendship when it was broken all to pieces. He had put her hand and Angela's together and said something crazy, and they had laughed and forgotten all about being mad. Why couldn't he do the same thing and fix her mother's and father's broken love?

In a little while, Mac came outside and stood beside her.
"We're going to throw the ball
around some," he said. "You
want to go?"

"Is Larry going?"

"Yeah, Larry's going," Mac
said, sounding mad.

"Well, I'm not going then," she
said.

Mac gave her a mean look and went on down the steps. And when Larry and Kim came out, Genny heard Larry's footsteps stop beside her for a moment, then move away. When she could no longer hear them, she turned and watched her brothers and her sister going down the street. She knew they were going over to the playground. And she knew they were taking along the red, sponge-rubber ball that they had had fun with ever since Kim was so little that she could only roll it.

But this was some old family now. Some old nothing break-up family. And everybody was mad. She was mad at Larry. Mac was mad at her. Kim was mad. And their mother and father didn't like each other any more.

Genny sat down on the steps, but she didn't stay there long. She got up and started walking toward Sixteenth Street. She felt like talking to somebody, and there was only one somebody she wanted to talk to. He ought to be home from church by now.

It was one of Mr. Parker's lonesome Sundays. Genny could tell as soon as she went in because he had been looking at pictures of his wife. The photo album was lying open on the sofa.

"Marlene not bringing the baby over today?" Genny asked.

Mr. Parker left the album open, but he slid it over to make room on the sofa for Genny. "She called last night," he said. "Said she was going out of town again. That's four Sundays in a row I haven't seen them. I guess my grandson will be a grown man before I get to see him again." He laughed, but it wasn't a happy laugh.

"Don't you get mad at Marlene?" Genny asked.

"I used to, Genetta," Mr. Parker said. "Used to get real mad, and hurt too. Took me a long time to understand that Marlene's giving as much as she's able to give. She's so wrapped up in her own life, her own problems, that she doesn't have much left to give anybody else. I understand that now. But I still get lonesome sometimes." He touched his wife's face in the album before he closed it. "What's on your mind today?" he asked Genny.

"Can I look at the lamps?" Genny said.

"Well, sure," Mr. Parker said, "if that's the way you want to spend a nice Sunday afternoon."

"I just want to see something," Genny said.

Mr. Parker led her to the room in the back that had been Marlene's when she was growing up. Now it was filled with lamps — floor lamps standing against the wall, table lamps, big and little, on a two-tiered wooden table in the middle of the room. Some of them were lying down because of their broken legs. A few had already been fixed and were waiting for their owners to come and get them.

Genny looked around at the lamps. Then she pointed to one with a big, ragged hole in the globe. "Can you fix that?" she asked.

Mr. Parker shook his head slowly the same way Larry had. "No, I sure can't," he said. "A shame, too."

"You might as well throw the lamp away, then," Genny said. Her voice sounded hard.

"Throw it away!" Mr. Parker laughed in a surprised way. "What in the world for?"

"It won't ever be the same, will it?" Genny said.

"Well, you're not the same as you were last year," Mr. Parker told her. "But we don't want to throw you away, do we? Look. I got a new globe for it. A different shape, but just as pretty, don't you think?"

"It's pretty, but —"

"But nothing!" Mr. Parker said. "This is a good lamp. The wiring is good. The switch is good. The base is strong. A good lamp." He frowned and gave Genny a close look. "I don't think we're really talking about this lamp. Are we?"

Genny didn't answer. She bit her lip and moved her shoulders up and back down again.

"Well, did I help you out any?" Mr. Parker asked.

Genny wasn't sure. "I don't know," she said. She turned to leave. It was time for her to go.

"I hope I did," Mr. Parker said.

He followed her out of the room. "You sure helped me a lot. Got me to talking. Think I'll go on over to Wilson's, see if I can get him in a good argument. But you come and get me, now, if you want to talk some more."

Genny walked fast up Fletcher Street and across the avenue. She wanted to get to the playground before Larry and Kim and Mac left. She was still angry, but not with Larry. Not with her not-magic brother.

It was her mother and father who were giving the family a different shape, and she was angry with them. Maybe later on she would understand, the way Mr. Parker did about Marlene, but right now she didn't want to.

Genny had some thinking to do. She kept walking fast, but she slowed down her thinking. She thought about the shapes of the families she knew. Lynn lived with her mother and her grandmother. Earl and his brothers lived with their married sister. Angela and Louis lived with their mother and father and aunt and uncle and cousins. Tony lived with his godmother and her children. Karen lived with her father and his new wife.

So many shapes. And the shapes were always changing. Somebody was born. Somebody died. Somebody moved in. Somebody moved out — the way her father was going to. Genny thought about her father going home from work and nobody being there to tell him jokes after he had taken his shower and was ready to talk. She didn't want him to be lonesome. He was still part of their family.

She said aloud, "Me and Kim and Mac and Larry and Mamma. Me and Kim and Mac and Larry and Daddy." Two

circles. Two circles linked together. That was their shape, for now. She would have to get used to it.

They weren't playing ball when she got to the playground. Larry and Kim were doing jumping jacks, and Mac was counting. Genny came up behind them.

"Hi," she said, but it didn't come out very loud. She said it again, and this time they turned around. They were glad to see her.

Mac had the ball. "Think quick!" he said. He threw the ball to her fast and she managed to catch it. But she didn't keep it. She threw it straight to Larry to say she was sorry.

Larry threw the ball high into the air. All four of them looked up, and all four of them put out their hands to catch it when it came back down. But they were laughing and bumping into each other, and nobody caught the ball. When it hit the ground, Mac kicked it, and they chased it across the playground.

In a little while, when they got tired of playing, they would talk. Sit on their favorite bench, the one in front of the giant stone frog, and talk about things. About making each other feel better. About understanding, and getting used to. About fathers and mothers and families and things.

And then they would go home.

AUTHOR

The story you have just read was taken from the book *Talk About a Family.* The author, Eloise Greenfield, is a well-known writer of biographies, stories, and poems for children. She was born in North Carolina and grew up in Washington, D. C. As a child, she loved to read what other people wrote, but it wasn't until she was married and had two children that she discovered she herself is a writer.

Ms. Greenfield's books have won many awards. Among them are the Carter G. Woodson Award for her biography *Rosa Parks.* *Mary McLeod Bethune,* another biography, was a runner-up for the Coretta Scott King Award. Eloise Greenfield herself has been honored by the Council on Interracial Books for Children.

Ms. Greenfield lives in Washington, D. C., where she is a member of the Black Writers' Workshop. She says of her books, "I want to give children words to love, to grow on."

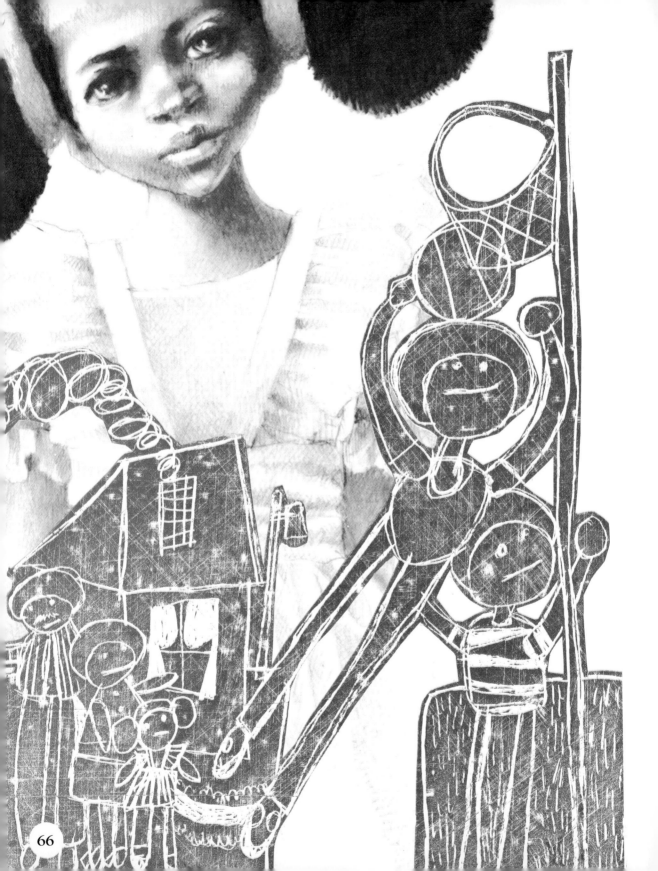

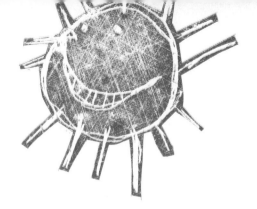

Reggie

by ELOISE GREENFIELD

It's summertime
And Reggie doesn't live here anymore
He lives across the street
Spends his time with the round ball
Jump, turn, shoot
Through the hoop
Spends his time with arguments
  and sweaty friends
And not with us
He's moved away
Comes here just to eat and sleep
  And sometimes pat my head
Then goes back home
To run and dribble and jump and stretch
And stretch
And shoot
Thinks he's Kareem
And not my brother

It's Sensational

As you read "The Search," couldn't you almost feel the cold that Smiley and his friend Puddin' Paint felt? One of your senses is the sense of touch, or feeling. That sense lets you feel whether things are hot or cold, rough or smooth, wet or dry. When you read a story, sometimes words or groups of words make you think you are feeling, seeing, smelling, or tasting what the author has written about. Feeling, hearing, seeing, smelling, and tasting are called the five senses.

Near the beginning of "The Search," you read, "The snow that had fallen during the night *glared* in the bright sunlight. I had to close my eyes to keep them from getting watery. . . ." Did the word *glared* help you to imagine a kind of blinding light? If it did, the word helped you think of your sense of sight.

Later on in the story, the author wrote, "More snow had fallen here. The trees *glittered;* the woods were so *still.*" In that sentence, the author helps you to think of two of your senses — the sense of hearing and the sense of sight. Did the word *glittered* help you "see" the sparkle of snow in the trees? Did the word *still* help you "hear" that there was no movement at all in the woods?

Do you remember that Smiley said, "Our feet *scrunched* the *crusted* snow as we walked"? *Scrunched* is a word that describes a sound — the sound made by Smiley's and Puddin' Paint's feet as they walked in the snow. When you say the word *scrunch*, it sounds like what the word means. If you stepped on an eggshell and broke it, the sound you would hear would be very much like the sound of the word *scrunch*. Words like this always appeal to your sense of hearing.

Now think about the word *crusted*. If something is *crusted*, it has a hard, crisp covering. Did you ever break a very hard roll? When you broke the crust, it probably made a little sound like "scrunch." The word *crusted* is one that appeals to two senses — the sense of touch and the sense of hearing.

The other two senses an author could help you to think about are the sense of taste and the sense of smell. As you continue to read books and stories, look for examples of words that appeal to these and the other three senses.

Carving in Stone

by SHAY RIEGER

As a sculptor I have worked with clay, plaster, wood, bronze, and stone. For me, carving in stone — because stone is so very hard — is the most exciting. When a block of marble is carved into a figure that is alive with form and feeling, I feel good.

Finding and Choosing Stones

Stones can be found everywhere. I have found them in the country, in city lots, and even in torn-down buildings. But most of the carving stones come from quarries. A quarry is a huge open hole in the earth from which stones are dug. The stones are then cut into different sizes and shipped to where they are needed. As a rule, I work with a stone I can handle. If a stone is very heavy, however, a pulley can be used for lifting and moving it.

Each stone has its own beauty. When choosing the right stone for my subject, I note the color and graining as well as the feel and shape of a stone. Sometimes the shape of a stone tells me what I should make. A piece of limestone that I found in a city lot was already formed like a snail. I carved it just a little, set it on a base, and had a finished piece. Most of the time, though, I pick a stone that looks nothing at all like what I want to make. I may just feel that the stone is beautiful or different.

Once the stones have been made into fish, insects, and other animals, they are sent to the art gallery. I believe that stone sculptures should be pleasant to the touch as well as to the eye. For this reason, there are no signs near my pieces that say "Do not touch."

Using Different Stones

The stones I use most often are marble, limestone, alabaster, and granite.

Granite is the hardest of all stone. It comes from deep inside the earth where it is so hot that the granite is a liquid. Over millions of years, the liquid rises to the surface of the earth. There it cools and becomes very hard. The colors of granite range from shades of pink and red to white and gray.

Limestone is a soft stone. It is the result of plants and the shells of sea animals having settled on the ocean floor and hardened. Limestone may be buff or white or gray.

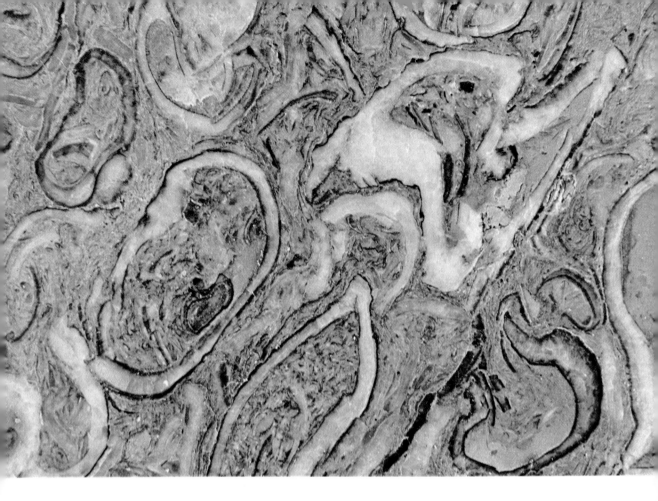

Marble was once limestone. It was changed over the ages by heat from deep under the sea and by the weight of rocks and water bearing down on it. Marble comes in many beautiful colors. There are oranges, purples, and reds. Some marble is as white as snow, and some is as black as coal. One kind of marble, called serpentine, is green and takes a high polish. It can be made as smooth as glass.

Alabaster is softer than most marble. Some alabaster stones are clear. Some are solid. Some have colorful patterns. The colors range from white, brown, and gold to soft pink with a shading of deep red.

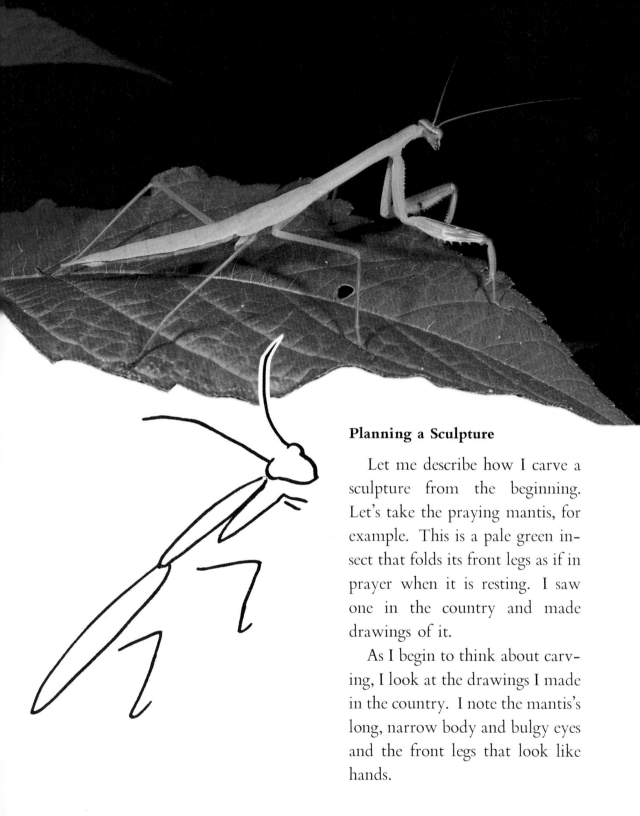

Planning a Sculpture

Let me describe how I carve a sculpture from the beginning. Let's take the praying mantis, for example. This is a pale green insect that folds its front legs as if in prayer when it is resting. I saw one in the country and made drawings of it.

As I begin to think about carving, I look at the drawings I made in the country. I note the mantis's long, narrow body and bulgy eyes and the front legs that look like hands.

I choose a serpentine stone because the shape and the jade green color seem right for the insect. Also, there is a hint of brown graining in the stone that reminds me of the earth.

Carving the Mantis

At the studio, everything is ready for work. These are the tools used for carving the stones. Hammers and chisels do most of the chopping. The files and electric sander are for shaping and smoothing. The goggles are for protection against the flying chips of stone. The mask is to keep the sculptor from breathing in the stone dust.

I now begin to carve the stone. In my left hand I hold the chisel. I aim it at the part of the stone I want to chop away. With my right hand, I hold the hammer and hit the top of the chisel. The chips start flying.

I chip away freely to rough out the shape of the mantis. At this stage, I pay little attention to detail.

I have cut away much of the stone. It is as though I were freeing the mantis that lay hidden within the rock.

The body of the insect has become quite clear now. I make tool marks to separate the base from the sculpture itself.

After much filing, rubbing, and sanding, the stone takes on a high polish.

I place two wires in the mantis' head. These are its antennae. Then I wipe away the stone dust with some clear oil.

After five weeks of work, the praying mantis is finished. It is set on a rosewood base. Then it is sent to the art gallery.

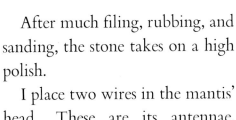

AUTHOR

While still a child, Shay Rieger began working with clay. Since then she has had all kinds of sculpture exhibited at galleries, libraries, schools, and museums. At one of her exhibits, she asked viewers to write down how they felt about her art. The questions children asked made Miss Rieger decide to write about how she forms her sculptures. That is how *The Stone Menagerie,* part of which you have just read, came to be written. Her books *Animals in Clay, Animals in Wood,* and *The Bronze Zoo* show the different materials with which she has worked.

Wrimples

by JACK PRELUTSKY

When the clock strikes five but it's only four,
there's a wrimple in your clock.
When your key won't work in your own front door,
there's a wrimple in the lock.

When your brand-new shoes refuse to fit,
there's a wrimple in each shoe.
When the lights go out and they just were lit,
that's a wrimple's doing too.

When you shake and shake but the salt won't pour,
there's a wrimple in the salt.
When your cake falls flat on the kitchen floor,
it's surely a wrimple's fault.

The way to fix these irksome works
is obvious and simple.
Just search and find it where it lurks,
and then . . . remove the wrimple.

During the late 1800's and early 1900's, thousands of people from Russia, Italy, and other countries came to America to build better lives. Many of these families made their homes in New York City.

In the book *The Witch of Fourth Street and Other Stories,* Myron Levoy tells eight slightly true but mostly fanciful tales about these wonderful people. The story you are about to read is one of these tales.

Mrs. Dunn's Lovely, Lovely Farm

by MYRON LEVOY

Mrs. Dunn had always wanted a farm. Back in the old country, she had lived in the great city of Dublin with its crowded streets and noisy carts over the cobblestones. She had made her husband promise that when they came to America, they would save every penny they possibly could.

And in time they could buy a farm — a lovely farm with chickens and cows and potatoes, with the smell of sweet clover and the giggle of a brook always beyond the door, where their children, Cathy and Neil, could have good fresh food, could grow and run and tumble — a lovely, lovely farm.

When they arrived in New York, with other thousands from Ireland and Italy and Hungary and Russia, they moved into a little apartment on the third floor of a building near Second Avenue. One of their neighbors was named De-Marco and another was named Kandel. In Dublin everyone had Irish names. This was something new and different, and a little frightening. But the neighbors said hello and smiled and warned them about Mr. Warfield, the terrible, horrible landlord. And Mr. and Mrs. Dunn felt much better because in Dublin the landlords had been terrible and horrible too. Things were becoming familiar very quickly.

The next task was for Mr. Dunn to find work. After much searching he found a job hauling coal. He helped send the coal roaring like a river down a metal chute into the basements of buildings. Sometimes he would stand on the pile of coal in the back of the truck and send it down through a square hole into the chute. And sometimes he would stand on the coal pile down in the cellar, clearing the coal away from the bottom of the chute so that more coal and still more coal could come roaring down into the coal bin.

Mr. Dunn would come home every night looking just like a great lump of coal himself. But after a good washing and a hot dinner, Mr. Dunn looked almost like Mr. Dunn again.

And though they could pay the rent and buy coats for the winter, and could buy a little more lamb and butter than they could in Dublin, they couldn't seem to save much money. After a year, Mrs. Dunn counted four dollars and ninety-two cents in her secret empty cereal box, and Mr. Dunn had eight dollars and twelve cents in his shaving mug.

At that rate, they would never have enough for a farm. There were new shoes needed, and a new blanket and a bigger stew pot, and this, and that, and the other. So Mrs. Dunn made a firm decision. They must buy their farm now, as much of it as they could, or the money would vanish like a mist over the chimneys of Dublin. And Mr. Dunn had to admit she was right.

That very next day, Mrs. Dunn bought a hen. They had told her at the market that it was a good laying hen, a Rhode Island Red, the best.

Mrs. Dunn wrapped the hen in a scarf, tucked it under her arm, and carried it five blocks back to her kitchen. Then she put the hen on the floor and watched it strut on the yellow linoleum.

The children named it Amelia for no good reason and fed it cereal and corn and crusts of bread. Mr. Dunn brought home scraps of wood from the coalyard and built a coop. Then with more wood and some chicken wire, he built a little barnyard filled with dirt and stones in which Amelia could scratch. And he took some old felt hats and shaped them into nice soft nests.

Soon, Amelia was joined by Agatha, and then Adeline. Now there were two eggs, sometimes three, every morning in the hat-nests. Cathy and Neil loved Agatha and Amelia and Adeline as if they were their own sisters. Each hen was different. Amelia was very, very proud and strutted as if she were a rooster. Agatha was a busybody, forever poking into everything. Adeline was shy and loved just to sit in the coop.

Soon, the other children in the building started bringing the three hens little presents. Aaron Kandel brought pieces of a huge, flat, dry cracker called *matzo* (maht′suh), which Adeline loved. Fred Reinhardt brought scraps of thick pumpernickel bread. And Vincent DeMarco brought dried seeds called chick peas. And sometimes, Mrs. Dunn would give one of the children a freshly laid egg to take home.

Now it was time for the vegetables, for who ever heard of a farm without vegetables? Mr. Dunn built large, deep boxes, filled them with earth, and planted seeds. Then he put them on the fire escape outside the bedroom window. When the fire-escape landing was covered with boxes, he put new boxes on the iron stairs leading up to the next landing. Soon, the fire escape was blooming with the green shoots of tomato plants, string beans, potatoes, onions, and parsley. And on every windowsill were pots of herbs: rosemary, thyme, mint, chives.

On weekdays, Mrs. Dunn carefully weeded and watered the fire-escape garden and fed the chickens. On Sundays, after he had tried to wash the last of the coal from his face and

hands for the third time, Mr. Dunn would repair the chicken wire, and hold up the growing vegetables with tall sticks and string, and build new boxes. Then he and Mrs. Dunn would walk from room to room, admiring the pots of herbs, the vegetables, the chickens and the mushrooms growing in flat boxes in the kitchen.

But one day, Mr. Warfield, the terrible, horrible landlord, came to collect the rents. As he was about to enter the building, a sun shower soaked his hat. He took off the hat and looked at it. There wasn't a cloud in the sky. Perhaps a tenant had spilled some water on him from above. He looked up and shook his fist toward the top of the building at the hidden enemy.

His mouth dropped in wonder, and he forgot to bring down his fist, for up above, three stories up, was a garden growing among the metal bars of the fire escape. A lady was watering the green mirage with a watering can. And some of the water had dripped down the fire escape from landing to landing until it finally splashed on Mr. Warfield's head.

"This is an outrage!" Mr. Warfield muttered to himself. "It's most unreasonable."

Then he plunged into the building and rushed toward the stairs.

"Ah, Mr. Warfield," said Mrs. Callahan at the first landing, "and when, tell me, are you going to fix m'stove? The divil of a thing's got only one burner working. Do you expect me to pay m'rent when I can't cook soup and stew at the same time?"

"I'll see you later," said Mr. Warfield. "I've got a madhouse here. A madhouse! Let me go by, Mrs. Callahan."

"And what might be the trouble, if I may ask?" said Mrs. Callahan.

"Somebody's growing a tree on the fire escape!"

"Ah, to be sure, to be sure." And with that, Mrs. Callahan nudged her little girl, Noreen, standing next to her. Without a word, Noreen turned and raced up the two flights of stairs to warn her friend Cathy Dunn that Warfield was on his way up. "And tell me now, Mr. Warfield, but how would a tree gain the necessary nourishment on a fire escape, do you know?"

"I intend to find out, Mrs. Callahan, if you'll let me get by!"

Meanwhile, up in the Dunns' apartment, people were flying back and forth. Cathy and Neil had each grabbed a chicken and raced out the door. One chicken went into the DeMarco apartment. The other clucked away in Mrs. Kandel's kitchen. But the chicken left behind, Amelia — or was it Adeline? — had gotten so excited from all the rushing about that she'd flown up to the ceiling and was now roosting comfortably on top of the chandelier in the living room. Mr. Dunn wasn't at home, but Mrs. Dunn took vegetable boxes off the fire-escape landing and slid them under the bed. And from the apartment above, Mrs. Cherney climbed out of her bedroom window onto the fire escape, took more boxes off the iron stairs, and hid them in her own apartment. But try though they did, there just wasn't enough time to hide everything.

Now Mr. Warfield had finally reached the third floor and was pounding at the Dunn's door. Three Rhode Island Reds answered with a shower of *berawk-bawk-bawks*. One was in Mrs. Kandel's kitchen, one in Mrs. De-Marco's bathroom, and one on Mrs. Dunn's chandelier. But Mr. Warfield knew they weren't chickens. That would not be possible. It was the children making noises at him.

Why did they all hate him? He was a good man — fair, reasonable. Wasn't he always reasonable? . . . But what was *this*? There were feathers in the hallway. Children having a pillow fight? Very likely. Ah well, children must play. No harm, Not like trees on the fire escape!

Then Mr. Warfield pounded on the door again. It was not the dainty tap-tap of a salesman, nor the thump-thump of a bill collector, but the shaboom-shaboom of a landlord. And again, from three apartments, three children in a superb imitation of three chickens, *berawk-bawk*ed away at Mr. Warfield.

"Why?" thought Mr. Warfield. "Why?" He had three children of his own, and they *loved* him. Didn't they? Of course they did.

At last the door opened a crack. Mrs. Dunn's hand appeared with an envelope holding the rent money. She waved

87

the envelope up and down at Mr. Warfield. Mr. Warfield took the envelope but also pushed firmly on the door.

"Mrs. Dunn, I'd like a word or two with you," he said.

"I'm feeling a bit ill today, Mr. Warfield, sir. Would you be so kindly as to stop back next week."

"Mrs. Dunn! There is a tree growing on your fire escape! I saw it with my own two eyes!"

"Mr. Warfield," said Mrs. Dunn rapidly, "you're blessed. There's many a blind man would trade this very building for your keen eyesight. But still, a tree cannot truly grow on a fire escape. Good day to you now."

"Good day, my foot! I demand to see the condition of that fire escape. As landlord, I have the right to enter and inspect the building at reasonable hours. I'm a reasonable man, and I would never come at an unreasonable hour."

"Why it's nearly four o' the clock. I've got to do m' husband's supper. 'Tis not a reasonable hour at all," said Mrs. Dunn.

"Either you let me in, Madam, or I'll call the police — *and* the fire department. A tree on the fire escape is a fire hazard. Let me in!"

"Tomorrow."

"NOW!" shouted Mr. Warfield. And with that, the chicken on the chandelier clucked again. "Did you hear that, Mrs. Dunn?"

"Sounded like a cuckoo clock. Cuckoo, cuckoo. 'Tis four o' the clock, you see."

"Nonsense. You have a *chicken* in there! My building has *chickens!*" At that, all three hens in all three apartments *berawk-bawk*ed again. "This isn't an apartment house! It's a zoo!" Then Mr. Warfield pushed his way past Mrs. Dunn and stormed into her living room.

"My chandelier!" shouted Mr. Warfield.

" 'Tisn't *your* chandelier. I've paid the rent. 'Tis *my* chandelier," said Mrs. Dunn.

Mr. Warfield rushed through to the bedroom and stared at the remains of the farm on the fire escape. "My fire escape!" His face was flushed. His eyes were bulging. "Unbelievable! Mrs. Dunn, what are these weeds supposed to *be?*"

"That? Why that's onions, Mr. Warfield."

"*This* is an *onion?*"

"Oh, you can't see it. The onion's beneath the dirt. Least I hope 'tis."

"And *this?*" he said, pointing.

"That's supposed to be potatoes. But I fear for them. The soil is not deep enough."

"Incredible!" he said. "Don't you like geraniums, Mrs. Dunn? I thought people liked to grow geraniums. Look out the window, across the street. See the window sills? There and there. And over there. Everyone *else* is growing geraniums."

"That's a good *idea,* Mr. Warfield." said Mrs. Dunn. "'Twould brighten up the house. I'll get some seed tomorrow."

"No, no. I didn't mean . . . Mrs. Dunn, look here. This is a firetrap! And that chicken ——"

"I have two more, visiting with the neighbors."

"Well, that, Mrs. Dunn, is a relief. I thought *all* the tenants had gone insane."

"No, 'tis only m'self. But I do think I'm as sane as you, if not a bit saner. Because you see, I shall have the freshest vegetables in the city of New York. I already have the freshest eggs."

"Those chickens in an apartment are a health hazard. You'll have to remove them! Sell them to a farmer or a butcher."

"I shan't. They stay right here."

"That's unreasonable. I'm a reasonable man, Mrs. Dunn. Say something reasonable, *ask* something reasonable, and I'll say, *That's* reasonable."

"Very well. Why don't you pretend that you hadn't come at all today. Then you wouldn't have seen anything, would you, and your mind would rest easy," said Mrs. Dunn.

"Completely unreasonable!" said Mr. Warfield. "And *that's* why you tenants don't like me — because I'm reasonable and you're all *un*reasonable. Simple as that."

"Oh, I like you, Mr. Warfield," said Mrs. Dunn.

"Nonsense."

"Any landlord who would offer me the use of his roof for a fine little garden must be a very likable *and* reasonable man."

"I didn't offer you any roof, Mrs. Dunn."

"You were going to; I saw it on the tip of your lips."

"My lips?"

"And you were going to say how much better 'twould be if the chickens had a much bigger coop up there on the roof."

"*I* was never going to say ——"

"Tut tut, Mr. Warfield." said Mrs. Dunn. "You've as good as said it. And I was going to answer that for such generosity you should surely receive some fresh string beans and onions and potatoes in season. And you were going to say, 'Ah, and how lovely the roof would look with greenery all about.' And I was about to answer, 'Yes, Mr. Warfield, and the tenants would surely look at you most affectionately.' Would they not, now?"

"*Hmm*," said Mr. Warfield, thinking.

"Reasonable or unreasonable?" asked Mrs. Dunn.

"*Hmm* . . . well . . . I'd have to give this some thought."

"But you're a man of *action*, Mr. Warfield. You pound on the door like a very tiger."

"Yes, well . . . it's not *un*-reasonable," said Mr. Warfield. "If you didn't already *have* any chickens or trees or onions, I would say no. But since you *do* have all this *jungle* of creatures and vines . . . I would, after careful consideration, being after all a human being, I would . . . *ahem, ahem* . . . say . . . *ahem* . . . yes."

"Oh, you are a darling man, Mr. Warfield. A darling, *darling* man."

"Here, Mrs. Dunn! Watch your language! I mean to say! *Darling* man?"

"Oh, back in the old country, it only means you're nice, that's all."

"Oh. Now do remember, Mrs. Dunn, a bargain's a bargain. I expect one tenth of everything you grow as my roof rent. Is that a deal?"

" 'Tis a deal, Mr. Warfield," said Mrs. Dunn.

"Except the onions. You can keep them all. I hate onions. My whole family hates onions."

And with that, Mr. Warfield slammed his hat on his head, only to find it was still wet from Mrs. Dunn's watering can. Without a word, he turned and stalked out to the living room. At that moment, Amelia — or was it Adeline up on the chandelier? —decided it was time to come down. For there, on top of Mr. Warfield's head, was her nest-shaped-like-a-hat, moving by. And down she came, wings beating, feathers flying, on top of Mr. Warfield's head. Mr. Warfield raced to the hallway with the chicken flapping on top of him.

"She likes you!" called Mrs. Dunn. "She knows you have a good heart! Chickens can tell right off!"

But Mr. Warfield didn't hear this very clearly, for as he raced out to the hallway and down the stairs, all three chickens started their *berawk-bawk*ing again. The loudest of all was the one on top of Mr. Warfield. He finally escaped by leaving his nest-shaped-like-a-hat behind.

And so Mrs. Dunn moved everything to the roof, and Mr. Dunn added still more boxes for vegetables. Cathy and Neil and their friends went up to the roof every afternoon to feed the chickens and water the plants. And Mrs. Dunn had her lovely, lovely farm — or at least she thought she did, which comes to the same thing in the end.

AUTHOR

Myron Levoy was born and grew up in New York City. He says of his childhood, "When I was very young, vegetables and ice were still sold from horse-drawn wagons, and chickens were still kept in some backyards. A ride on the Second Avenue el, above the push-carts and crowds, was a trip across the known world. In our apartment building, seven languages were spoken: Russian, Italian, German, Yiddish, Lithuanian, Hungarian, and Polish. Oh, yes, and English, with a half-dozen accents." All this has found its way into Mr. Levoy's first book for young readers, *The Witch of Fourth Street,* from which this story was taken.

Besides being a writer, Mr. Levoy is an aerospace engineer who has helped develop an atomic engine for rockets and spaceships.

SKILL

Dictionary: Pronunciation

Sometimes as you read, you come to a word you have not seen before. You know that you can get the meaning for a word from reading the other words and sentences around it or you can use a glossary or dictionary. What do you do if you do not know how to pronounce the word? You can use a dictionary to find the pronunciation of a word too.

What is a special spelling?

Each entry word in a glossary or dictionary is printed in syllables. There is a small dot between each syllable. After each entry word is a special spelling that shows you how to pronounce the word. Here is the way the word *telephone,* a word you know, usually looks in a glossary or dictionary with its special spelling:

tel·e·phone (tĕl′ə fōn′)

The **special spelling** of a word shows the sounds of letters and letter combinations in that word. The consonants in a special spelling stand for the sounds that you know for those consonants. For example, in the special spelling, **tĕl′ə fōn′,** the **t, l, f,** and **n** stand for the sounds you know for those letters. To get the sounds for the vowels in a special spelling, you need to learn how to use a pronunciation key.

Grateful acknowledgment is made for permission to reprint the pronunciation key from *The American Heritage School Dictionary.* Copyright © 1972, 1977, Houghton Mifflin Company. Adapted by permission of *The American Heritage School Dictionary.*

What is a pronunciation key?

A **pronunciation key** is a section placed at the bottom of every page or every other page of a glossary or dictionary to show you how to pronounce some letters in the special spelling. The glossary in this book uses this pronunciation key:

ă pat / ā pay / â care / ä father / ĕ pet / ē be / ĭ pit / ī pie / î fierce / ŏ pot / ō go / ô paw, for / oi oil / o͝o book / o͞o boot / ou out / ŭ cut / û fur / *th* the / th thin / hw which / zh vision / ə ago, item, pencil, atom, circus

Look again at the special spelling for *telephone.* You know what the **t** stands for. After **t** is **ĕ.** To find the sound that **ĕ** stands for, look at the pronunciation key. The word p**e**t comes right after ĕ. That is the **key word** for the sound of ĕ in a special spelling. Always listen for the sound of the heavy, dark letter in a key word. Say p**e**t to yourself and listen for the sound of **ĕ.** That is the sound of the first *e* in *telephone.*

In the middle of the special spelling for *telephone,* you see this mark: ə. This mark is called a **schwa.** Find the schwa in the pronunciation key. After ə are five key words: **a**go, it**e**m, penc**i**l, at**o**m, and circ**u**s. Notice that a different letter is in heavy, dark type in each key word. The letters in heavy, dark type are different, but they all stand for the same sound. Say each key word to yourself and listen for the sound of the heavy, dark letter in each. That sound is the one that you hear in the second syllable of *telephone.*

Look at the last part of the special spelling, **tĕl'ə fōn'.** Notice that the sound for f is the sound *ph* stands for in *telephone.* In a special spelling, the consonant or consonants used to show a sound may be different from the one or ones used in the regular spelling of the word.

Now find the ō in the pronunciation key. The key word g**o** after the ō tells you the ō in the last part of the special spelling has the same sound as the letter **o** in the word g**o**.

Notice that the regular spelling of *telephone* has an *e* at the end of it, while the special spelling, **tĕl′**ə fōn′, does not. If the final *e* in the regular spelling of a word is not sounded, there is no symbol for it in the special spelling.

There is one more thing that you need to know to be absolutely sure what the word *telephone* should sound like. You need to know how to read the stress marks in the special spelling of the word.

What are primary and secondary stress marks?

When you say a word that has more than one syllable, you say one of those syllables with more stress, or force, than the others. Now look again at the special spelling of *telephone,* **tĕl′**ə fōn′. The heavy, dark mark after the first part (′) is called a **primary stress mark.** It tells you that **tĕl** is said with more stress than the other parts of the word.

In some words, more than one syllable is stressed. Usually one of those syllables has a weaker stress than the other stressed syllable. In the special spelling, the part with the weaker stress is shown by a secondary stress mark (′). That mark is not as heavy and dark as the primary stress mark. Look at the secondary stress mark after the last part of **tĕl′**ə fōn′.

Say *telephone* quietly to yourself. Notice that the first part, **tĕl′**, is said with the most stress. Notice that the last part, fōn′, is said with more stress than the second part, ə, but not with as much stress as the first part, **tĕl′**.

Most dictionaries have the stress mark after the part that should be stressed. Some dictionaries place the stress mark before the stressed part. Before you use a dictionary, read in the front part the explanation of the marks used in that dictionary to find out how that dictionary uses stress marks.

REVIEW

Now review what you have learned about using a dictionary to get pronunciation. To do this, read the question that is the first heading. Then answer that question to yourself in your own words. Do the same thing with the other two heading questions.

USING A DICTIONARY TO GET PRONUNCIATION

Use the pronunciation key on page 95 to get the correct pronunciation of the word shown in heavy, dark type in each of the numbered sentences below. You have probably heard these words, but you may not have seen them in print. On a separate paper, write the number of each sentence and the answer to the question that follows the sentence.

1. Jane will **advertise** (ăd′vər tīz′) in the newspaper that she has three puppies for sale.
   Which key word in the pronunciation key tells you the sound of *a* in *advertise*?

2. Will you **guarantee** (găr′ən tē′) that this bicycle will be in working order for at least a year?
   Which key word in the pronunciation key tells you the sound of *ee* in *guarantee*?

3. If you use the large glass to **magnify** (măg′nə fī′) the small print, you can read the sentence.
   Which key word in the pronunciation key tells you the sound of *y* in *magnify*?

4. The **engineer** (ĕn′jə nîr′) showed us drawings of bridges that she had planned.
   Is the secondary, or weaker, stress on the first or last syllable of *engineer*?

The Wolf and the Boy

by E. C. FOSTER
and SLIM WILLIAMS

During a spring thaw, a young Alaskan Inuit boy is caught on floating ice with a young wolf. By the time they get back to shore, having drifted far to the south, they are firm friends. The boy — he will choose his own name when he is ten — and the wolf, Agorek, spend the summer together traveling through strange territory as they make their way toward home.

Where the wolf hunted, the boy followed. And the wolf hunted where the quarry led. So, even though their goal lay just to the west of north, the trail they used went every way — west, south, west down a stream for fish, then around all points of the compass after a fast and clever rabbit that doubled back on its tracks. Between side trips, they tried to move fairly straight into the north.

So the warm days passed as they wandered and played. Most days were sunny, though sometimes there were clouds

and a whisper of coming cold. Most of the time they feasted. Sometimes they went hungry.

One day the wolf smelled game and raced off to follow the smell. He was not really hunting, just having fun. Before long he came loping back. The boy paid no attention.

But when the wolf stopped dead still some way off, the boy looked up to see why. For a moment the wolf stood very still. Then he came on, slowly, carefully. He stopped again, his eyes fixed past the boy, who turned to see where the wolf was looking.

There, quite close by, was another wolf. The boy wasn't frightened. The strange wolf was a young one, a little smaller than the boy's companion. And neither animal was paying the smallest attention to the boy.

Agorek raised his head very high. He held his ears back, close against the sides of his head. This made his head look very narrow and very long from the sharp tips of his ears to the sharp point of his nose. Then he started forward again, walking on his very tiptoes, raising each paw high at every step.

The strange wolf stood perfectly still, its nose a little raised, almost as if it didn't care. But its eyes never left the prancing Agorek.

As he came near, the smaller wolf sat down on its haunches, silent, still, not unfriendly, just watching. And the bigger wolf fairly danced on his tiptoes as he circled the smaller one.

A quick thought of how he himself had sometimes acted when She-Who-Came-With-the-Flowers was present, crossed the boy's mind.

At last understanding came to him. The strange wolf was a young female. Agorek was just acting like a boy showing off in front of a girl.

The boy thought it was funny. But he was polite, staying quietly just where he was. He grinned, but he didn't laugh out loud. The two wolves saw nothing but each other.

From the west, the direction from which the little wolf had come, a long, high, wolf song sounded. Boy and wolves turned toward the song. On top of a high chain of hills, a line of wolves was outlined against the sky. Two of them were very big.

The little wolves beside the boy perked up their ears. The boy felt a quick pain of sorrow. Agorek might leave him and go back to his own kind.

The pack on the hilltop started down, and the little female ran to meet them. But Agorek ran to the boy and nudged him off in the other direction. The wolf's eyes were wide with fear.

In panic, the two ran as fast as they could until the boy could barely keep going. They soon saw that running was the worst thing they could have done. Neither of them could match the speed of the full-grown wolves.

As they ran, a narrow gully split the earth before them. The boy ran to one side of it, the wolf to the other. Instantly the pack moved toward the wolf, away from the boy.

"Agorek, stay with me!" the boy screamed. Then he jumped across the narrow crack. They ran on some little way, but the boy was slowing down.

The pack was close behind them when they neared a rocky place. Boulders piled up twelve or fifteen feet high.

They ran to a little V-shaped cleft between high rocks and turned on the pack. Agorek snarled to keep up his courage, and the boy, his jade ax in one hand and his driftwood harpoon handle in the other, stood ready to lash out at any wolf who came within range.

But when Agorek and the boy stopped running, so did the pack. They arranged themselves in a half circle some way off. The chase stopped while both decided what to do next.

The boy had heard that wolves love the young of any kind and will take them in and care for them if they are left alone and helpless. He and Agorek were young, certainly, but, he guessed, not young enough. Nobody could call them babies. He remembered his father saying he had never heard of a wolf attacking a person. But he had heard of wolves killing a strange wolf caught hunting within their range. It was Agorek who was in danger, then. It was clearly up to the boy to protect the little wolf.

The boy tried to keep the wolf behind him, but the wolf, wanting to protect the boy, stayed between him and the attackers.

At the center of the half circle were two huge wolves, the parent wolves of the pack. To either side of them crowded two almost full-grown wolves, two half-grown, and three from last year's litter. One of these three was the little female they had seen first. They were a family. The boy knew the pack is always a family, unless there is a lone wolf who has lost its mate. His father had said a wolf never mates a second time.

The boy's ax and stick were ready, but he was sure the pressing pack would not attack as long as he stayed alert. He

was afraid, however, that the instant he dropped his guard, the pack would come at his friend.

One of the younger wolves climbed up the rocks and howled down at Agorek from high above. But at a growl from an older one, he came back down. They all stayed a careful distance away from the boy. That puzzled him. It wasn't that they were afraid of him. He was sure they weren't afraid. It was more as if they thought him no fit enemy. He was outside the range of their anger.

He knew how he might gain a little help, but he needed time. Evergreeen scrub grew thickly in cracks between the rocks, and there was a deep covering of dry needles on the ground all around. He scraped together as much as he could with the side of his foot and kicked the needles into a heap out past the rocks.

The wolves had settled down, sitting back on their haunches. With their enemy trapped, the pack was content to wait the boy out.

The boy was glad for this, for he could use the time it gave him. Agorek had stopped panting, but he was far from settling down. He knew his danger. The boy took the jade arrowhead from his pocket. With the wolf standing guard above him, he crouched over the heap of dried needles.

He held the jade ax close to the needles and struck it sharply with the jade arrowhead. Nothing happened.

Every eye in the wolf pack watched him. The young wolf who had scrambled up the rocks moved in a step closer. The boy struck rock on rock again. Still nothing happened.

The eager young wolf inched in more. One of the parent wolves growled, and the eager one inched back. Again the boy struck jade on jade. This time the dry needles flashed into quick flames, and the wolves tumbled back before this strange new danger.

The boy looked about him as the flames flared and died. There was dead wood from the evergreen scrub all around. Without going too far from the hollow, he could keep a small fire going for some hours.

So they sat and waited. Presently all the wolves of the pack lay down. The big ones watched wide-eyed. Some of the younger ones curled up asleep.

It was very quiet. The sun had come more than two-thirds of the way down from its highest point, and all the birds and animals who lived on the tundra were sleeping.

The only sounds were the slow crackle of the little fire and the boy speaking softly to the wolf.

"Agorek, you must understand, I am in no danger. The wolves won't hurt me. I am in no danger. But you must stay behind me, so I can protect you. The fire will keep them off while we rest. Then we'll think of some way out. I'm sure we will."

He stroked his friend's fur. "Only stay close to me," he said. "I wish I could make you promise."

But Agorek did not seem to believe that the boy was safe from the pack. And the boy knew the wolf would fight to the death to protect his friend from danger.

The warm summer day wore on. Except for watching, Agorek lay quiet beside the boy in their spot between the rocky cliff and the fire.

The red sun dropped below the horizon, and it was twilight across the tundra. The boy added a few sticks to the fire and tried to shake off sleep. It was only a few hours to midnight, and soon after that, the sun would start up again.

Then the birds would waken and the animals would be up and about their business, the boy told himself. It wouldn't be so hard to stay awake. Just now, he was weary. But he must not sleep! He must not!

The fire died down until its glow was hidden under gray ash. The boy's head dropped. Agorek got to his feet and silently placed himself in front of the sleeping boy. For a brief time there was no sound. All the tundra was quiet.

But the active young wolf of the pack was awake. He watched the fire die. Then he saw his enemy move out. He couldn't hold himself back.

The boy awakened at Agorek's angry roar and saw the two young wolves leap at each other. He hit out with his driftwood stick and tried to get between wolf and wolf.

The one from the pack, trying to reach Agorek, knocked the boy to the ground, almost into the ashes. His kicking feet stirred the ashes as he struggled up. The fire blazed again, and the young wolf rolled back away from it. His nose was smarting from the crack of the boy's stick. The sting of Agorek's teeth marks was in his throat.

He ran back to the pack and was scolded with growls. But when he crept up close to the parent wolves, head down and tail drooping, they stopped their scolding, and the female bent her head and licked the smarting nose.

The excitement was over almost before it began. There was no sleep in the boy's eyes now. He had never been more wide awake. The angry fur stood up around Agorek's neck.

"We'll have to leave here," the boy said. "We can't stay."

They couldn't hunt. They had no water. It was better to go back than to stay where they were. They were safe from attack, perhaps, but they were held in what was really a trap.

The boy looked out over the tundra. Already there was a hint of the glow of dawn to the east of the northern horizon. He heard the first sleepy honk of a goose off somewhere behind the rocks.

His driftwood harpoon handle had cracked when he had hit the little wolf. He would have to get another one. But the handle was still much longer than any of the branches of

the low evergreen scrub, so he held it in the dying fire until the end was burning.

Then, with Agorek tense and shaking, the two moved out from the little hollow. They moved along beside the cliff, keeping the shelter of the rocks at their backs as long as they could.

The wolves were quickly on their feet, keeping close watch on the two. But they made no sudden forward move, for the fire followed the boy and Agorek.

Wherever dry leaves or evergreen needles or caribou moss were within reach, the boy set fire to them, and he and the wolf ran as the pack held back before each quick blaze.

"It's wicked to burn the caribou moss," the boy said. "But we need the fire right now more than the caribou need the moss."

His fear for Agorek made him wish the whole of the spreading tundra would flame up. But in his heart he hoped only as much would burn as was needed for their escape.

It was still too early for the ground plants or the leaves of the willows to be dry, but there were enough fallen leaves and needles and woody stalks from the dead growth of other years to keep a trail of blazes between the pair and the pack.

They passed a drift of dead willows in a dry creek bed. The boy chose several long branches and broke them out. He lighted one of them and threw what was left of his burning driftwood handle into the bare dried-out trees.

With that big blaze between them and the pack, they hurried ahead to where the ground appeared to slope down. When they looked back, they could see the course of the dry creek bed across the tundra by the line of burning trees. No wolves had yet crossed that line.

When they reached the beginning of the gentle slope, the plants and shrubs were greener ahead of them. They went doggedly on, not knowing how far the wolves might track them. In the distance there were thickly growing trees, not very tall. The trees ahead must surely mean water. And the boy thought — hoped — a stream might mark the edge of the land the wolves thought of as their range. Soon there were trees on each side of them as well as in front, and when they reached the water, the boy found they were on a long peninsula in the deep bend of a broad river.

The river was much too wide to cross, and it looked deep. They would have to go back. But first the boy threw himself down on the river edge, and the wolf waded into the cold water. The two drank long and thirstily.

They started to return the way they had come. But there, just coming into view above the long slope, was the wolf pack. If the two tried to go back across the neck of land, the pack would be too close for them to find another way across the river.

There was nowhere to go. The coarse fur at the wolf's neck and back rose in anger. He growled deep in his throat. The boy knew the wolf would fight courageously to his last breath. He wouldn't give in. The boy wouldn't give in either, but his fear was for the wolf.

Fire had helped them before. Again it was their only chance. The boy ran among the trees, breaking off dead branches and gathering up dried underbrush and leaves. Fuel was plentiful.

He was glad he had stopped to light a new length of wood each time the one he carried burned short. The sparks had caught on the third try in the dry needles back at the V-shaped hollow in the rocks. But sometimes it took a long time to draw fire from stone. It took even longer to draw it from wood on wood.

They soon had a generous fire blazing near the land end of the peninsula. Now they were fairly safe from any of the pack coming on to their long tongue of land.

The area they held was too limited to promise any hunting. From time to time a bird might fly in, and the river was big enough to provide plenty of fish. Even so, they could stay only a short time.

The boy cut down a young willow tree and fashioned a new handle for his harpoon. They might as well eat something while he figured out how to get across the river. He was sure they'd be safe on the other shore.

Of course, Agorek could swim across to safety. But the boy knew they'd have to go together or not at all. The brave and loyal wolf would never leave him to face the pack alone.

So while they fished and feasted, the wolf kept watch and the boy tried to figure out what to do. From time to time, he gathered more wood and fed the fire. Close to the river's edge, he found a big driftwood log, bent and forked like a wide letter Y.

Seeing the log gave him the beginning of a plan. A straight log will roll in the water, but a crooked log will float with the same side always on top. The branch forking out on this one would make this log lie flat.

The sun was dropping to the west again, and birds and wolves were appearing to settle down to sleep. Only the whole pack never slept. One or two at least were always awake and ready.

The boy shivered a little. He wished he might wait until the next day, but he knew better than to chance falling asleep again as he had the night before.

He cut several long thin willow whips and heated them over the flames. Then he slipped out of his parka and pants and mukluks, folded his clothes carefully, and tied everything to the Y-shaped log with the hot soft willow whips.

He placed a tall, burning stick upright in the notch of the fork when everything else was ready. As long as they were anywhere near the pack, he didn't dare be without the defense of fire.

"Now, Agorek," he said, "Please come help me swim."

He launched the log from the far tip of the peninsula. The water was bitterly cold to the naked boy. He shivered until his teeth rattled, but he held tightly to Agorek's fur with one hand and clung to the log with the other.

They did well until they got out into the middle of the

river. Here the current was unexpectedly fast and strong. Try as he would, Agorek couldn't keep the boy and the log from being swept downstream.

This brought them in close to land again, past the fire, and very near the place from which the wolves were watching. The pack moved toward the river's edge.

They were closing in when the boy's feet touched bottom.

"Over here, Agorek," he cried, but as soon as the boy's fingers loosened, the wolf swam to the downstream side of the raft. The boy gave a mighty push to start them out into the current again.

This time, with the wolf pushing at the log to keep it on course, they were able to struggle through the current around the peninsula. After what seemed a long, cold time to the boy, they landed safely downstream on the far shore.

While the wolf shook the water from his fur, the boy climbed gratefully back into his warm, dry clothes.

He looked back across the river and was glad to see no wolves along the shore. Only two of the pack were in sight, going away up the green slope. As the boy had hoped, the river marked the edge of the pack's range.

Thankfully, tired boy and weary wolf sank down on the river bank. It was very late. The sun had begun a new day, and the birds and animals were already up and about their business.

In the book **The Friend of the Singing One** *by E. C. Foster and Slim Williams, you can read about other adventures the boy and the wolf have before they finally reach their home area.*

AUTHORS

Elizabeth C. Foster and Clyde (Slim) Williams together wrote two books on Alaskan life, *The Friend of the Singing One,* part of which you have just read, and *The Long Hungry Night.* The authors were working on a third story set in Alaska when Mr. Williams died in 1974.

Mrs. Foster, who has lived in Illinois, Tennessee, and Florida, enjoys gardening, needlework, traveling, and especially reading. She says that she carries a book with her everywhere she goes.

Mr. Williams went to Alaska when he was eighteen, and he stayed for thirty-two years. In 1932, upset by the harm being done to fish and animals there, he drove a dog team from Alaska to Washington, D.C., to ask President Hoover to protect Alaskan wildlife.

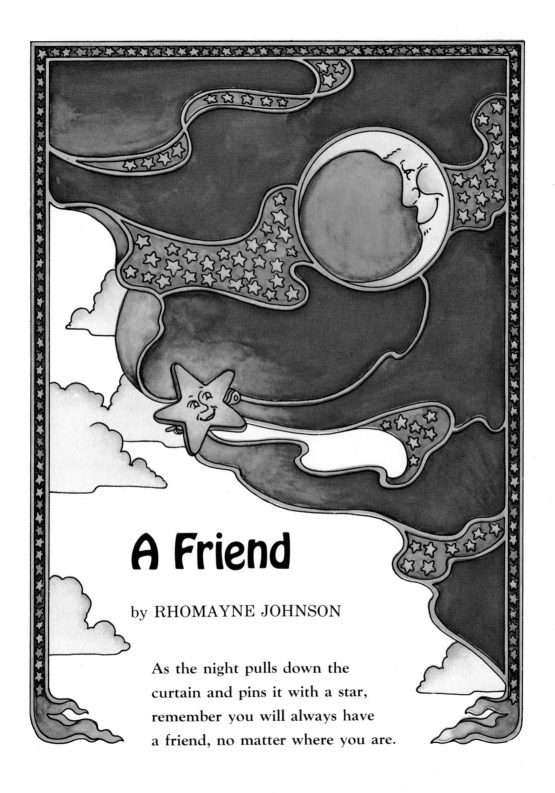

A Friend

by RHOMAYNE JOHNSON

As the night pulls down the
curtain and pins it with a star,
remember you will always have
a friend, no matter where you are.

from

Little House on the Prairie

by LAURA INGALLS WILDER

The book *Little House on the Prairie* tells about the adventures of a pioneer family who traveled west in a covered wagon and settled on the grassy prairie of Kansas. The author, Laura Ingalls Wilder, really was the little Laura in the story.

After traveling for many days across the prairie, Laura's father finally found a good spot near a creek to build their new home. Mr. Edwards, who lived two miles away and was their nearest neighbor, helped her father build a log cabin. The cabin wasn't completely finished right away because a stable had to be built for the family's horses, Pet and Patty. But even though the cabin was without a fireplace, had no door or windows, and had only the bare ground for a floor, Laura and her family felt snug and safe inside it.

The story you are about to read is only a part of the book. In it, Mrs. Wilder tells about an exciting time when she and her family were especially grateful for the safety that their little house on the prairie provided.

The Wolf Pack

All in one day, Pa and Mr. Edwards built the stable for Pet and Patty. They even put the roof on, working so late that Ma had to keep supper waiting for them.

There was no stable door, but in the moonlight Pa drove two big posts well into the ground, one on either side of the doorway. He put Pet and Patty inside the stable, and then he laid small split logs one above another, across the door space. The posts held them, and they made a solid wall.

"Now!" said Pa. "Let those wolves howl! I'll sleep tonight."

In the morning when Pa lifted the split logs from behind the posts, Laura was amazed. Beside Pet stood a long-legged, long-eared, wobbly little colt.

When Laura ran toward it, gentle Pet laid back her ears and snapped her teeth at Laura.

"Keep back, Laura!" Pa said sharply. He said to Pet, "Now, Pet, you know we won't hurt your little colt." Pet answered

him with a soft whinny. She would let Pa stroke her colt, but she would not let Laura or Mary come near it. When they even peeked at it through the cracks in the stable wall, Pet rolled the whites of her eyes at them and showed them her teeth. They had never seen a colt with ears so long. Pa said it was a little mule, but Laura said it looked like a jack rabbit. So they named the little colt Bunny.

When Pet was on the picket line, with Bunny frisking around her and wondering at the big world, Laura had to watch Baby Carrie carefully. If anyone but Pa came near Bunny, Pet squealed with rage and dashed to bite that little girl.

Early that Sunday afternoon, Pa rode Patty away across the prairie to see what he should see. There was plenty of meat in the house, so he did not take his gun.

He rode away through the tall grass, along the rim of the creek bluffs. Birds flew up before him and circled and sank into the grasses. Pa was looking down into the creek bottoms as he rode. Perhaps he was watching deer browsing there. Then Patty broke into a gallop, and swiftly she and Pa grew smaller. Soon there was only waving grass where they had been.

Late that afternoon Pa had not come home. Ma stirred the coals of the fire, laid chips on them, and began to get supper. Mary was in the house, minding the baby, and Laura asked Ma, "What's the matter with Jack?"

Jack was walking up and down, looking worried. He wrinkled his nose at the wind, and the hair rose up on his neck and lay down, and then rose up again. Pet's hoofs suddenly thudded. She ran around the circle of her picket rope and stood still, whickering a low whicker. Bunny came close to her.

"What's the matter, Jack?" Ma asked. He looked up at her, but he couldn't say anything, Ma gazed around the whole circle of earth and sky. She could not see anything unusual.

"Likely it isn't anything, Laura," she said. She raked coals around the coffeepot and the spider and onto the top of the bake oven. The prairie hen sizzled in the spider; the corn-cakes began to smell good. But all the time, Ma kept glancing at the prairie all around. Jack walked about restlessly, and Pet did not graze. She faced the northwest, where Pa had gone, and kept her colt close beside her.

All at once Patty came running across the prairie. She was stretched out, running with all her might, and Pa was leaning almost flat on her neck.

She ran right past the stable before Pa could stop her. He stopped her so hard that she almost sat down. She was trembling all over and the black coat was streaked with sweat and foam. Pa swung off her. He was breathing hard too.

"What is the matter, Charles?" Ma asked him.

Pa was looking toward the creek, so Ma and Laura looked at it too. But they could see only the space above the bottomlands, with a few treetops in it, and the distant tops of the earthen bluffs under the High Prairie's grasses.

"What is it?" Ma asked again. "Why did you ride Patty like that?"

Pa breathed a long breath. "I was afraid the wolves would beat me here. But I see everything's all right."

"Wolves!" she cried. "What wolves?"

"Everything's all right, Caroline," said Pa. "Let a fellow get his breath."

When he had got some breath, he said, "I didn't ride Patty like that. It was all I could do to hold her at all. Fifty wolves, Caroline, the biggest wolves I ever saw. I wouldn't go through such a thing again, not for a mint of money."

A shadow came over the prairie just then because the sun had gone down, and Pa said, "I'll tell you about it later."

"We'll eat supper in the house," said Ma.

"No need of that," he told her. "Jack will give us warning in plenty of time."

He brought Pet and her colt from the picket line. He didn't take them and Patty to drink from the creek, as he usually did. He gave them the water in Ma's washtub, which was standing full, ready for the washing next morning. He rubbed down Patty's sweaty sides and legs and put her in the barn with Pet and Bunny.

Supper was ready. The campfire made a circle of light in the dark. Laura and Mary stayed close to the fire and kept Baby Carrie with them. They could feel the dark all around them, and they kept looking behind them at the place where the dark mixed with the edge of the firelight. Shadows moved there, as if they were alive.

Jack sat on his haunches beside Laura. The edges of his ears were lifted, listening to the dark. Now and then he walked a little way into it. He walked all around the campfire and came back to sit beside Laura. The hair lay flat on his thick neck and he did not growl. His teeth showed a little, but that was because he was a bulldog.

Laura and Mary ate their corncakes and the prairie hen's drumsticks and listened while Pa told Ma about the wolves.

He had found some more neighbors. Settlers were coming in and settling along both sides of the creek. Less than three miles away, in a hollow on the High Prairie, a man and his wife were building a house. Their name was Scott, and Pa said they were nice folks. Six miles beyond them, two bachelors were living in one house. They had taken two farms and built the house on the line between them. One man's bunk was against one wall of the house, and the other man's bunk was against the other wall. So each man slept on his own farm, although they were in the same house and the house was only eight feet wide. They cooked and ate together in the middle of the house.

Pa had not said anything about the wolves yet. Laura wished he would. But she knew that she must not interrupt when Pa was talking.

He said that these bachelors did not know that other settlers were in the country. They had seen only Indians. So they were glad to see Pa. And he stayed there longer than he had meant to.

Then he rode on, and from a little rise in the prairie, he saw a white speck down in the creek bottoms. He thought it was a covered wagon, and it was. When he came to it, he found a man and woman and five children. They had come from Iowa, and they had camped in the bottoms because one of their horses was sick. The horse was better now, but the bad night air so near the creek had given them fever 'n' ague. The man and woman and the three oldest children were too sick to stand up. The little boy and girl, no bigger than Mary and Laura, were taking care of them.

So Pa did what he could for them, and then he rode back to tell the bachelors about them. One of them rode right away to fetch that family up onto the High Prairie, where they would soon get well in the good air.

One thing had led to another, until Pa was starting home later than he had meant. He took a shortcut across the prairie, and as he was loping along on Patty, suddenly out of a little draw came a pack of wolves. They were all around Pa in a moment.

"It was a big pack," Pa said. "All of fifty wolves, and the biggest wolves I ever saw in my life. Must be what they call buffalo wolves. Their leader's a big gray brute that stands

three feet at the shoulder, if an inch. I tell you my hair stood straight on end."

"And you didn't have your gun," said Ma.

"I thought of that. But my gun would have been no use if I'd had it. You can't fight fifty wolves with one gun. And Patty couldn't outrun them."

"What did you do?" Ma asked.

"Nothing," said Pa. "Patty tried to run. I never wanted anything worse than I wanted to get away from there. But I knew if Patty even started, those wolves would be on us in a minute, pulling us down. So I held Patty to a walk."

"Goodness, Charles!" Ma said under her breath.

"Yes. I wouldn't go through such a thing again for any money. Caroline, I never saw such wolves. One big fellow trotted along, right by my stirrup. I could have kicked him in the ribs. They didn't pay any attention to me at all. They must have just made a kill and eaten all they could.

"I tell you, Caroline, those wolves just closed in around Patty and me and trotted along with us. In broad daylight. For all the world like a pack of dogs going along with a horse. They were all around us, trotting along, and jumping and playing and snapping at each other, just like dogs."

"Goodness, Charles!" Ma said again. Laura's heart was thumping fast, and her mouth and her eyes were wide open, staring at Pa.

"Patty was shaking all over and fighting the bit," said Pa. "Sweat ran off her, she was so scared. I was sweating too. But I held her down to a walk, and we went walking along among those wolves. They came right along with us, a quarter of a mile or more. That big fellow trotted by my stirrup as if he were there to stay.

"Then we came to the head of a draw running down into the creek bottoms. The big gray leader went down it, and all the rest of the pack trotted down into it behind him. As soon as the last one was in the draw, I let Patty go.

"She headed straight for home, across the prairie. And she couldn't have run faster if I'd been cutting into her with a rawhide whip. I was scared the whole way. I thought the wolves might be coming this way and they might be making better time than I was. I was glad you had the gun, Caroline. And glad the house is built. I knew you could keep the wolves out of the house with the gun. But Pet and the colt were outside."

"You need not have worried, Charles," Ma said. "I guess I would manage to save our horses."

"I was not fully reasonable at the time," said Pa. "I know you would save the horses, Caroline. Those wolves wouldn't bother you, anyway. If they had been hungry, I wouldn't be here to —"

"Little pitchers have big ears," Ma said. She meant that he must not frighten Mary and Laura.

"Well, all's well that ends well," Pa replied. "And those wolves are miles from here by now."

"What made them act like that?" Laura asked him.

"I don't know, Laura," he said. "I guess they had just eaten all they could hold, and they were on their way to the creek to get a drink. Or perhaps they were out playing on the prairie, and not paying any attention to anything but their play, like you do sometimes. Perhaps they saw that I didn't have my gun and couldn't do them any harm. Or perhaps they had never seen a man before and didn't know that men can do them harm. So they didn't think about me at all."

Pet and Patty were restlessly walking around and around inside the barn. Jack walked around the campfire. When he stood still to smell the air and listen, the hair lifted on his neck.

"Bedtime for little girls!" Ma said cheerfully. Not even Baby Carrie was sleepy yet, but Ma took them all into the house. She told Mary and Laura to go to bed, and she put Baby Carrie's little nightgown on and laid her in the big bed. Then she went outdoors to do the dishes. Laura wanted Pa and Ma in the house. They seemed so far away outside.

Mary and Laura were good and lay still, but Carrie sat up and played by herself in the dark. In the dark Pa's arm came from behind the quilt in the doorway and quietly took away his gun. Out by the campfire, the tin plates rattled. Then a knife scraped the spider. Ma and Pa were talking together.

The house was safe, but it did not feel safe because Pa's gun was not over the door and there was no door; there was only the quilt.

After a long time, Ma lifted the quilt. Baby Carrie was asleep then. Ma and Pa came in very quietly, and very quietly went to bed. Jack lay across the doorway, but his chin was not on his paws. His head was up, listening. Ma breathed softly, Pa breathed heavily, and Mary was asleep too. But Laura strained her eyes in the dark to watch Jack. She could not tell whether the hair was standing up on his neck.

Suddenly she was sitting straight up in bed. She had been asleep. The dark was gone. Moonlight streamed through the window hole and streaks of moonlight came through every

crack in that wall. Pa stood black in the moonlight at the
window. He had his gun.

Right in Laura's ear a wolf howled.

She scringed away from the wall. The wolf was on the
other side of it. Laura was too scared to make a sound. The
cold was not in her backbone only; it was all through her.
Mary pulled the quilt over her head. Jack growled and
showed his teeth at the quilt in the doorway.

"Be still, Jack," Pa said.

Terrible howls curled all around inside the house, and
Laura rose out of bed. She wanted to go to Pa, but she knew
better than to bother him now. He turned his head and saw
her standing in her nightgown.

"Want to see them, Laura?" he asked softly. Laura couldn't
say anything, but she nodded and padded across the ground to

him. He stood his gun against the wall and lifted her up to the window hole.

There in the moonlight sat half a circle of wolves. They sat on their haunches and looked at Laura in the window, and she looked at them. She had never seen such big wolves. The biggest one was taller than Laura. He was taller even than Mary. He sat in the middle, exactly opposite Laura. Everything about him was big — his pointed ears, and his pointed mouth with the tongue hanging out, and his strong shoulders and legs, and his two paws side by side, and his tail curled around the squatting haunch. His coat was shaggy gray and his eyes were glittering green.

Laura clutched her toes into a crack of the wall, and she folded her arms on the window slab, and she looked and looked at that wolf. But she did not put her head through the empty window space into the outdoors where all those wolves sat so near her, shifting their paws and licking their chops. Pa stood firm against her back and kept his arm tight around her middle.

"He's awful big," Laura whispered.

"Yes, and see how his coat shines," Pa whispered into her hair. The moonlight made little glitters in the edges of the shaggy fur, all around the big wolf.

"They are in a ring clear around the house," Pa whispered. Laura pattered beside him to the other window. He leaned his gun against that wall and lifted her up again. There, sure enough, was the other half of the circle of wolves. All their eyes glittered green in the shadow of the house. Laura could hear their breathing. When they saw Pa and Laura looking out, the middle of the circle moved back a little way.

Pet and Patty were squealing and running inside the barn. Their hoofs pounded in the ground and crashed against the walls.

After a moment Pa went back to the other window and Laura went too. They were just in time to see the big wolf lift his nose till it pointed straight at the sky. His mouth opened, and a long howl rose toward the moon.

Then all around the house, the circle of wolves pointed their noses toward the sky and answered him. Their howls shuddered through the house and filled the moonlight and quavered away across the vast silence of the prairie.

"Now go back to bed, little half-pint," Pa said. "Go to sleep. Jack and I will take care of you all."

So Laura went back to bed. But for a long time, she did not sleep. She lay and listened to the breathing of the wolves on the other side of the log wall. She heard the scratch of their claws on the ground and the snuffling of a nose at a crack. She heard the big gray leader howl again and all the others answering him.

But Pa was walking quietly from one window hole to the other, and Jack did not stop pacing up and down before the quilt that hung in the doorway. The wolves might howl, but they could not get in while Pa and Jack were there. So at last Laura fell asleep.

Laura felt a soft warmth on her face and opened her eyes into morning sunshine. Mary was talking to Ma by the camp-fire when Laura ran outdoors in her nightgown. There were no wolves to be seen; only their tracks were thick around the house and the stable.

Pa came whistling up the creek road. He put his gun on its pegs and led Pet and Patty to the creek to drink as usual. He had followed the wolf tracks so far that he knew they were far away now, following a herd of deer.

The mustangs shied at the wolves' tracks and pricked their ears nervously, and Pet kept her colt close at her side. But they went willingly with Pa, who knew there was nothing to fear.

Breakfast was ready. When Pa came back from the creek, they all sat by the fire and ate fried mush and prairie-chicken hash. Pa said he would make a door that very day. He wanted more than a quilt between them and the wolves next time.

AUTHOR

Laura Ingalls Wilder was born in 1867 in a log cabin on the edge of a Wisconsin forest. From there, with her parents and sisters, she journeyed in a covered wagon across Minnesota, Iowa, and Missouri to Kansas, where the family built a cabin on the prairie.

Next they moved to Minnesota, where they lived for several years on a farm on the banks of a creek. Then, when Laura was thirteen, they went west again to the shores of a lake in Dakota Territory. During the very cold winters, they lived in the little town of DeSmet. At the age of fifteen, Laura began to teach school, and three years later she married Almanzo Wilder.

Mrs. Wilder told the story of her own childhood and of growing up in the early West in an award-winning series of books for children. They are *Little House in the Big Woods, Little House on the Prairie, On the Banks of Plum Creek, By the Shores of Silver Lake, The Long Winter, Little Town on the Prairie,* and *These Happy Golden Years.* In *Farmer Boy* she wrote about the childhood of the farm boy, Almanzo, whom she later married.

After their marriage, the Wilders lived, with their daughter Rose, on a farm in Mansfield, Missouri. At the age of sixty-five, Mrs. Wilder wrote the first of her "Little House" books. Her last one was published when she was seventy-six. Laura Ingalls Wilder died in 1957.

Adding Spice

Many cooks use spices to make food taste more interesting. In the same way, words can be used to add spice to what you read, write, and say.

Walk is a simple word — and a very useful one. *Walk* means "to go forward on foot." Think of all the ways people and animals "go forward on foot." They go quickly or slowly. They go carefully or carelessly. They take big steps or small ones. There are as many words to describe the ways that people and animals walk as there are ways of walking.

133

The authors of the story "The Wolf and the Boy" used some words that described ways of walking. At the beginning of the story, you read that "the warm days passed as they [the wolf and the boy] *wandered* and played." The word *wander* means "to walk without going anywhere in particular." It is a *way* of walking. The authors could have said, "The warm days passed as they *walked* and played." If they had, the picture that you would have imagined would not have been the same. The word *wandered* "spiced up" the sentence.

Later in the story, the authors wrote that the wolf "came *loping* back." *To lope* means "to go forward in a steady, easy way, taking very long steps." You've probably seen people *lope*. They swing their arms as they walk. Their bodies seem to sway from side to side. The word *loping* adds more flavor, or spice, than the word *walking* would have.

Do you remember that when Agorek first saw the strange, small wolf, he "fairly danced on his tiptoes as he *circled* the smaller one." The word *circled* tells us that Agorek walked around the small wolf. By using the word *circled* instead of the words *walked around,* the authors make the wolf's action much clearer.

Wander, lope, and *circle* are a few words that have been used in place of the word *walk* to add spice to a story. There are many words, such as *walk,* that people use too often because they don't take the time to think of more interesting words. Check yourself as you speak and write. Think of words that will add spice to what you want to say. For a start, think about words you could use in place of *glad.* It is a word that is used far too often! How could you say "I was *glad* to see her" in a more interesting way?

Books to Enjoy

Chooki and the Ptarmigan by Carol Codd
Chooki is an Inuit girl who cares for a helpless young bird that later saves her life.

Me and the Man on the Moon-Eyed Horse
by Sid Fleischman
In this humorous Old West adventure, young Clint helps to catch a band of robbers, the Step-and-a-half Jackson Gang.

Mary McLeod Bethune by Eloise Greenfield
This biography tells how Mary McLeod, a black girl of long ago, became a famous educator and the founder and president of a college in Florida.

Lu Pan: The Carpenter's Apprentice by Demi Hitz
Here is the unusual true story of a boy of ancient China who became a famous architect and inventor.

A Very Young Gymnast by Jill Krementz
Large photographs and a lively text tell the true story of a ten-year-old girl who is training to be a gymnast.

Sidewalk Fossils by Robert Sommer and Harriet Becker
This book tells about the interesting tracks and prints that can be found in the cement sidewalks of the city, such as footprints, leaf prints, and names of streets and contractors.

Gateways

MAGAZINE TWO

Contents

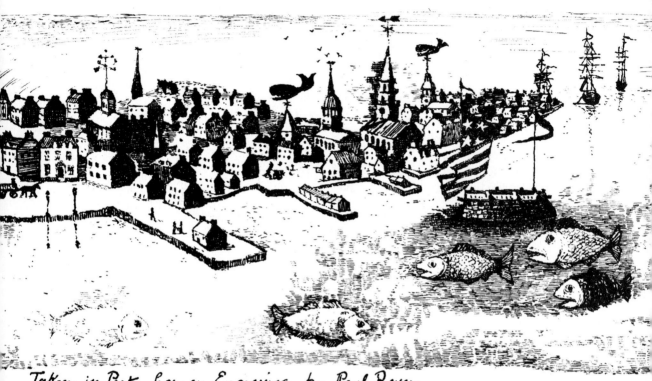

Taken, in Part, from an Engraving by Paul Revere

Paul Revere's Big Ride

by JEAN FRITZ

In 1735 there were in Boston 42 streets, 36 lanes, 22 alleys, 1,000 brick houses, 2,000 wooden houses, 12 churches, 4 schools, 418 horses (at the last count), and so many dogs that a law was passed prohibiting people from having dogs that were more than 10 inches high. But it was difficult to keep dogs from growing more than 10 inches, and few people cared to part with their 11- and 12-inch dogs, so they paid little attention to the law. In any case, there were too many dogs to count.

Along with the horses, streets, and alleys, there were, of course, people in Boston —more than 13,000. Four of them lived in a small wooden house on North Street near Love Lane. They were Mr. Revere, a goldsmith and silversmith; his wife, Deborah; their daughter, Deborah; and their young son, Paul Revere, born the first day of the new year.

Of all the busy people in Boston, Paul Revere would turn out to be one of the busiest. All his life he found that there was more to do, more to make, more to see, more to hear, more to say, more places to go, more to learn than there were hours in the day.

And there was plenty for Paul to do. When he was fifteen years old, his father died, and Paul took over the silversmithing business. He made beads, rings, lockets, bracelets, buttons, medals, pitchers, teapots, spoons, sugar baskets, cups, porringers, shoe buckles, and candlesticks. Once he made a silver collar for a man's pet squirrel.

To make extra money, he took a job ringing the bells in Christ Church. Sometimes at a moment's notice, word would come that the bells were to be rung. Off Paul would run, his hat clapped to his head, his coattails flying.

In 1756, when Paul was twenty-one, he married Sarah Orne, and they began filling up the house with children. There were Deborah, Paul, Sarah, Mary, Frances, and Elizabeth (in addition to two babies who died young). Then his wife, Sarah,

died, and Paul married Rachel Walker. Along came Joshua, Joseph, Harriet, Maria, and John (in addition to three more babies who died young).

Paul kept putting up new chairs at the kitchen table, and now in addition to making buckles, spoons, cups, and all the other silver items, Paul had to find new ways to make money. So he engraved portraits, produced bookplates, sold pictures, made picture frames, brought out hymnbooks, and became a dentist. "Artificial Teeth. Paul Revere," he advertised. "He fixes them in such a Manner that they are not only an Ornament, but of real Use in Speaking and Eating."

You would think that with all Paul Revere did, he would make mistakes. But he always remembered to put spouts on his teapots and handles on his cups.

The false teeth that he whittled out of hippopotamus tusk looked just fine.

Most of the time when he did arithmetic in his daybook, he got the right answers.

Of course, sometimes there were so many different things to do that he forgot what he was doing. In the beginning of a new daybook, he wrote, "This is my book for me to —" But he never finished the sentence.

Sometimes he was in such a hurry that his writing looked sloppy. At the end of a letter he'd write, "Pray excuse my scrawl."

Still, Paul Revere wasn't always at work. Occasionally he just

dreamed. There was one page in his daybook that he used simply for doodling.

But beginning in 1765, there was no time for doodling. The English were causing trouble. They were telling the colonies they couldn't do this and couldn't do that. And they were slapping on taxes, one after another. First there was a tax on printed matter. When this was taken off, there was a tax on tea, glass, printers' colors, and paper. The one tax that England would never give up was the tax on tea.

And what did Paul Revere do about it?

He became a leader of the Sons of Liberty, a secret club that found interesting ways to work against the English.

One of Paul's busiest nights was December 16, 1773. He picked up his ax and joined other Sons of Liberty, all pretending to be Indians.

They were going to make sure that no one in Boston would pay taxes on the three shiploads of tea

that had just arrived from England. So they marched on board the ships, hauled the chests of tea onto the decks, broke them open, and dumped the tea — ten thousand pounds of it — into Boston Harbor. It was all done in an orderly fashion. No one was hurt. No other cargo was touched. The ships were not harmed. (Only one small thing went wrong. A man found stuffing tea into the lining of his coat had to be punished.)

When the Sons of Liberty finished, they marched home, washed their faces, and went to bed.

But not Paul Revere. Someone had to ride to New York and Philadelphia and spread the news. And Paul was picked to do it.

So off he galloped, his hat clapped to his head, his coattails flying. From Boston to Philadelphia and back he went — sixty-three miles a day.

He was back in Boston on the eleventh day. This was long before anyone expected him.

Paul Revere became Massachusetts's Number One express rider between Boston and Philadelphia. He also became a secret agent. In the winter of 1774 it looked more and more as if the English soldiers in Boston meant to make war on America. Paul's job was to try to find out the English plans.

He rode the streets at night, delivered messages to Philadelphia, and kept himself ready at all times to warn the countryside.

But all his rides, Paul knew, were small compared to the Big Ride that lay ahead. Nothing should go wrong with this one. In the spring, everyone agreed, the

English would march into the countryside and really start fighting. And when they did, Paul Revere would have to be ahead of them.

On Saturday, April 15, 1775, spring, it seemed, had arrived. Boats for moving troops had been seen on the Charles River. English scouts had been seen on the road to Lexington and Concord. A stableboy had overheard two officers making plans.

At 10:45 on Tuesday night, April 18, Dr. Joseph Warren, who was directing Patriot activities in Boston, sent for Paul Revere. Other messengers had been sent to Lexington and Concord by longer routes. Paul was to go, as planned, the same way the English were going — across the Charles River. He was to alarm the citizens so they could arm themselves. And he was to inform John Hancock and Samuel Adams, Boston's two Patriot leaders who were staying in Lexington. And he was to leave now.

He had already arranged a quick way of warning the people of Charlestown, across the river. Two lanterns were to be hung in the steeple of the North Church if the English were coming by water. One lantern was to be hung if they were coming by land.

So Paul rushed to the North Church and gave directions. "Two lanterns," he said. "Now."

Then he ran home, flung open the door, pulled on his boots, grabbed his coat, kissed his wife, told the children to be good, and off he went — his hat clapped to his head, his coattails flying. He was in such a hurry that he left the door open, and his dog got out.

On the way to the river, Paul picked up two friends who had promised to row him to the other side. Then all three ran to a dock near the Charlestown ferry, where Paul had kept a boat hidden during the winter. Paul's dog ran with them.

The night was pleasant, and the moon was bright — too bright. In the path of moonlight across the river lay an armed English transport. Paul and his friends would have to row past it.

Then Paul realized his first mistake. He had meant to bring cloth to wrap around the oars so the sound would be muffled. He had left the cloth at home.

That wasn't all he had left behind. Paul Revere had started out

for his Big Ride without his spurs.

Luckily, one of Paul's friends knew a lady who lived nearby. He ran to her house, called at her window, and asked for some cloth. This lady was not a time-waster. She stepped out of the pet-

ticoat she was wearing and threw it out the window.

Then for the spurs. Luckily, Paul's dog was there, and luckily, he was well trained. Paul wrote a note to his wife, tied it around the dog's neck, and told the dog to go home. By the time Paul and his friends had ripped the petticoat in two, wrapped each half around an oar, and launched the boat, the dog was back with Paul's spurs around his neck.

Paul and his two friends rowed softly across the Charles River. They slipped carefully past the

English transport with its sixty-four guns, and they landed in the shadows on the other side — safely. There a group of men from Charlestown who had seen the signal in the church steeple had a horse waiting for Paul.

And off Paul Revere rode on his Big Ride, beating on doors as he went, waking up the citizens. At Lexington he woke up John Hancock and Samuel Adams and advised them to leave town. He had a quick bite to eat, and then, in the company of two other riders, he continued to Concord, warning farmers along the way.

For a while all went well. And then suddenly from out of the shadows appeared six English officers. They rode up with their pistols in their hands and ordered Paul to stop. But Paul didn't stop immediately.

One of the officers shouted, "If you go an inch farther, you are a dead man."

Paul and his companions tried to ride through the group. But they were surrounded and ordered into a pasture at one side of the road.

In the pasture six other officers appeared with pistols in their hands.

One of them spoke like a gentleman. He took Paul's horse by the reins and asked Paul where he came from.

Paul told him, "Boston."

The officer asked what time he had left Boston.

Paul told him.

The officer said, "Sir, may I crave your name?"

Paul answered that his name was Revere.

"What! *Paul* Revere?"

Paul said, "Yes."

Now, the English officers certainly did not want to let Paul Revere loose, so they put him, along with other prisoners, at the center of their group, and they rode off toward Lexington. As they approached town, they heard gunfire. "What was that?" the officer asked.

Paul said it was a signal to alarm the countryside.

With this piece of news, the English decided they'd like to get back to their own troops in a hurry. Indeed, they were in such a hurry that they no longer wanted to be bothered with prisoners. So after taking the prisoners' horses, they set them free.

And then what happened?

Paul Revere felt bad, of course, to be on his Big Ride without a horse. He felt uneasy to be on a moonlit road on foot. So he struck out through the country, across stone walls, through pastures, over graveyards, back into Lexington to see if John Hancock and Samuel Adams were still there.

They were. They were just preparing to leave town in John Hancock's carriage. Paul and Hancock's clerk, John Lowell, went with them.

All went well. They rode about two miles into the countryside, and then suddenly John Hancock remembered that he had left a trunk full of important papers in a Lexington tavern. This was a mistake. He didn't want the English to find those papers.

So what happened?

Paul Revere and John Lowell got out of the carriage and walked back to Lexington.

It was morning now. From all over the area, farmers were gathering on Lexington Green. As Paul crossed the green to the tavern, there were between fifty and sixty armed men preparing to take a stand against the English. The troops were said to be near.

Paul went into the tavern, had a bite to eat, found the trunk, and carried it out, holding one end while John Lowell held the other. As they stepped on the green, the troops appeared.

And then what happened?

Paul and John held on to the trunk. They walked right through the American lines, holding on to the trunk. They were still holding on when a gun was fired. Then there were two guns, then many guns firing back and forth. Paul did not pay any attention to who was firing or who fired first. He did not stop to think that this might be the first battle of a war. His job was to move a trunk to safety, and that's what he did.

The battles of Lexington and Concord did, of course, begin the Revolutionary War. And Americans have talked ever since about Paul Revere's ride.

After the war, when Paul was forty-eight years old, he went back to silversmithing and opened a hardware store too. Later he made bells — 398 of them. Some still ring today. Paul Revere died in 1818, when he was eighty-three years old.

AUTHOR

Jean Fritz is a distinguished author of children's books, many of which have won awards. She has written about many things, but Mrs. Fritz says that her greatest joy has been writing historical fiction and that her favorite period is the Revolutionary one.

Even as a child in Hankow, China, where she was born of missionary parents, she dreamed about America and its history, and she began to put her dreams into writing. When she was thirteen, she came to America, where she continued to write. Her lively, humorous stories about America's patriots such as Paul Revere, Sam Adams, Ben Franklin, and John Hancock make history fun.

Mrs. Fritz says that she likes art, yard sales, beaches, and any place or thing that is new, for then she feels that she is on the edge of some lovely surprise.

What Ever Happened to Main Street?

by DAVID WEITZMAN

Does your town have a Main Street, a Center Street, a First Avenue, or an "A" Street? If it does, I'll bet it's the oldest-looking street in town. And, if you were to look for dates on the buildings along that street, you'd find some of the first buildings ever built in your city.

Why do those streets have names like that? People hardly ever walk along them. Chances are they're not main streets anymore. But they once were.

Adapted from *My Backyard History Book*, by David Weitzman. Copyright © 1975 by the Yolla Bolly Press. Used by permission of Little, Brown and Co.

The city may have made plans to tear down that old part of town. It seems so dull compared to the new downtown. Perhaps there are already empty lots between the old buildings, filled with the broken bricks and rubble of what was once there. So before it's too late, take a walk down your Main Street or Center Street or First Avenue or "A" Street, and go into the past.

Close your eyes and imagine the old sights and sounds. Hear old cars putt-putting and beep-beeping their way down streets filled with the noise of horses, clanging trolley cars, and bumping carts. On the sidewalks, see the women in long skirts and high-top shoes. Notice the rushing of workers in overalls. Look at the clerks in stiff collars and vests. You can begin to understand something of your town's history if you watch carefully for the small bits of the past. Look for cobblestones showing through the pavement. Find traces of old trolley tracks. Discover an iron drinking trough for horses with a little bubbling fountain for people. See fancy cast-iron lampposts and gas lamps poking out from old brick building fronts. Notice the little fire hydrants.

This is where it all began. Perhaps, being here, you can discover by yourself how your town began.

Like people, towns are born, grow, and get old. Like people, towns have personalities. They are serious. They laugh. Cared for, they are healthy. Not cared for, they become weak and die.

But unlike people, who usually grow in every direction at once, towns often start at one point and grow outward.

There are any number of ways a town gets started. Lots of towns have railroad tracks running right through them. The old yellow-and-brown railroad station just off Main Street played an important part in the way the town grew.

Seventy or a hundred years ago, that station stood alone. There was nothing for miles around. Nothing, that is, until the cattle drives began, and thousands of head of cattle arrived to be shipped by train to the slaughterhouses in the big city.

Then, over the years, things changed. Bigger cattle pens were built. Hotels and restaurants popped up. General stores and banks opened. Businesses that bought and sold cattle grew. And, of course, houses for all the people running these businesses had to be built.

Soon factories began to spring up to take advantage of the nearby railroad. The town slowly became a large transportation and manufacturing center, with more houses and stores. And it was always growing out and away from its beginning — the railroad tracks.

Other cities began as transportation centers, too, but of a different kind. They became shipping centers. They grew around docks along rivers or around natural harbors on the seacoast. Even today, you can see the way these cities grew. As you walk away from the docks, you notice how the city becomes newer and newer the farther out you get.

Still another kind of city started at a crossroads. It began with a gas station. Then there came a restaurant and bus stop. Then a general store was built. And then — when a lot of the people who got off the buses didn't get back on — some houses, churches, and schools were built.

There are still other kinds of beginnings for cities. There are college towns, manufacturing cities, county seats, state capitals, and mining towns. Whole cities have grown around places for recreation. There are retirement communities too.

Now, does that give you any ideas about how your town began and why?

AUTHOR

David Weitzman grew up in Chicago, where he learned a kind of history on the city streets. He walked through old Polish, Greek, Swedish, German, and Chinese neighborhoods. He paid special attention to old buildings, old bridges, and the great steam locomotives of the time. He says that what he learned led him later to write *My Backyard History Book,* part of which you have just read.

Mr. Weitzman teaches social studies in an elementary school in California. He is also the author of a social studies textbook series.

FIRST SNOW

by HELEN COUTANT

Everyone was expecting the snow. It was the second week in December, and the hills around the small New England town were such a dull brown that Liên ached for them to be covered over. Only the first snow could do that.

It was not so long ago that Liên and her family had come from Vietnam. They arrived in summer, so at first the weather seemed little different from that comforting heat of the tropics they had always known. But with the passing of summer into fall, the cold grew stronger. As the days shortened, Liên's grandmother, already old and weak, fell sick. The doctor came often. Liên knew her parents were worried and wished for the warm days to return.

Yet though she loved her grandmother and knew the cold weakened her, Liên could not help longing to see the snow. When she went shopping with her mother, she looked at the clean wooden sleds eager children had already put out on their porches. The gleaming runners on the sleds made Liên shiver. It seemed to her that the sleds waited for the snow too.

Liên spent the dark, late afternoons showing her grandmother pictures of snow in a big book. Together they ran their fingers over the pictures until Liên's hands almost felt the cold and her ears filled with the roar of an icy wind. The thought that any day now the snow might really come made her heart beat faster.

Finally on a gray and heavy morning, the doctor, who had come more often than usual this week to see Liên's grandmother, said that snow would surely fall before dark.

He liked Liên and before leaving would always stop to speak to her. But today, as he turned up his collar against the bitter cold and pressed her father's arm, his face was less cheerful than before. Her father and mother had followed him to the front door. Now they stood silently. Liên watched through the curtains as he hurried away. Then she heard her father say to her mother, "Grandmother is dying."

"Dying?" wondered Liên. It was a word she had not paid much attention to before. Looking out the window at the frozen ground and the gray clouds, she asked herself if Grandmother's dying had something to do with the coming snow.

She ran between her parents. "What does it mean that Grandmother is dying?" she cried. Hardly had she spoken than Liên felt herself picked up and held by them both. But though they pressed her close, stroking her hair, Liên could see that their thoughts were far away. No answer came from them. There was nothing for Liên to do but tiptoe back to the front window and wait.

The cold, thick glass of the window burned her fingers like ice. By now the clouds had fallen so low that they hid the top of the nearest hill. She wondered what the garden would look like after the snow came and made everything white. If she went for a walk, would her hair turn white too, as though she had suddenly grown old? Only her grandmother's hair would not be changed by

the snow, for it had been white as long as Liên could remember. Yet today, something about her grandmother
had changed. She was dying.

"Grandmother will know what dying means," Liên
decided. She ran softly from the hall to the small corner
room off the kitchen, where her grandmother lived in
order to be near the family all day long. The room was
hardly big enough for more than a bed, yet Liên thought
of it as large and sunny. White and yellow chrysanthemums bloomed in pots on the windowsill.

Grandmother was lying on a wooden bed. Her long
white hair had been neatly fastened with dark pins. A
heavy quilt was pulled up to her chin. Many nights Liên

had slept under the same quilt with her grandmother. Now she sat down on the bed, dropped her shoes to the floor, and pulled some of the warm quilt over herself. Then she looked her grandmother in the eyes.

"What does it mean that you are dying, Grandmother?" asked Liên. Her grandmother remained silent, but she reached out from under the quilt and took Liên's hand in hers. "The doctor said the snow will come today," Liên said.

"So . . ." her grandmother whispered, "I think it has come just for us, Liên." Gently she turned Liên's head toward the window. Together they looked past the flowers into the winter sky. "This morning it is cold, my child, is it not? Heavy clouds are hanging over the pine trees. It seems that the whole sky is ready to fall and cover us with snow." She stopped suddenly. For a long time, Liên waited, wondering if the peaceful breathing of her grandmother meant she was falling asleep. Then in a clear voice, her grandmother went on. "Now listen carefully. If you go out into the garden and hold your hand up to the sky and are patient, you will have an answer to your question. You will discover for yourself what dying means."

"Then I am right!" cried Liên, sitting up, sure now that her grandmother's dying had something to do with the first snow. She pulled her legs out from under the quilt, slipped into her shoes, and kissed her grandmother.

"Dress warmly, my child," her grandmother said. "And go right away. It would be a pity to be late."

The buttons on her jacket were hard to fasten. But at
last Liên had closed the front door behind her and was
running to the middle of the garden.

It was a bitter day. All morning the sun had cut
through the clouds only once or twice. Overnight the
cold had cracked the bare earth, and the little brook had
frozen over. The air stung Liên's face and her breath
went up in white puffs like smoke. She looked up at the
dark clouds that filled the sky.

Far above the tops of the tallest pine trees, tiny snow-
flakes had begun to fall. At first they circled lazily, but
when the damp lower air ruffled their edges, the snow-
flakes began to grow and fall faster.

When she saw the snow-
flakes coming, Liên remembered what her grandmother
had said. She held her hand up
to the sky. "The snow!" she
cried. She stretched her arm as
high as the thick jacket would
allow. A rush of wind blew
through her hair. Then one
snowflake landed on the tip of
her longest finger. It stayed
there, and Liên stared at it, not
daring to breathe. This was
not the cold, hard snow of the
pictures but a tiny, fleeting
thing, beautiful and delicate.

Then the sun broke through the clouds and shone for an instant on the snowflake, causing its white edges to burst into a thousand tiny rainbows. "Is this what dying means?" marveled Liên, remembering why she was standing there. But as if that thought had made a change, the snowflake got smaller. "Come back, oh please come back!" Hardly had she said this than the snowflake was gone. A tiny drop of water rolled down into her hand.

Liên stared at her hand, at the drop that was just water. Then it, too, began to change. It seemed to get bigger in the sunlight.

"Look, Grandmother," Liên called, turning toward the house. But as she moved, her hand trembled. The drop of water, lighter than sunshine, rolled off. It fell to the ground and was gone.

"Oh," cried Liên, going down on her knees. Searching for the beautiful drop, she scraped away layers of dead and frozen leaves. Her fingertips stung from the cold. But she kept looking until something poked against her

hand. Where the water had fallen, a tiny pine tree now stood up in the sudden light. No bigger than her thumb, this little tree already smelled of deep, rich forests.

At that moment Liên thought she knew what dying meant. The drop of water had not really gone. It had only changed, like the snowflake, into something else. "You will change too," Liên spoke to the tiny tree, "but not yet." Carefully she covered the little tree with its blanket of leaves.

Now as she stood up, Liên's hands stung. She pushed them deep into her pockets and looked again at the sky. On her cheeks, a new snowflake landed and melted, then another. "I understand, Grandmother," Liên cried, running toward the house.

The window of her grandmother's room looked gray and cold as Liên stared up, too small to see over the sill. But the chrysanthemums bloomed as always, so yellow and clear they seemed to be out in the snow with her.

A tap on the glass startled Liên. At first she could see only the darkness above the flowers. Then slowly, as if it were being drawn on the glass, her grandmother's face appeared.

Now she put one hand gently against the pane. Liên's hand rose to meet it from the other side. A quiet smile trembled on her grandmother's face.

"I'm coming, Grandmother," Liên cried, raising her arms as if to fly inside.

"I'm coming!" she said. And suddenly the whole sky was filled with falling snow.

AUTHOR

First Snow was Helen Coutant's first book for children. It grew out of a belief that this American author shared with her Vietnamese artist husband, Vo-Dinh: Ancient ideas from another land can have meaning for today's children. For the cause of peace, she and her husband have worked together on pamphlets, newsletters, and an adult book.

Besides being a writer, Helen Coutant is a translator and a teacher of English. She and her husband and their daughters, Katherine Phuong-Nam and Hannah Linh-Giang, live in an old stone house in Maryland.

Growing Crystals
by JOHN WAUGH

With either a cup of salt or a cup of alum, you can grow crystals in your own kitchen. Those made of salt will be shaped like blocks and be a little cloudy. Those made of alum will have many sides and will be clear and sparkling. Here's what to do.

Put two cups of water in a small pot and heat it over a low flame. Slowly add the salt or alum and stir. If all of it doesn't dissolve in this amount of water after a few minutes, add more water a bit at a time until it does.

Let the liquid cool. Then pour it into a clean bowl. (It will be easier for you to see your crystals if you do not use a white bowl.) Cover the bowl with a piece of cloth to slow down the evaporation of the water. Put the bowl in a place where no one will touch it. Leave it there for a week or so. But begin looking for change the day after you set the liquid.

As the water slowly evaporates, the salt or alum is left behind. Crystals form on the sides and bottom of the bowl. Some may also form on top of the water. They will be hard to see at first, so look carefully every day. Then select the best-

formed crystal, and remove the others with a spoon. Leave the best one in the water, checking it twice a day. Turn it from time to time so that it doesn't become flat where it rests on the bottom of the bowl. If smaller crystals begin to form on the bigger one, knock them off with a sharp, pointed knife. Remove them from the bowl. By doing this, you cause the salt or alum to grow on the single crystal, making it bigger. Always remember to put the cover back on the bowl.

Soon the water level will go down, and the top of your big crystal will be sticking out above the water. You may want to take it out and dry it. But you may want to make it even bigger. If you do want to make it bigger, repeat the first part of these directions. Use salt or alum, water and a *second* bowl. Don't cover the second bowl. When crystals begin to form on the bottom of it, empty the contents of the second bowl into the first bowl. Cover the first bowl, and remove small crystals when you turn the big one.

When your crystal has grown as large as you like, take it out and enjoy it!

AUTHOR

John C. Waugh is an earth-science teacher who enjoys studying the stars, playing the guitar, going camping, bicycling, and scuba diving. He and his wife and children live on a large farm in New York.

SKILL

Index

When you want to find the information a book has on a certain subject, use the index at the back of the book to find that information quickly. The index is a list of the main topics and subtopics that the book tells about. Beside most topics in the list is a page number or numbers telling where the information begins and ends.

What are main topics?

Look at the part of the index of a book on the next page. The words that are printed in heavy type and begin farthest to the left in each column are called **main topics.** They name people, places, and things that the book tells about.

The main topics of an index are arranged in alphabetical order, just as words are arranged in a dictionary. For example, you can see that **Apples** is listed before **Arizona** and that **Bats** is listed before **Boston.**

If the main topic is a person, that person's name is listed with the last name first. Find the name Jim Bottomley. It is listed as **Bottomley, Jim,** isn't it?

What are subtopics?

After many main topics in an index, you will find **subtopics.** In most indexes, subtopics, too, are arranged in alphabetical order. Subtopics tell what kinds of information the book gives about the main topic.

Find the main topic **Atomic power.** After it you can see two subtopics for that main topic. The subtopics *how discovered* and *uses of* are in alphabetical order after their main topic. The first subtopic shows you that the book has information about how atomic power was discovered. The second subtopic shows you that the book also has information on the uses of atomic power.

What do the page numbers tell?

After most main topics and each subtopic, you will find one or more page numbers. These numbers tell you the pages in the book on which information is given about the topic. If more than one page number is given after a topic, the numbers will be separated by a comma or a dash. If they are separated by a comma, information about that topic will be found on each of the pages shown. However, if the page numbers are separated by a dash (–), you will find information on the pages listed and on all the pages between them.

For example, find the main topic **Brazil** in the sample index. After it, you will find the subtopic *cities* and the numbers 222, 224. The comma between those numbers tells you that you could find information about the cities in Brazil on pages 222 and 224 but not on page 223.

Now look at the subtopic *products* after the main topic **Brazil.** After it you will find the numbers 225–227. The dash between those numbers tells you that there is information about the products of Brazil on pages 225, 226, and 227.

When no subtopics are given after a main topic, the numbers listed are the numbers of the pages on which information is given about the main topic. For example, notice that in the sample index, no subtopics are listed after **Amazon River.** You could find information about that main topic on pages 210, 211, 212, and 229.

What are key words?

Sometimes when you use an index, you are simply looking for all the information that you can find on a certain subject. The **key word** is the name of the subject that you would look for among the main topics in an index. For example, if you were looking for all the information that a particular book has about Alaska, you would look for the key word **Alaska** among the main topics of the index.

Sometimes, though, you may have a question in mind when you use an index. For example, you may want to answer the question *Who was the inventor of the telephone?* or the question *What do squirrels eat?* You would choose a key word from each question that names most exactly what the question is about. You would look for that word among the main topics. The question *Who was the inventor of the telephone?* is about the telephone, so *telephone* would be the key word that you would pick. The question *What do squirrels eat?* is about squirrels, so *squirrels* would be your key word.

Notice that if you used the word *inventor* as a key word for the first question, your subject would be very broad and general. If you did find **Inventor** as a main topic, it might have little or no information about the exact inventor in whom you were interested, the inventor of the telephone.

A question may have more than one word that should be used as a key word. For example, you may want to answer the question *What heavy work do elephants do in a circus?*

If you use only the word *elephants* as a key word, you may find only part of the information that the book gives on the question. You may need to use the word *circus* as a key word also in order to find the rest of the information that the book gives on the question.

REVIEW

Survey the headings of this lesson. Think about the answer to each heading question, and recite the answers to yourself. Review your answers. You should be ready to find main topics in an index.

USING AN INDEX

Use the part of an index on page 169 to answer the questions that follow. On a sheet of paper, write the number of each question. Beside the number, write the page or pages on which you would expect to find help in answering the question.

1. Is baseball the most popular sport in Japan?
2. For what purposes can atomic power be used?
3. What are the jungles like along the Amazon River in Brazil?
4. When was Dame Judith Anderson born?
5. What national parks are located in Arkansas?
6. Is Boston the largest fishing port in the United States?
7. What is the largest city in Australia?
8. Is baseball popular among children in Mexico?

My Name Is Toliver, Sir

by ESTHER WOOD BRADY

After her grandfather sprains his ankle, ten-year-old Ellen Toliver must disguise herself as a boy to carry a very important message to General Washington across the bay to Elizabeth-town, New Jersey. The message is hidden in a small metal box baked inside a loaf of bread. The owner of the Jolly Fox Tavern in Elizabeth-town will be expecting the bread. Ellen plans to find a farmer's boat or an oyster catcher's boat to take her across the bay. But from the start, nothing goes as planned.

Long before Ellen reached Front Street, she heard the beat of army drums and the shrill piping of the fifes. Trim lines of red-coats marched up and down the streets and formed in companies on all the docks.

The East River was filled with small sloops and riverboats. But nowhere could Ellen see the fat broad-beamed boats of the farmers or the oyster boats from Jersey.

Near the Market-House, she stopped a thin little man pushing a wheelbarrow with only two small pumpkins in it.

"Where are the oyster boats," she asked anxiously, "or the farmers' boats from Elizabeth-town?"

"Oh," he said, "not many of them came over today. Not much food to sell and the oyster catch was poor. Those who came started back a few moments ago."

"Back!" cried Ellen. "'Why, they can't have gone yet. It's too early for them to leave."

"Well, they have!" he said. "Only British boats are here now."

"You must be mistaken," Ellen said. "They must be at another dock." She'd have to hurry to find them.

"Look for yourself, boy," the man called after her. "They say twenty British boats are taking troops over to Elizabeth-town today."

With her heart pounding wildly, Ellen ran from one dock to another all up and down Front Street. She raced among the chests and barrels and heavy ropes as she looked at every boat tied up there. She darted among the soldiers and the sailors, but no one stopped her or noticed her.

The man was right. There were only British boats filling up

with soldiers, all along the waterfront. The men sat on planks and were crowded together as closely as kernels of corn on a cob.

"What can I do now?" she thought, her mind racing. "There isn't anyone to ask for a ride." She fingered the coins in her pocket. "If I dared to ask," she said to herself.

It was plain to see that nothing could be done. She'd have to tell Grandfather what had happened. Surely he would understand there was nothing she could do. . . .

Perhaps she could get to Elizabeth-town on one of the red-coats' boats. It would be dangerous, but it would be better than going home to face Grandfather's disappointment. Perhaps, since no one seemed to notice her now, she could slip on board quietly and hide herself under a seat. No one would find her there.

"You could do it," she said to herself. "You could make yourself do it." She stood there staring at the boats, trying to get up enough courage to start. All at once, one of the redcoats leaned across the side of the boat and grinned at her.

He was a husky man with dirty, scraggly hair beneath his black hat. "What're you hugging so tight?" he asked her. "It smells right good." His fat red cheeks shook when he spoke.

"Oh, don't bother the boy, Dow," said the sad-faced soldier who sat beside him. His mouth dropped at the corners and looked as tired as his eyes. Then he leaned across Dow and said, "I've got a boy back home in London who looks like you. What's your name?"

"Ellen Toliver, sir," she answered.

"How's that?"

Ellen gasped. She had forgotten how she was dressed. But with all the noise, he had not heard her. Raising her voice she said, "I said my name is Toliver, sir."

"My boy's name is Tom. But he looks like you. Same pale face. Same big eyes. It makes me homesick to see a boy who favors Tom," he said sadly.

Ellen could see by his face that he really was homesick. He also looked kind. Perhaps she dared ask him if she could just ride across the bay with them.

But these were British soldiers. How could she trust the enemy?

Before she could decide what to do, she felt a tug at her blue bundle. It was the man called Dow. "Smells like fresh bread there," he said. Quickly, Ellen snatched the bundle away. Then suddenly she felt herself grabbed around the waist by two big hands and whisked across the side of the boat. She was too surprised and frightened to make a sound.

The man with the red cheeks laughed as he set her down on the bench beside him. "No noise from you," he growled.

What was happening to her? This wasn't what she had meant to do. She stared at the wet brown planks of the deck.

The man looked down at her and grinned. Under his bushy eyebrows his blue eyes were laughing at her. "Surprised, are you?" he asked.

The sad-faced soldier on her other side said impatiently, "What're you doing that for, Dow?"

"Because I'm hungry as a bear in spring. That's why. Nothing but salt biscuits and dried fish, day after day."

Hungry! Ellen gasped at the thought of it. But it was too late to get back to the dock. She could tell the sloop was being cast off. The sails were raised and flapped loudly in the breeze. Then they smoothed out as the boat came about in the river and turned into the wind. She felt it rock as it headed into the waves.

The thin man with the sad face looked at her sharply. "Are you all right, boy?" he asked with concern. "My friend is a joker."

"A joker!" snorted the other. "I'm hungry." Then he turned to Ellen. "Dow's my name. And this is Higgins. He's homesick for his boy in London. And you're Toliver, you say."

Ellen nodded her head. She turned to look at the ships in the harbor. They were sailing past seven great warships anchored there. Grandfather said the British had brought in seven hundred ships last summer. And thirty thousand soldiers had camped on Staten Island. Thirty thousand soldiers! That was almost twice as many soldiers as there were people in New York.

"Are we going to Elizabeth-town?" she asked the homesick Mr. Higgins.

He shrugged. "That's what our orders are," he said.

Dow smiled at her as he took a knife from his belt and pulled it from its case. "Now that we are friends" — he coughed politely — "now that we are friends, I'll just share your fresh bread."

He leaned down and quickly snatched Ellen's blue bundle from her mittened hands.

"Oh, sir!" she cried as she reached for the blue kerchief, "I can't share it. It's for an old man's birthday present!"

"I could smell that good fresh bread when you stood there on the dock," said Dow as he slapped her hands away. "I said to myself, 'That boy will be happy to share his bread with a soldier of the King.'"

"But it's for my grandfather's friend!" cried Ellen. "Please give it back to me."

"Too bad for your grandfather's friend," Dow barked as he fumbled with the knot in the kerchief.

Ellen stared at his knife. The bright, gleaming blade in Dow's rough hands seemed more awful than a sword at her throat. In a moment he would cut into the bread and find the small metal box. Then he'd open the box and find Grandfather's message to General Washington. Soon he'd know that she was helping a spy. Grandfather had told her to say she didn't know anything about it. But they'd find out where she lived and who she lived with. Grandfather would be caught! She knew well enough what would happen then.

Suddenly, without thinking what she did, she snatched the blue bundle from Dow's hands so quickly that he lost his grip. In an instant she tucked it under her jacket, doubled up, and locked her arms beneath her legs.

The sad-faced Higgins laughed so hard his tall black hat almost fell from his head. "You're a quick one, Toliver."

Dow's fat cheeks shook with anger. "Why, you little rascal," he snarled as he tried to pry her arms loose. "Give me back that bread!"

"No!" cried Ellen. Her arms were locked in fear so tightly she could not have moved them if she'd tried.

"Give me that bread!" Dow barked as he pulled at her pigtail.

"No," said Ellen. She winced from the pain at the back of her head.

The redcoats sitting on the bench in front of them turned

around. They started to laugh at the sight of a small boy trying to fight off big old Dow.

"Hang on, boy!" they shouted.

Ellen could hear Higgins laughing until he began to hiccup and gasp for air. "He's like an oyster shell!" Higgins could hardly catch his breath. "You'll have to pry him open!"

"I haven't had fresh bread for weeks," Dow complained, tugging at Ellen's arms with his fat red hands. "And so I mean to have it!" The more he pulled, the more the soldiers laughed.

Ellen's arms felt as strong as iron. "You won't have my bread. I won't give it to you," she whispered. Then she remembered that her mother had given her some corncakes. "There are some good corncakes in my pocket, sir. Take all of them, all. And welcome."

From the stern of the boat, a voice roared at them, "Stop that racket! You'll send us all into the waves!"

Everyone became quiet at once. In the silence, Ellen heard only the waves banging along the sides of the sloop.

At last Dow shrugged and said from the side of his mouth, "You little scamp. I'll take those corncakes."

"They're in my pocket. Take them all, sir."

Dow cut a piece of corncake and put it in his mouth. "That bread is squashed flat by now. So keep it! I hope the old man likes squashed bread."

Higgins nudged her with his elbow. "Not bad, Toliver! You're a spunky one. But then all you Yankees are spunky."

Ellen glanced up at Higgins. He seemed to mean what he said. No one had ever called her spunky. She kept her arms tightly locked across her bundle as she carefully sat up.

"Spunky!" snapped Dow. "Just plain fools. Foolish enough to fight the King. And in winter yet!"

"This war will be over soon," said Higgins. A smile spread over his sad face. "And we'll be going home! Why, it's got to be over soon. They can't hold out much longer. We took three thousand prisoners when we took Fort Washington up there on Hudson's River."

"And a hundred and fifty cannon," Dow reminded him, "when we took Fort Lee on the Jersey side. Sent them running like rabbits over to Pennsylvania! Ragtag army!" Dow said, laughing. "Some wear old jackets. Some wear farmers' smocks. I never in my life saw an army that looked like that!"

"They can shoot, though," Higgins said gloomily.

"Oh, they can shoot all right," said Dow, "when they're not running away the way they did at Kip's Bay." He gave Ellen a nudge. "We saw nothing but their backs at Kips Bay. They are all a bunch of cowards!"

"No!" Ellen cried. "They are not cowards!"

Dow looked closely at her. "You know what? You're mighty pretty for a boy. Almost as pretty as a girl."

"I am not!" Ellen ducked her head to hide her alarm. "But they are not cowards," she said stubbornly.

"Oh, ho! A rebel we have!" said Dow as he looked at her from under heavy eyebrows. "A little rebel boy."

A big soldier with a scar across his forehead turned around. "Throw the rebel overboard," he said roughly. "There'll be one less rebel to fight."

Ellen tightened her arms around the bundle inside her jacket and ducked her head to make herself as small as possible. She felt as cold as ice. Yet her face was damp with sweat. If they threw her overboard, she'd take the loaf of bread down with her. They'd never, never get the box away from her.

Higgins threw back his head and started to sing in a loud voice, "Come all you soldiers bold, lend an ear, lend an ear." Immediately the men around him sang out a loud chorus, "Lend an ear, lend an ear!"

Higgins sang verse after verse, and the men joined in the chorus. Ellen was glad because it took their minds off her. By the time they had sung "Hearts of Oak" and "Old King Cole," she felt more relaxed.

At length they came to the narrow channel, where the river carried them swiftly along. With sails set wide, the boat was now skimming across the water instead of fighting its way through the waves.

On either side of them, the shores were close enough to see. To the left were snowy fields and orchards and little brown farmhouses. Ellen decided that this must be Staten Island. She remembered the map in her father's schoolhouse.

She was glad that her brother, Ezra, had explained the map to her. It was easy to guess that this swampy land on the right, with all the pine trees, would be New Jersey — and the end of her journey! Soon she'd be jumping off the boat and racing for the Jolly Fox Tavern. She'd be safe inside with her grandfather's friends. At the thought of it, she could feel the load of worry rise up from her shoulders and float away. She felt so happy that she started humming.

"What's wrong with you?" Dow barked at her.

Ellen shrank back. She didn't want any trouble with Dow.

"You scare the boy," Higgins spoke up sharply. "He didn't ask to come along, did he?"

"What's he afraid of?" Dow asked. "Me? Are you afraid of me, boy?"

"Well, maybe — a little," Ellen confessed.

"Why" — Dow made his eyes look round and innocent —"I'm as gentle as a morning in May."

Higgins snorted. Then for a long time he sat staring off at the clouds in the sky. At last he said to Ellen, "When I was a boy, I had a brother who bothered me like that. I had to learn to talk back to him. Funny thing was — when he saw I wasn't afraid of him, he left me alone." He turned and smiled. "Bullies are like that."

After a long silence Ellen said quietly, "Are you ever afraid of anything now, Mr. Higgins?"

Higgins did not answer her question right away. At last he leaned down and said in a low voice that only she could hear, "Well, son, I'll answer you true as I would answer my own son back home. Sometimes."

He nodded his head. "Sometimes I am afraid — everyone is. Being afraid is nothing to be ashamed of." He glanced over at her. "But when something has to be done," he said firmly,

"don't wonder and wonder about being afraid. If it's important to you — do the best you can."

Ellen stared up at the white sails. This trip was important. At first it had been important to her because it was very important to Grandfather. But now she had seen the British soldiers with their guns — hundreds of them — going to fight the Patriots' army. Now she was eager to help General Washington. Now she was glad to be part of the chain of people who wanted the Patriots to win.

On the right she could see the church steeples and the snowy roofs of a town, white against the pine trees. Several buildings

lined the street that ran along the waterfront. As the boat drew closer, she strained her eyes to see a sign of the Jolly Fox Tavern.

"I hope the Shannons have a roaring fire and a hot meat pie," Ellen thought.

With sails flapping loudly, their boat headed toward a dock and glided in for a landing. Ropes were tossed to the dockhands who waited to pull them in.

"All ashore!" shouted the officer in the stern. "Step lively."

The men stood up and stretched. Ellen quickly scrambled up on the dock. When she was well out of Dow's reach, she turned and laughed at him. "Good-by, Mr. Dow!" she cried happily.

"Hold your tongue, boy," snapped Dow.

"Good-by, Mr. Higgins," she called. "I'll remember the things you told me."

"I'll remember you, Toliver."

Ellen's brown eyes were shining, and her cheeks were as red as winter apples. She slipped the blue bundle out of her jacket, swinging it around her head as she turned to run.

"Fresh little beggar," Dow said to Higgins. "Too pretty for a boy, to my mind."

But Ellen didn't hear that. She was racing to the Jolly Fox Tavern.

AUTHOR

When Esther Wood Brady was a little girl, she decided that she would write books for children when she grew up. She says that she started writing when she was in the second grade. Although she had a reading problem then — she often copied and spelled words backwards — she was able to overcome it. This problem, however, caused her to develop an interest in the reading problems of others. As an adult, she worked in the public schools tutoring children. All this while, she kept ideas for a book in her mind. Many years later, while sick in bed for a month, she began to write *Toliver's Secret,* her first published book. The story you have just read was taken from that book.

Mrs. Brady once took an around-the-world trip by freighter and spent some time in China, Japan, and the Philippines.

She and her husband live in Washington, D. C.

Cinder Ellie

by JAMES S. AYARS

During the school year, Elinor Morgan was a runner on the girls' track team at her school in the city. Because she spent so much time running on cinder tracks, she was nicknamed Cinder Ellie.

Now the Morgans — Ellie, her brother, her parents, and her lively grandmother — were spending the summer at the beach at Lonesome Point. An all-day summer festival would be held at the old fairgrounds in a nearby town. The big day would include a hundred-yard dash for boys and a hundred-yard dash for girls. The boys on the Lonesome Point track team — Ray Olsen, Ernie Andersen, Tommy Tilbury, and others — would be there. Ellie wanted to be there, too, to run in the girls' race. When the day of the festival arrived, Grandma Morgan drove Ellie to the fairgrounds.

Ellie and Grandma Morgan arrived at the fairgrounds before any events had begun and before all the good seats in the grandstand had been taken. They sat down on a bench close to the exit. From there Ellie could slip out easily when the time came for her race.

The woodchopping contest began. Ellie wondered at the speed with which the yellow chips flew and seemed to fill the air.

Before the last woodchopper had cut through the last log and had his time announced by the judges, Ellie slipped out of the grandstand for her warm-up.

"The next event is the pie-eating contest," said the announcer. "After that, we'll have the hundred-yard dash for girls and the hundred-yard dash for boys. Following that is the tug of war. Pie eaters, report now to the platform across the track from the grandstand. Runners, report to the starter, the man with the white cap. He's on the track to the west of the grandstand."

Ellie took her spiked shoes and starting blocks out of her grandmother's car. She saw boys running toward the starter from all directions. Boys, boys everywhere — some in track suits, some in blue jeans and blue shirts, some in blue jeans and no shirts. Some wore rubber-soled shoes. A few wore spiked track shoes. But most were barefoot. A few carried starting blocks. Ellie joined the circle of boys crowded around the starter.

"The next event is the hundred-yard dash for girls," the starter said. "But where are the girls? Oh, yes, I see one." He had spotted Ellie at a far edge of the circle.

He spoke to the announcer, who put a megaphone to his lips and aimed it at the grandstand. Twice he shouted, "Last call for the hundred-yard dash for girls. Last call for the hundred-yard dash for girls."

The starter looked hopefully toward the grandstand and waited for half a minute, a minute, two minutes. Then, with a shrug of his shoulders, he turned toward the announcer.

"One girl. What'll we do? Doesn't seem right for her to come out here expecting to run and find no one to run against. Should we let her run with the boys if she wants to?"

"I don't know what people here will think about that," said the announcer. "Maybe it's all right. Why not ask her and then ask the boys?"

The starter looked at Ellie.

"There are no other girls to run the hundred," he said. "Should we just give you the blue ribbon to take home?"

Ellie shook her head.

"Not if I haven't earned it. I'd like to run."

"You mean run with the boys?" the starter asked.

"If there aren't any girls to run, I could run with the boys. I do at home."

The starter raised his voice enough to reach the whole group.

"We'll have to skip the hundred-yard dash for girls. The next event is the hundred-yard dash for boys. We'll start it as soon as we can after the pie-eating contest is over.

"We have about forty boys reporting for the hundred," he went on. "That's about three times as many as this track has room for. We'll have to run three heats and a final. The first four runners in each heat will qualify for the final."

He pointed at Ellie.

"This girl came to the meet prepared to run. No other girls

have shown up, and we've had to call off her race. She wants to run the hundred with you. What do you say?"

"Let her run," said half a dozen boys near the front of the group.

"No!" shouted three or four others. Ray Olsen's voice was the loudest.

"Sure! Let her run. We'll show her we can beat her," called a boy from the far edge of the circle.

The starter smiled.

"Let's settle it this way. The girl will run in the third heat. Any of you who don't want to run against her can go in the first or second heat. Then maybe you won't have to run against her at all."

The starter counted the boys — thirty-nine — and divided them into three groups: thirteen in each of the first two heats, thirteen and Ellie in the third.

"Most of you don't have starting blocks," he said. "So nobody will use them. You'll all take standing starts. Run in any shoes you choose — spiked shoes or rubber-soled shoes — or no shoes at all."

The starter blew his whistle.

"Runners in the first heat —" The starter waited while thirteen boys sorted themselves out of the group and lined up across the track. "Go to your marks. Get set." *Bang!*

In the ten minutes that had gone by since the end of the pie-eating contest, Grandma Morgan had been growing more impatient by the second. She had kept looking toward the starting line and trying to make out what was happening there. She had seen a group of boys around a man with a white cap. Once she had seen Ellie. But where were the girls Ellie was supposed to run against?

Grandma Morgan was hardly aware of the sound of the gun or of the boys strung out across the track, kicking up soft, gray dust. She did not notice the cheers in the grandstand as the boys crossed the finish line. She didn't know — or care — which boy won.

"Well!" she exclaimed in an angry tone. She had come to watch Ellie run. And Ellie hadn't run at the time scheduled for her race.

Bang!

Grandma Morgan turned again toward the starting line. Again she saw boys strung out across the track and kicking up gray dust. Again she heard cheers as the boys crossed the finish line.

She wondered who was manager of this meet. She'd like to give him a piece of her mind. She shaded her eyes against the sun and again looked toward the starting line. More boys milling around and getting ready for the next race!

Where was that manager?

Grandma Morgan stood up.

"Down in front!" bellowed a man behind her.

Grandma Morgan turned to give the bellower a piece of her mind.

Bang!

The grandstand suddenly filled with a rushing sound like that of a strong gust of wind, the sound of many people rising to their feet.

"Run, girl! Run!" shouted the bellower.

"Yeah!" The crowd exploded in a great roar.

"Come on, girl! Run! Come on!" people shouted.

A man standing beside Grandma Morgan bent almost double as he slapped his legs and haw-hawed.

"Come on, girl! Come on! Beat 'em, girl! Beat 'em!" The shouts grew louder.

Grandma Morgan turned toward the track. Down there, right in front of the grandstand, was Ellie, running smoothly and at full speed. Ellie, with her brown hair streaming behind her, was leading a pack of boys, their feet digging the dust, their arms pumping, their heads bobbing, toward the finish line.

"Run, Cinder Ellie, run!" shouted Grandma Morgan.

The bellower took up the cry as Ellie broke the yarn stretched across the finish line. "Run, Cinder Ellie, run!"

"Ellie, Ellie, Cinder Ellie!" the people chanted as Ellie walked off the track.

Two minutes later, Ellie slid onto the bench beside Grandma Morgan.

"No other girls to run," she panted. "The starter was awfully nice. He let me run with the boys. I'll have to run in the final as soon as the tug of war is over."

"Where are your track shoes — your spikes?" asked Grandma.

"I put them back in the car with the starting blocks. I didn't use them because only two boys in my heat had spikes, and I didn't want an unfair advantage over the others. We couldn't use blocks. Had to use a standing start. I got a poor start. Guess I made up for it at about the twenty. I'm going down to get ready for the final."

Ellie slid off the bench and disappeared as suddenly as she had appeared.

Ray Olsen had won the first heat. Ernie Andersen had placed fifth in the third heat and was not in the final.

"You'll have to run top speed all the way," Ernie told Ray as the two boys rested in the shade of a tree near the starting line. "That girl can run! I saw her heels all the way down the track."

"She shouldn't have run," Ray said angrily. "She shouldn't have been allowed to run. She's a girl, and the race was for boys."

"But her race was called off," Ernie reminded him. "It was only fair to let her run with us. Most of the boys agreed to let her run."

"I didn't."

"You were one of maybe three or four."

Just then, Tommy Tilbury walked into the shade of the tree. He had a sheet of paper in one hand and a pencil in the other hand.

"You'll have to run the final faster than you ran your heat," he told Ray.

"I don't know why," said Ray. "I ran faster in my heat than the boy who won the second heat."

"The girl's the runner you'll have to beat," said Tommy. "She won her heat by several yards."

"I can beat her easily," said Ray.

"Maybe," said Tommy. "But I think you ought to know what I've just discovered. I didn't believe my ears when I heard the times of the heats announced. I checked with the timers. That girl ran the hundred three-tenths of a second faster than you did and half a second faster than the winner of the second heat."

Tommy looked at the sheet of paper in his hand.

"According to my figures, if you and Ellie run the final in the times you ran the heat, Ellie will beat you by more than two yards."

"Something's wrong with those timers or their watches," Ray said. "That girl didn't run faster than I did. I watched her run."

"She runs so easily, she doesn't look as if she's running fast," said Ernie. "But I think you better not do any loafing after the gun is fired."

Ray didn't do any loafing after he heard the bang. But the final was like the third heat. The crowd shouted, "Ellie! Ellie! Cinder Ellie!" Their new hero had crossed the finish line more than two yards ahead of Ray, who came in second.

Tommy and Ernie found Ray breathing hard and walking in small circles on a grassy spot be-hind the grandstand.

"Well, you said it. She can run," Ray admitted with a sad, crooked smile.

"You were ahead of her for the first fifteen or twenty yards," said Ernie.

"She got a poor start," said Ray. "I could see that. I was right next to her — on her left. She's not used to standing starts."

"You were awfully close to her when she passed you," said Tommy.

"I know," Ray said. "We were so close that we almost bumped, but Ellie went right by me. I guess those timers were right about Ellie's speed. That girl can really run!"

Cinder Ellie and the boys on the Lonesome Point track team go on to train for the big state meet in August. But this time Ellie and the boys are to run on the same team. You can find out what happens at the meet by reading the rest of the book **Track Comes To Lonesome Point.**

AUTHOR

James S. Ayars has been writing about sports for many years, and for a long time he worked for the *Athletic Journal* in Chicago, Illinois. He says that he wrote *Track Comes To Lonesome Point,* from which "Cinder Ellie" was taken, for his daughter, Rebecca Jean, who was the original Cinder Ellie. Mr. Ayars and his wife, Rebecca Caudill, who is an author also, drove Becky Jean to many track meets. It was there that they learned about track. Becky Jean was once a member of the United States Olympic track team.

In addition to his interest in sports, Mr. Ayars enjoys the outdoors, gardening, and photography. He and his wife live in Urbana, Illinois, but they spend winters in Tucson, Arizona.

The McIntosh Apple

by JANIS NOSTBAKKEN
and JACK HUMPHREY

If *A* is for *apple,* then *M* is for *McIntosh.* In the world, the apple is more widely grown than any other fruit. In Canada, the McIntosh is more widely grown than any other apple. Because of the McIntosh, Canada is one of the world's great apple-producing nations. And it all started back in 1811 on a little farm in Dundas County, Ontario. . . .

John McIntosh, who had recently settled in Canada, was hard at work clearing his land when he discovered the remains of a deserted farmhouse. Hidden among the bushes nearby were several young apple trees growing wild. This was an important find for McIntosh. In those days, the apple was a major part of a farmer's diet. It was often the only fruit grown on farms, and it had many uses: It could be eaten fresh, dried for use in pies and preserves, or even pressed into cider. It could also be stored through the winter in a cool fruit cellar. So John replanted the young trees in a fenced-in piece of land near his home. Then he waited for the time when the trees would bear fruit. To his delight, the apples from one of the trees were extra juicy, crisp, and sweet. They were the best he'd ever tasted.

Neighbors from far and wide soon heard about this hearty apple and wanted to grow it too. But there was a problem. A seed from an apple will most likely grow into a tree if it is planted carefully. However, the apples from this tree will often be smaller and poorer than the apple from which the seed was taken. They may even be a different kind of apple altogether. This meant that the neighbors (and the McIntosh family) couldn't plant seeds and get more trees having the same apples. It seemed there could be only *one* "McIntosh apple" tree.

But then a wandering farm hand was hired to work at the McIntosh farm.

During his travels from farm to farm, the hired hand had learned about grafting. He fitted and tied a branch from the McIntosh tree onto another apple tree. Now this apple tree would bear McIntosh apples.

The hired hand taught Alan McIntosh, John's son, about grafting. Soon, Alan was selling branches from the McIntosh apple tree and showing other farmers how to graft them onto their own apple trees. Branches were later cut from those trees. Orchards of McIntosh apple trees began springing up. Ontario became an apple-producing region. Soon after, all of Canada did too.

To this day, every McIntosh Red that is grown is a descendant of a tree found on a little farm in Dundas County, Ontario, almost two hundred years ago.

AUTHOR

Janis Nostbakken and Jack Humphrey are Canadian authors. Ms. Nostbakken helped create several Canadian children's TV programs. Mr. Humphrey has been a writer and producer in both radio and TV.

Apple Song

by FRANCES FROST

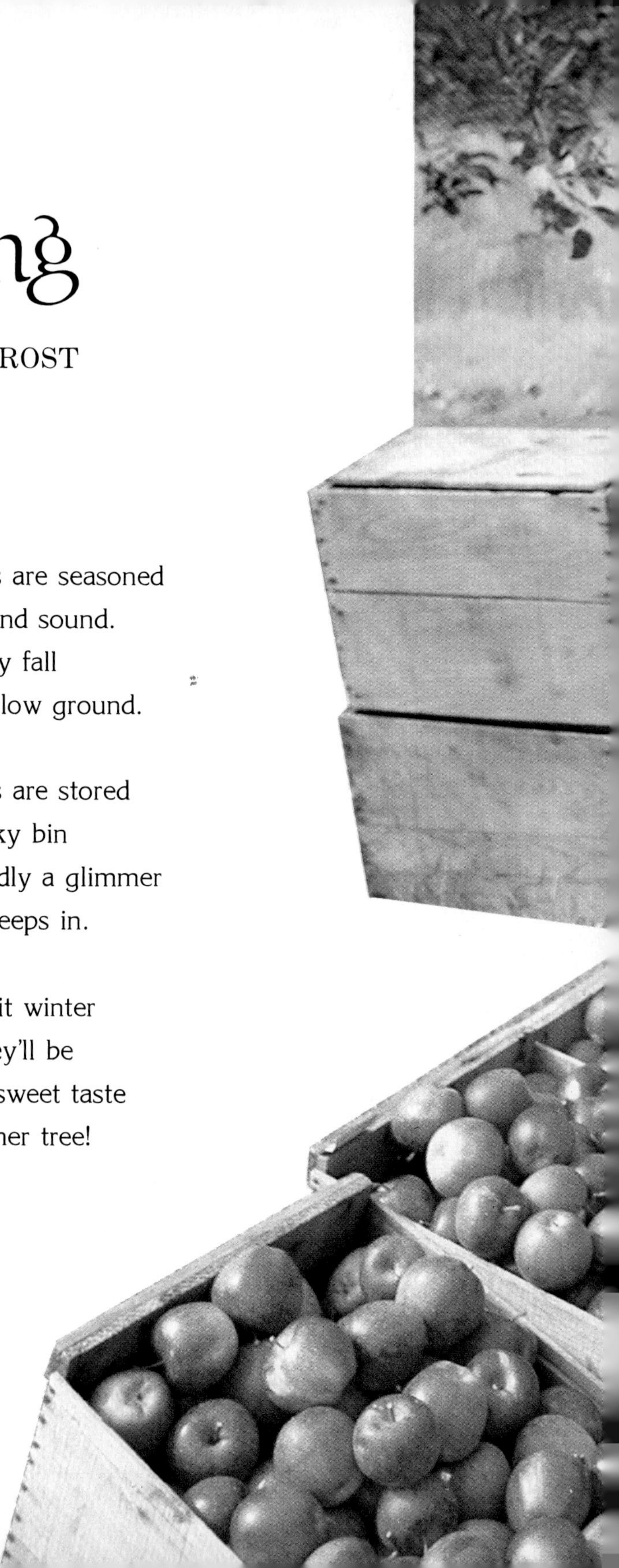

The apples are seasoned
And ripe and sound.
Gently they fall
On the yellow ground.

The apples are stored
In the dusky bin
Where hardly a glimmer
Of light creeps in.

In the firelit winter
Nights, they'll be
The clear sweet taste
Of a summer tree!

What's in a Name?

Recently you read that the *McIntosh* apple is named after John McIntosh, a Canadian farmer. Many words, some of them very common, were once people's names.

One common word is *sandwich*. You may have heard how that word came to be. One day many years ago in England, a man called the Earl of Sandwich was too busy to stop to eat his dinner. He asked a servant to bring him a piece of meat between two slices of bread. From that time on, whenever something to eat was placed between two slices of bread, it was called a sandwich.

Have you ever gone to the store and asked for a sixty-*watt* bulb? Every time you ask for a light bulb in this way, you are using the name of James Watt, a famous inventor.

The next time you drink a glass of milk, thank Louis Pasteur, a scientist. He discovered a way to destroy the harmful germs in milk. That way of treating milk is now called *pasteurization*, named for Mr. Pasteur.

When you see the words *sandwich, watt,* and *pasteurization* in print, you might not think they came from people's names. Why not? They do not begin with capital letters as people's names do.

Many words that come from people's names are written with a small letter at the beginning of the word. However, other such words do begin with capital letters, such as *Braille* and *Morse* code. *Braille* is a style of printing that can be read by people who are blind. It was invented by Louis Braille. *Morse* code is a way of sending messages by sound patterns, flashes of light, written dots and dashes, or wigwags of a flag. It was invented by Samuel F. B. Morse.

You have probably seen or had a ride on the *Ferris* wheel at an amusement park. That ride was invented for the 1893 World's Fair in Chicago, Illinois, by George G. W. Ferris, an engineer.

Have you ever heard of Queen Victoria of Great Britain? She was a very famous ruler. A four-wheeled carriage in which she often rode — the *victoria* — was named for her. But something much more important than the carriage carries Queen Victoria's name. The time in history when she was queen is called the *Victorian* Age. Even today, you still hear of *Victorian* furniture, *Victorian* manners, and so on.

People's names are everywhere. Certain flowers have been named for people. Pieces of clothing have been named for people. Many cities, towns, and states are named for people too. Perhaps you could find out if yours is one of them.

The Arrival of Paddington

by ALFRED BRADLEY and MICHAEL BOND

Characters

Mr. Henry Brown

Mrs. Mary Brown

Paddington Bear

Jonathan Brown

Refreshment Man

Judy Brown

Mrs. Bird

Props

At Paddington Station:

Cardboard boxes for parcels
and luggage.

Sign saying "Paddington Station"

Suitcase

Jar of marmalade — almost empty

Tea trolley or tray

Cakes on paper plates

Plastic or paper cups

Drinking straw

Cake wrapper

At No. 32 Windsor Gardens:

Table and chairs

Tray with teapot and cups

Towel

Possibly some cushions and
anything else that helps make
the set look like the Browns'
living room.

Scene One

When the play begins, **Paddington** *is concealed behind an assorted pile of parcels and luggage.* **Henry** *comes onto the platform, closely followed by his wife.*

Mr. Brown: Well, Mary, after all that rushing about, we're here early.

Mrs. Brown: What's the time now?

Mr. Brown: It's just a quarter past four, and Judy's train doesn't arrive until half past.

Mrs. Brown: Are you sure?

Mr. Brown: She told me in her letter, and she doesn't usually make mistakes.

Mrs. Brown: I'll just go and check which platform . . . *(Goes off)* *(Left to himself,* **Mr. Brown** *strolls around the platform.* **Paddington,** *hidden behind the parcels, pops up like a jack-in-the-box and quickly down again.* **Mr. Brown** *is looking surprised.* **Mrs. Brown** *returns.)*

Mrs. Brown: It's platform five. And you're quite right. The train doesn't arrive until half past four.

Mr. Brown: Mary, you won't believe this, but I've just seen a bear.

Mrs. Brown: A what?

Mr. Brown: A bear.

Mrs. Brown: A bear? On Paddington Station? Don't be silly, Henry. There can't be.

Mr. Brown: But there is. I distinctly saw it. Over there. Behind those parcels. It was wearing a funny kind of hat. Come and see for yourself.

Mrs. Brown *(Humoring him):*   Very well. *(She peers behind the parcels.)* Why Henry, I believe you were right after all. It is a bear!

*(***Paddington** *stands up suddenly. He is wearing a bush hat with a wide brim and has a large luggage label around his neck.)*

Paddington: Good afternoon. *(He raises his hat.)*

Mr. Brown: Er . . . good afternoon.

Paddington: Can I help you?

Mr. Brown: Well . . . no . . . er, not really. As a matter of fact, we were wondering if we could help you.

Mrs. Brown *(Taking a closer look):*   You're a very unusual bear.

Paddington: I'm a very rare sort of bear. There aren't many of us left where I come from.

Mr. Brown: And where is that?

Paddington: Darkest Peru. I'm not really supposed to be here at all. I'm a stowaway.

Mrs. Brown: A stowaway?

Paddington: Yes. I emigrated you know. I used to live with my Aunt Lucy in Peru, but she had to go into a Home for Retired Bears.

Mrs. Brown: You don't mean to say you've come all the way from South America by yourself?

Paddington: Yes. Aunt Lucy always said she wanted me to emigrate when I was old enough. That's why she taught me to speak English.

Mr. Brown: But what ever did you do for food? You must be starving.

Paddington *(Opening his suitcase and taking out an almost empty jar):*   I ate marmalade. Bears like marmalade. And I hid in a lifeboat.

DINGTO
FARES POSTED INSIDE
PLEASE LOOK AFTER THIS BEAR THANK YOU

Mr. Brown: But what are you going to do now? You can't just sit on Paddington Station waiting for something to happen.

Paddington: Oh, I shall be all right . . . I expect.

Mrs. Brown: What does it say on your label?

Mr. Brown (*Reading it*): "Please look after this bear. Thank you."

Mrs. Brown: That must be from his Aunt Lucy. Oh, Henry, what shall we do? We can't just leave him here. There's no knowing what might happen to him. Can't he come and stay with us for a few days?

Mr. Brown: But Mary, dear, we can't just take him — not just like that. After all . . .

Mrs. Brown: After all, what? He'd be good company for Jonathan and Judy — even if it's only for a little while. They'd never forgive us if they knew you'd left him here.

Mr. Brown: It all seems highly irregular. I'm sure there's a law against it. (*Turning to* **Paddington**) Would you like to come and stay with us? That is, if you've nothing else planned.

Paddington (*Overjoyed*): Oooh, yes, please. I should like that very much. I've nowhere to go and everyone seems in such a hurry.

Mrs. Brown: Well, that's settled then. And you can have marmalade for breakfast every morning. . . .

Paddington: Every morning? I only had it on special occasions at home. Marmalade's very expensive in Darkest Peru.

Mrs. Brown: Then you shall have it every morning starting tomorrow.

Paddington (*Worried*): Will it cost a lot? You see I haven't very much money.

Mrs. Brown: Of course not. We wouldn't dream of charging you anything. We shall expect you to be one of the family, shan't we Henry?

Mr. Brown: Of course. By the way, if you *are* coming home with us you'd better know our names. This is Mrs. Brown and I'm Mr. Brown.

Paddington *(Raises his hat twice):* I haven't really got a name, only a Peruvian one which no one can understand.

Mrs. Brown: Then we'd better give you an English one. It'll make things much easier. *(Thinking hard)* It ought to be something special. Now what shall we call you? I know! We found you on Paddington Station, so that's what we'll call you . . . Paddington.

Paddington *(Savouring it):* Paddington. Pad-dington. Paddington. It seems a very long name.

Mr. Brown: It's quite distinguished. Yes, I like Paddington as a name. Paddington it shall be.

Mrs. Brown: Good. Now, Paddington, I have to meet our young daughter Judy off the train. I'm sure you must be thirsty after your long journey, so while I'm away Mr. Brown will get you something to drink.

Paddington: Thank you.

Mrs. Brown: And Henry, when you get a moment, take that label off his neck. It makes him look like a parcel. **(Paddington** *doesn't much like the thought of looking like a parcel.)* I'm sure he'll get put in a luggage van if a porter sees him. *(She goes off almost bumping into a man pushing the refreshment cart.)*

Mr. Brown *(Removing the label):* There we are. Ah! The very thing. Now I can get you something to drink.

(Paddington *puts the luggage label into his suitcase.)*

Man: What would you like — tea or coffee?

Paddington: Cocoa, please.

Man *(Annoyed):*   We haven't got any cocoa.

Paddington: But you asked me what I would like. . . .

Man: I asked you what would you like — *tea* or *coffee!*

Mr. Brown *(Hastily, trying to avoid an argument):*   Perhaps you'd like a cold drink?

Man: Lemonade or orangeade?

Paddington: Marmalade.

Mr. Brown *(Before the man loses his temper):*   I think some orangeade would be a good idea — and a cup of tea for me, please. *(The man serves them.)* And perhaps you'd like a cake, Paddington?

Paddington: Oh, yes, please.

Man: Cream-and-chocolate, or cream-and-jam?

Paddington: Yes, please.

Man: Well, which do you want?

Mr. Brown: We'd better have one of each. *(The man puts them on a plate.* **Mr. Brown** *pays him and hands the plate to* **Paddington.***)* How's that to be going on with?

Paddington: It's very nice, thank you, Mr. Brown. But it's not very easy drinking out of a beaker. I usually get my nose stuck.

Mr. Brown: Perhaps you'd like a straw. *(He takes one from the man and puts it into Paddington's beaker.)*

Paddington: That's a good idea. *(He blows through the straw and makes a noisy bubbling sound.)* I'm glad I emigrated. *(He takes a bite from one of the cakes.)* I wonder what else there is? *(He puts the plate of cakes on the floor in order to peer at the trolley, and promptly steps on the cake. In his excitement he upsets the rest of the cups on the* *trolley, scattering them in all directions. Trying to steady himself, he knocks Mr. Brown's tea out of his hand, slips over and ends up sprawled on the platform. As* **Mr. Brown** *bends to help him up,* **Paddington** *staggers to his feet. They collide and Paddington's cream cake ends up plastered all over Mr. Brown's face. Just at this moment,* **Mrs. Brown** *returns with* **Judy.)**

Mrs. Brown: Henry! Whatever are you doing to that poor bear? Look at him! He's covered all over with jam and cream.

Mr. Brown: *He's* covered with jam and cream! What about me? *(He begins to tidy up the mess.)*

Mrs. Brown: This is what happens when I leave your father alone for five minutes.

Judy *(Clapping her hands):* Oh, Daddy, is he really going to stay with us? **(Paddington** *stands up, raises his hat, steps on the cake and falls over again.)* Oh, Mummy, isn't he funny!

Mrs. Brown: You wouldn't think that anybody could get into such a state with just one cake.

Mr. Brown: Perhaps we'd better go. Are we all ready?

Judy: Come along, Paddington.

(Paddington *picks up his suitcase and puts the remains of the cakes in it. The cake wrapper sticks to his paws, but he doesn't notice it.)* We'll go straight home and you can have a nice hot bath. Then you can tell me all about South America. I'm sure you must have had lots of adventures.

Paddington: I have — lots. Things are always happening to me. I'm that sort of bear. *(He goes off with* **Judy.)**

Mr. Brown *(To his wife):* I hope we haven't bitten off more than we can chew.

Man: Well, if you have, you'll just have to grin and *bear* it. *(He laughs loudly at his own joke and goes off.)*

Scene Two

(This scene takes place at No. 32 Windsor Gardens. **Judy** *and* **Paddington** *have just walked into the living room.)*

Judy: Here we are. Now you are going to meet Mrs. Bird.

Paddington: Mrs. Bird?

Judy: Yes. She looks after us. She's a bit fierce sometimes, and she grumbles a bit. But she doesn't really mean it. I'm sure you'll like her.

Paddington *(Nervously):* I'm sure I shall, if you say so.

(The door opens and **Mrs. Bird** *appears.)*

Mrs. Bird: Goodness gracious, you've arrived already, and me hardly finished the washing up. I suppose you'll be wanting tea?

Judy: Hello, Mrs. Bird. It's nice to see you again. How's the rheumatism?

Mrs. Bird: Worse than it's ever been. *(She stops abruptly as she sees* **Paddington.***)* Good gracious! Whatever have you got there?

Judy: It's not a whatever, Mrs. Bird. It's a bear. His name's Paddington.

(Paddington *raises his hat.)*

Mrs. Bird: A bear . . . well, he has good manners. I'll say that for him.

Judy: He's going to stay with us. He's come all the way from South America, and he's all alone with nowhere to go.

Mrs. Bird: Going to *stay* with us? How long for?

Judy: I don't know. I suppose it *depends!*

Mrs. Bird: Mercy me! I wish you'd told me he was coming. I haven't put clean sheets in the spare room or anything.

Paddington: It's all right, Mrs. Bird. I didn't have any sheets in the lifeboat. I'm sure I shall be very comfortable. *(He shakes hands with her. When he lets go, the cake wrapper is sticking to her hand. She tries in vain to get it off, and finally it sticks to her other hand.)*

Judy: Let me help, Mrs. Bird. (**Judy** *takes it from her but then finds that it is glued to her own hand. At this moment,* **Mr. and Mrs. Brown** *arrive with* **Jonathan.**)

Hello, Jonathan. *(She shakes hands with* **Jonathan** *and passes the sticky paper on to him.)* You haven't met Paddington yet, have you? Paddington, this is my brother, Jonathan.

Jonathan: How do you do?

Paddington: Very well, thank you.

(**Paddington** *shakes hands with* **Jonathan** *and collects the sticky paper.)*

Mrs. Bird: Whatever's going on?

Paddington: I'm afraid I had an accident with a cake, Mrs. Bird. It's left me a bit sticky.

Mrs. Bird: I think a good hot bath will do you the world of good.

Judy *(Confidentially):*   She doesn't mind really. In fact, I think she rather likes you.

Paddington: She seems a bit fierce.

Mrs. Bird *(Turning around suddenly):*   What was that?

Paddington: I didn't hear anything.

Mrs. Bird: Where was it you said you'd come from? Peru?

Paddington: That's right. *Darkest* Peru.

Mrs. Bird: Humph. Then I expect you like marmalade. I'd better get some more from the grocer. *(She leaves the room.)*

Judy *(Happily):*   There you are! What did I tell you? She *does* like you.

Paddington: Fancy her knowing that I like marmalade.

Judy: Mrs. Bird knows everything about everything.

Mrs. Brown: Now, Judy, you'd better show Paddington his room.

Judy: Come on. It used to be mine when I was small. There's a bathroom as well so you can have a good cleanup.

Paddington: A *bathroom.* Fancy having a special room for a bath. (**Paddington** *and* **Judy** *leave the room.*)

Mr. Brown: I hope we're doing the right thing.

Mrs. Brown: Well, we can hardly turn him out now. It wouldn't be fair.

Mr. Brown: I'm sure we ought to report the matter to someone first.

Jonathan: I don't see why, Dad. Besides, didn't you say he was a stowaway? He might get arrested.

Mr. Brown: Then there's the question of pocket money. I'm not sure how much money to give a bear.

Mrs. Brown: He can have twenty pence a week, the same as Jonathan and Judy.

Mr. Brown: Very well, but we'll have to see what Mrs. Bird has to say about it first.

Jonathan: Hurrah!

Mrs. Brown: *You'd* better ask her then. It was your idea.

(**Mrs. Bird** *comes in with a tray of tea, followed by* **Judy.***)*

Mrs. Bird: I suppose you want to tell me you've decided to keep that young Paddington.

Judy: May we, Mrs. Bird? *Please.* I'm sure he'll be very good.

Mrs. Bird: Humph! *(She puts the tray on the table.)* That remains to be seen. Different people have different ideas about being good. All the same, he looks the sort of bear who means well.

Mr. Brown: Then you don't mind, Mrs. Bird?

Mrs. Bird: No. No, I don't mind at all. I've always had a soft spot for bears myself. It'll be nice to have one about the house. *(She goes.)*

Mr. Brown: Well, whoever would have thought it?

Judy: I expect it was because he raised his hat. It made a good impression.

Mrs. Brown *(Pouring the tea):* I suppose someone ought to write and tell his Aunt Lucy. I'm sure she'd like to know how he's getting on.

Mr. Brown: By the way, how *is* he getting on?

(There is a loud gurgling noise from the bath, followed by a tremendous splashing sound. **Paddington** *begins to sing.)*

Judy: Oh, all right, I think. At least, he seemed all right when I left him.

(Mr. Brown *suddenly feels his head.)*

Mr. Brown: That's funny. I could have sworn I felt a spot of water.

Mrs. Brown: Don't be silly, Henry. How could you?

Mr. Brown *(Another drop lands on his head.):* It's happened again!

Jonathan *(Looks up at the ceiling):* Hey! *(He nudges* **Judy**.) Look!

Judy *(Looks up too):* Oh, my! The bath!

Jonathan: Come on!

Mr. Brown: Where are you two going?

Judy: Oh . . . *(Pretending to be casual)* We're just going upstairs to see how Paddington's getting on. *(She bundles* **Jonathan** *out of the room.)* Quick!

Mrs. Brown: What was all that about, I wonder?

Mr. Brown: I don't know, Mary. I suppose they're just excited about having a bear in the house. . . .

Judy *(Calls offstage):*   Are you all right, Paddington?

Paddington: Yes, I think so.

Judy: Oh, oh! Look at this mess!

Jonathan: Why on earth didn't you turn the tap off? No wonder all the water overflowed.

Paddington: I'm afraid I got soap in my eyes. I couldn't see anything. *(As he is led back into the room by* **Jonathan** *and* **Judy,** *he squeezes water out of his hat.)*

It's a good thing I had my hat with me. I used it to bail the water out. I might have drowned otherwise.

Mr. Brown: No wonder I thought I felt some water.

Judy: Now you just dry yourself properly, or you'll catch cold. *(She drapes a towel round him.)*

Paddington *(Proudly as he looks at himself):*   I'm a lot cleaner than I was.

(Mrs. Bird *enters.)*

Mrs. Bird: You'd better give me your hat, Paddington. I'll put it on the line.

Paddington *(Puts his hat back on):*   I'd rather you didn't, Mrs. Bird. I don't like being without it. It's my special bush hat, and it belonged to my uncle.

Mrs. Brown: In that case, perhaps you'd like to tell us all about yourself and how you came to emigrate.

Paddington *(Sits down in an armchair and makes the most of his audience):*   Well . . . I was brought up by my Aunt Lucy. *(He closes his eyes.)*

Jonathan: Your Aunt Lucy?

Paddington *(Sleepily):*   Yes. She's the one who lives in the Home for Retired Bears in (SNORE)ima. . . .

Mr. Brown *(Puzzled):* In (SNORE)-ima! Where's that?

Paddington: It's in Peru, Mr. Brown. (SNORE) *Darkest* Peru.

Judy: Paddington . . . wake up.

(**Paddington** *gives a longer snore.* **Mr. Brown** *pokes him gently.*)

Mr. Brown: Well I never. I do believe he's fallen asleep.

Mrs. Brown *(Drapes the towel round him to make him more comfortable):* I'm not really surprised. I don't suppose there are many bears who've had quite such a busy day!

Jonathan and **Judy** *(In chorus):* Especially from (SNORE)-ima.

CURTAIN

AUTHOR

British author Michael Bond wrote his first short stories, magazine articles, and radio and television plays for grownups, not for children. His first children's book, *A Bear Called Paddington*, was written as the result of his buying a small toy bear as a present for his wife. He named the bear after the subway station near their London, England, apartment, and, just for fun, began writing stories about the bear. After the first, there were several other books about Paddington, including *Paddington on Stage*, from which the play you have just read was taken. Mr. Bond has also written puppet plays for British radio and television.

Alfred Bradley has produced many children's plays in England. He put some of the Paddington stories into play form.

Velvet Whiskers

by MAXINE KUMIN

I wanted to give
A horse I knew
A sugar lump
That he could chew.

He snuffed my hair.
It made him sneeze.
He didn't say,
Excuse me, please.

He whiffed around
My curled-up fist.
He nuzzled all
Along my wrist.

But when I dared
To spread my hand,
His yellow teeth
Were smooth as sand.

He didn't nip
My thumb, or chew
A single finger
Off. He knew

A way to slurp
The sugar up,
Like too-hot cocoa
From a cup.

And as he crunched,
I felt his nose,
Soft as a
New baby's toes.

Soft as velvet
Gloves would fit.
His whiskers grew
Right out of it.

Velvet whiskers!
But of course —
He was a very
Special horse.

SKILL

The Main Idea of a Paragraph

You know that authors group sentences into paragraphs. Authors put ideas together in this orderly way so that what they write will be clear to you. You have learned that the one thing that most of the sentences in a paragraph tell about is called the topic of the paragraph. The most important idea that a paragraph gives about its topic is called the **main idea.** The main idea is stated in a sentence.

How do you find the main idea?

You often find the main idea of a paragraph by deciding which sentence best sums up what all the sentences say about the topic. Read the following paragraph:

> One of the most interesting and unusual animals in the world today is the duck-billed platypus. This creature has fur like that of an otter or a weasel. Its tail looks like the tail of a beaver. Its feet are webbed. It has a bill like a duck.

The topic of this paragraph is *The duck-billed platypus* because all the sentences say something about that animal. The first sentence sums up what the others say about the duck-billed platypus. That sentence tells the main idea of the paragraph.

What are supporting details?

Supporting details are those sentences or ideas that support the main idea. *To support* means "to add strength to something or someone; to help." The main idea of the paragraph on page 228 is that the duck-billed platypus is an interesting and unusual animal. Now think about how the other sentences in the paragraph support the idea that the duck-billed platypus is interesting and unusual. One interesting detail is that its fur is like that of an otter or a weasel. Another is that its tail looks like the tail of a beaver. Its webbed feet and its bill like a duck's are unusual. All the other sentences in the paragraph support the main idea that the duck-billed platypus is an interesting and unusual animal.

Where can you find the main idea?

When the main idea is stated in a sentence, it may be found anywhere in the paragraph. The main idea may be stated at the beginning, in the middle, or at the end of a paragraph.

Read the paragraph that follows, and find the sentence that states the main idea:

Scientists who study the cold continent of Antarctica have found coal and fossils of fern and coral beneath the thick ice. They know that coal begins to form in warm, swampy places. They know that ferns and coral grow only in warm places. These facts have made scientists begin to feel that Antarctica was not always the cold continent it is today.

In this paragraph, the last sentence sums up what all the other sentences say. The first three sentences tell about things found in Antarctica that could have formed or grown only in warm places. They support the main idea: *These facts have made scientists begin to feel that Antarctica was not always the cold continent it is today.*

When the main idea is located in the middle of the paragraph, it is sometimes harder to find. Read the following paragraph, and find the main idea:

There are study centers on land in Antarctica where scientists record the thickness and movement of the ice sheet. They also study the seals and penguins that live near the edge of the land. Scientists study Antarctica both on land and from the sea. Scientists work in study centers on ships off the coast of Antarctica and sail around the continent. They write down the temperatures of the air and water. They also collect sea creatures to study.

The first part of the paragraph tells about what the scientists on the land of Antarctica study. The last part of the paragraph tells about what they study from the sea. One sentence in the middle of the paragraph, *Scientists study Antarctica both on land and from the sea,* sums up what all the sentences are about.

REVIEW

Look over the headings of this lesson and recite the answers to the questions they ask. Now you are ready to try to find the main idea of some paragraphs.

CHOOSING THE MAIN IDEA OF A PARAGRAPH

Read each of the following paragraphs carefully. Select the sentence following the paragraph that best expresses the main idea. On a sheet of paper, write the letter of that sentence beside the number of the paragraph.

1. Greenland is more than fourteen hundred miles long. In some places it is over seven hundred miles wide. It is about one quarter of the size of the United States. It is much larger than Denmark, the small country that owns Greenland. Greenland is the largest island in the world.

    a. Greenland is more than fourteen hundred miles long.

    b. Greenland is the largest island in the world.

    c. It is much larger than Denmark, the small country that owns Greenland.

2. Most people think of an artist as someone who paints or draws pictures. Many people do not know that an artist is someone who practices any of the fine arts. They may not know that a sculptor is an artist. They may never have thought of a great musician as an artist. When some people read a fine poem, they may not know that they are reading the work of an artist.

a. When some people read a fine poem, they may not know that they are reading the work of an artist.

b. Most people think of an artist as someone who paints or draws pictures.

c. Many people do not know that an artist is someone who practices any of the fine arts.

The Spider, the Cave, and the Pottery Bowl

by ELEANOR CLYMER

In a certain place in the desert there is a cave, and sometimes outside the cave you can see a spider in its web. And on the shelf in my grandmother's house there is a pottery bowl. All these things are connected, and this is what I am going to tell about. But first I must tell about myself.

I am Indian. My name is an Indian word meaning "One Who Dips Water." But in school they call me Kate. In winter I live with my father and mother and brother Johnny in a town near the edge of the desert. My father works in a store. There is a garage next to the store, and he helps there too. We have a garden and peach trees. We have a wooden house. We have running water and electricity. We

aren't rich, but we have those things.

But in summer Johnny and I go back to the mesa where my grandmother lives. We used to live there too, but we moved away. Grandmother's house is part of a village built of stone, with many small rooms, all connected, like a wall of houses around an open place. It's a small village. Some of the houses have other houses that were built on top of them when more rooms were needed. The village is very old, many hundreds of years old.

When you drive across the desert, you can see the mesa, like a high wall of rock ahead of you. And on top is the village.

I love it on the mesa. It is windy, hot in the sun but cool in the shade of the houses, and you can see far out over the desert — the Painted Desert they call it because it looks as if it were painted. It is beautiful on the mesa, but it is hard to live there. There is no water. The people must carry water up from springs down below. They must carry up everything they need, and they must go down to tend their gardens and walk a long way through the desert to find grass or plants for their sheep to eat. It is hard work.

That is why some people moved away. My father doesn't mind hard work, but he needed to earn money for us. So we had to go away to the town.

But every summer we came back, my mother and my brother and I. We stayed in my grandmother's house. My mother helped Grandmother with the summer work. And I helped too. We went down below and worked in the garden, and we dried the corn and squash for the winter. We gathered peaches from the orchard at the foot of the mesa, and we dried them. My brother played with his friends and rode the burros that live in the corral.

We gathered firewood for the stove and for the fireplace and piled it up for the winter. We plastered the walls to make the house look clean. And we went a few miles away and brought home clay for the pottery.

The pottery is what I love most of all. I love to work the cool, wet clay between my hands. When I was little, my grandmother gave me pieces of clay to play with, and I made things out of them. I made little animals: sheep and donkeys and birds.

Then when I got bigger, I watched my grandmother make bowls and jars. She made a flat piece for the bottom. Then she rolled pieces of clay into long rolls between her hands and coiled them on top of the flat piece till she had built up a jar. She smoothed it with a stone or a piece of shell and shaped it in beautiful curves. When it was dry, she painted it with lovely designs. I watched her hand holding the brush of yucca leaves, slowly painting birds and leaves around the curving sides of the bowl. When she had enough bowls and jars, she built a fire and baked them hard.

People came to buy them, and

my father took some to sell in the store where he works. But one bowl was never for sale. It stood on the shelf in the corner. It had been there for as long as I could remember.

But this summer was different. My mother could not go to Grandmother's. She had to stay behind and work in a hotel to earn extra money.

She said to me, "Kate, you are big. You will help Grandmother. And Johnny is big enough to bring wood and water."

I promised to help. Johnny was hoping he could go with the big boys to herd sheep. He thought he was big enough this year.

My father drove us to the mesa in the truck. The mesa is about forty miles from our town. We rode across the desert, between red and black and yellow rocks, and between sand dunes covered with sage and yellow-flowered rabbit brush.

At last we saw the houses and the store and the school at the foot of the mesa. We took the narrow, rocky road up the side of the mesa, and at last we came out in the open space on top.

It was good to be there. We jumped out of the truck and ran to see our friends. My best friend, Louisa, was there with her mother. She lives on the mesa all the time. I was so glad to see Louisa that we hugged each other. Summer is the only time we can really be together.

My grandmother was waiting for us in the doorway of her house. When I saw her, I was surprised. She looked much older than the last time I had seen her. I had always thought of Grandmother as a strong, plump woman with black hair. This year she looked smaller, thinner, and her hair was gray.

Father noticed too. He said to her, "Are you all right?"

Grandmother said, "Yes, I am well."

Father carried in the basket of food we had brought and the boxes with our clothes.

Father asked about Grandmother's garden. But she said she had not planted a garden this year. Then he asked if she had any pottery for him to take back, and she said, "No, I have not made any."

Father said good-by then. As he was leaving, he said to me, "Remember, if you need Mother or me, go down to the store and telephone, and we will come."

The first days passed. I did everything I could think of. I tried to grind corn on the *metate* (the grinding stone), thinking it would please Grandmother. But I did not really know how to do it, and it was easier to cook the ready-made cornmeal. I washed the cups and bowls and shook out the bedding. I swept the house. Grandmother did not do much. She rested most of the time.

Nearly every day some tourists came. When the tourists asked for pottery, I had to say that we had none. I wondered when we were going to make some, but I did not like to ask.

Then one day I did ask. There had been lots of tourists, all looking for pottery. When they went away, I said, "Grandmother, when will we make some?"

She said, "There is no more clay."

I knew there was none in the storeroom. Always before, there had been chunks of the grayish clay there, waiting to be ground up and soaked in water and shaped into bowls.

Grandmother used to carry it herself from a place she knew, a mile or so from the mesa. Later on, Father had brought it in the truck. But this year she had not asked him to get any.

"The bed of clay is used up," she said.

I said, "But there are other beds. Louisa's mother and the other women know where to get clay. I can go with them and get some."

She said, "The clay that I used was very fine. It needed nothing mixed with it to keep it from cracking."

I knew what she meant. Some kinds of clay will crack in the firing unless they are mixed with sand or ground-up bits of old pottery. But the kind she liked was good enough to be used alone. And there was no more of it.

I said, "Well, I will get some other kind, and you can show me what to do."

She nodded and said, "Perhaps. Perhaps later."

So there was nothing to be done, except to do my work and remind Johnny to do his. But most of the time he was nowhere in sight.

Johnny was disappointed too. There were no big boys for him to go herding with, and none of the men wanted to take him to the cornfields. So all he did was play with the burros.

One day Louisa and I went to get some firewood on the mesa top, beyond the village. We took cloths along and piled juniper twigs in them. It was hot; there

was no shade to protect us from the sun. The wind blew, but that only made it hotter.

As we walked back with our firewood, I felt hot and dusty, and I would have liked to have had a bath. But on the mesa there was no water for bathing.

As we came toward the village, there was a loud noise: boys' voices shouting and burros' hoofs clattering on the stone. Johnny and three other boys had come running into the plaza. They had let the burros out of the corral and were trying to lasso them. It made a terrible dust, and people began running out of the houses, shouting at them.

In the middle of all this, there were some tourists in a big white car. The people inside the car looked scared.

Louisa's mother came out with a broom and chased the burros away. She told Johnny to go home, and she shouted at the other boys to drive the burros back to the corral.

After I said good-by to Louisa, I went home with my firewood and put it down beside the stove. Johnny was sitting at the table.

Then there was a knock at the door. It was one of the old men of the village.

"Please come in," Grandmother said.

He entered and looked at Johnny. He said, "You and your friends must be more polite. Those strangers are our guests. If you are not careful, the *kachinas* will whip you. *Kachinas* are the spirits that take care of people. They bring rain for the cornfields, and they bring gifts for good children and punishment for bad ones."

Johnny looked frightened.

After the old man went away, I wanted to talk about something else to make Johnny feel better, so I went over to the shelf in the corner, lifted the pottery bowl down, and held it.

"Be careful!" said Grandmother.

Johnny asked, "Where did that come from?"

Grandmother said, "It belonged to the Old Ones, our ancestors. Long ago your grandfather was working with some white men in the ruins on the other side of the mesa. He brought it home to me. It was in a cave. There were other bowls, but only this one was perfect. I learned from studying it how to make my own pottery."

Johnny got up and looked into the bowl. There were some smooth stones in it. We both knew what they were. They were Grandmother's polishing stones, the ones she used for rubbing her pottery to make it smooth and shiny. Johnny reached in and took them out and felt them with his fingers.

Grandmother said, "Your grandfather found them in the bowl. A woman used them long ago, and I have used them all these years."

With his finger Johnny traced the design on the bowl. It was a bird with a pointed beak and outspread wings.

"It's pretty," he said.

Then he went to put the stones back into the bowl. In doing so, he pushed my arm. The bowl fell to the floor and smashed.

We both stood there staring at the pieces on the floor. Then we looked at Grandmother. What would she say? I was sure she would be very angry. Maybe the *kachinas* would whip both of us. After all, I had taken the bowl down, so it was my fault just as much as Johnny's.

But Grandmother did not scold us. She only looked very sad for a moment. Then she said, "Pick up the pieces and put them into a basket. Perhaps we can mend it."

I didn't think we could, but I picked them up and put them with the polishing stones into a basket.

When I looked up, Johnny was gone. I thought, "I guess he feels pretty bad. I'll leave him alone for a while."

And I began to get supper ready. When it was done, I went out to call Johnny, but he didn't answer. I asked some of the boys if they had seen him, and they said, "Yes, up by the corral." So I went up there, and he was standing patting his favorite burro. She had her nose on his shoulder as if she were sympathizing with him.

I told him to come home and eat, and he said he wasn't hungry. But I said it was time to come anyhow, so he came with me. I had cooked bacon and corn bread, and we had peaches and cake that I had bought at the store. I noticed Johnny ate quite a lot, though he had said he wasn't hungry.

After supper Grandmother lay down on her bed, but instead of going to sleep, she began to tell stories.

She told some we had heard before, ones we liked to hear again. She told the story about where our people came from. She told about the Spider Woman, the grandmother of us all, who took care of the people and showed them where to live. That was why we must never kill a spider, because it could be Grandmother Spider herself.

Then she told us a story I had never heard before. She said, "On the far side of the mesa, there is a path that leads to the fields below. And beside the path there is a spring. It is not the spring we all use. It is a very small, secret spring. There is a hollow place nearby, under the rocks. That is where Grandmother Spider lives. It is her secret house. If you see her there, spinning her web, you must not stop. You must lay a stick of firewood beside the path for the Spider Woman and hurry on. If you stop to talk to her, she may invite you into her house. Once you go in, you may have to stay there. So be careful, and do not go that way."

Then she closed her eyes, and I could tell from her breathing that she was asleep. Johnny was almost asleep. I pulled him up and led him over to his bed, and he fell onto it and was sound asleep in a minute.

Then I went to bed myself. I thought about the stories. Why did Grandmother tell us those stories? Especially the one about the spring. Which spring was it? Could it be the one where Louisa and I sometimes went for water? No, it couldn't be. It must be one somewhere else.

I had a strange dream. I dreamed that out of the fireplace came something small and gray. It was a spider. It looked all around and waved its little feet in the air as if it was looking for something. It ran up the wall to the shelf. I looked, and there was the pottery bowl where it had always been. I thought, "Oh, I'm so glad it wasn't broken after all." The spider ran inside the bowl and disappeared, and then I woke up and it was daylight.

Sometimes dreams fade away as soon as you wake up, but this dream was as clear as if it had been real life. The first thing I did was to jump out of bed to look at the shelf to see if the bowl was there but of course it wasn't.

Then I saw something else. Johnny wasn't there. I thought it was strange that he should be out so early. Most days it was hard to get him out of bed. I looked outside the door, but he was not in sight. I wondered if he had gone for water, but the pails were empty. So I put my clothes on and went myself.

At the top of the path, I met a couple of men who were going to work in their fields. I could tell where they were going because they had their hoes.

One of them was angry. He was saying, "I don't see how she could have gotten out."

I said, "Good morning. Did you lose something?"

He said, "Yes, my burro. She got out of the corral somehow. I don't know how, because the others aren't out. Did you see her?"

I said, "No, but I'll look for her." I hurried home. Grand-

mother was awake. I said, "Did you see Johnny?"

She hadn't seen him. I was sure he had something to do with the burro. It was the one he liked so much.

I said to Grandmother, "One of the neighbors' burros is missing. Maybe Johnny has taken it, not knowing the man wanted it for work this morning. I will go and see if I can find him."

Grandmother nodded and said, "He is troubled about the bowl. Tell him it does not matter. I am not angry. Last night I was sad, but now I think that perhaps it had to be. The Old Ones may have wanted it back."

I was just going when she said, "Wait. Eat first and take some food and water with you. Never go out in the desert without food and water." So I put some cornbread and a bottle of water into a basket.

Then I went to the corral. It was true that the little female burro was gone. But which way did she go? I looked around on the ground and found some little hoofmarks. Then I looked to see which way they went.

Back of the village, the mesa top stretches out for miles. Desert plants grow on it — juniper and sagebrush and some cactus. I started to walk away from the village, and I could see where twigs and leaves had been broken, and I thought that must be the way Johnny went.

I found a path where there were some little hoofprints. I followed them as fast as I could.

The mesa has valleys in it like big cracks in a table top. We call them washes, because when there is a thunderstorm, the water washes down them like a flood.

I looked up at the sky and thought, "I'm glad it's not going to rain today," though we had all been hoping for rain for many days because it was so dry. But there were only white clouds in the blue sky, the fluffy kind that never do anything.

I was coming to one of those washes. The path led down the slope into the valley. It wasn't steep like the edge of the mesa where the village is; still, it was pretty far down. I squinted my eyes, and yes, down in the valley

I saw a boy on a burro. They looked very tiny. I yelled, "Johnny!" But of course he couldn't hear. So I started down. The ground had a lot of loose sand and stones, and I slid partway down, holding on to bushes as I went. At last I got to the bottom.

I was getting tired, and I thought, "Why am I hurrying? Johnny knows the way back, and besides, he has the burro."

But then I looked up at the sky, and I saw that there was good reason to hurry. Instead of the fluffy white clouds, all of a sudden there were thunderclouds, tall gray clouds standing like mountains in the west. The sun was still bright, and as long as the clouds did not cover the sun, I did not feel frightened. But they were moving. In the desert a storm can come up in a few minutes. I began to run and to shout, "Johnny!"

He heard me and stopped, and then turned the burro and came toward me. I ran as hard as I

could and pointed to the sky, and he understood. At last I caught up to him. I was out of breath and couldn't talk, but I climbed on the burro and beat her with my heels to make her run. Johnny ran on ahead. We were in the middle of the valley, and it was maybe half a mile to the opposite side, to a higher spot where we would be safe. We got there just in time.

In a few minutes we heard thunder. Then the cloudburst came. The rain poured down, and in no time the wash was running like a river. Mud and rocks and tree branches came tumbling down in the roaring water.

Then I heard Johnny yell, "Come up here!"

He had found a cave, really an overhanging arch in the rock, and was standing there out of the rain. I pulled the burro and went up there too, and we sat down and watched the rain fall. We sat for a long time. We ate the bread and drank the water I had brought.

I asked, "Where were you going?"

But he wouldn't tell. I said, "Maybe you were going to look for Grandmother Spider."

Then he laughed and said, "No."

I said, "Well, then what?"

He said, "If I tell you, you'll laugh at me."

I promised not to laugh. Then he said, "Grandfather found that bowl in the ruins where the Old Ones used to live. I broke it, so I was going to find another."

I said, "But Johnny, there aren't any left. The white people took them all away long ago."

He said, "White people couldn't find them all. I would find one that they didn't see."

We stood up and looked around at the rock shelter we were in. It might have been a good place for the Old Ones to live, though if their houses had ever been there, they had crumbled away. But at the back, under one end of the arch, there was a crack, really a hole in the rock, partly filled with stones and sand, and we noticed that a trickle of water ran out of it and down the slope.

"There must be a spring in there," I said.

"Let's go in," Johnny said. "It looks like a deep hole. Maybe there are some ruins inside."

Just then I noticed something. Near the entrance, a spider web was stretched across the branches of a little bush. I would not have seen it if the sun hadn't come out and made drops of water on the threads sparkle in the light. In the middle of the web was the spider. Some little flies were buzzing about. One of them hit the web and was trapped. At once the spider pulled in all her legs and jumped on the fly. I thought how clever she was to make her web by the spring where the flies would come.

Then I thought, "Maybe it's the Spider Woman!" And I shouted to Johnny, "Don't go in!" But it was too late. He was inside the hole. "Now," I thought, "the Spider Woman will get him, and he will have to stay in her house forever."

I felt frightened. But I could not let him go in there alone. I tied the burro to a bush and crawled in after Johnny.

It was pretty dark inside. At first I couldn't see anything. Then my eyes got used to the darkness, and I saw Johnny at the back of the cave. The cave was larger inside than I had thought it would be. Its floor was damp with the water that trickled down from the wall. I guess the water flowing for many years had hollowed out the cave.

"Did you find anything?" I asked.

"Yes," said Johnny, "an old basket and a stick."

I went to the back of the cave to look. Somebody had been digging there and had gone away and left the things behind. I tried to lift the basket, but it was heavy. I dragged it to the entrance and looked inside.

Johnny said, "It's just a lot of dirt. I wanted to find pottery."

I said, "Johnny, you did!"

He thought I was joking. He said, "It's only sand."

I said, "It's not sand. It's clay. There's clay in this cave. We can make pottery with it."

The clay was between two layers of rock in the wall at the back of the cave. We took the old digging stick and dug it out. We put it in Johnny's shirt to carry it. We wanted to take the clay we had found in the old basket, but it was heavy. Besides, the basket was rotted with dampness, and I was afraid it would break, so we left it there.

We took as much clay as we could carry and went outside. The sky was blue. The water was still running down the wash, but we could cross it. We loaded our clay on the burro and started home.

Johnny led the burro down the slope, but I stayed behind. I went back to the place where the spider web hung. The spider was waiting for another fly.

I bent down and said, "Thank you, Grandmother Spider. I saw you last night in my dream. I thought you were telling me something. Now I think I understand." Then I looked around for a piece of firewood to lay beside the spring. I couldn't find one, so I laid down the digging stick that I had in my hand.

I ran to catch up with Johnny, and we led the burro down the slope. We climbed the other side of the wash and walked across the mesa to the village. It was getting toward evening. We had been gone a long time.

Grandmother was sitting inside the door waiting for us. She looked sad and small and very old.

I said, "Here we are."

She said, "So you found him. Where did you go?"

I wanted to say, "To Grandmother Spider's house." But I was afraid she would think I was joking. You must not joke about such things. So I just said,

"Across the wash. We've brought you a present from there."

I laid Johnny's shirt on the floor and untied it. She bent down and took a handful and felt it with her fingers.

"Clay!" she said. "The best kind of clay!" She smiled at me. "Where did you get it?"

I told her, "Across the wash there is a kind of cave, really just a hole in the rocks, with water trickling from it. We found a basket of clay and a digging stick."

Grandmother said, "I know that place. A woman was digging there. She had her child with her, and the child was playing outside. There was a storm, and she ran out to save the child and never went back."

I asked, "Did she save the child?"

She said, "Yes, the child is grown up now. But we never went back. We thought it was bad luck. But you see, after many years it is time for good things to happen. It doesn't hurt to wait." Then she looked at Johnny and asked, "Why did you run away? And why did you take the burro?"

He looked a little scared because he knew he shouldn't have taken the burro without permission. But he was brave.

He said, "I was sorry I broke the bowl. I wanted to find another bowl in the place where the Old Ones lived. But I didn't know how far it would be, so I took the burro. But I didn't find a bowl. Kate says there are no more left. She says the white people took them all away."

Grandmother said, "They could not take them all. There are still many left, but they are buried in the earth. You would have to dig deep to find them. But what you did find is better. We will make our own bowls now."

AUTHOR

Eleanor Clymer, who has written over fifty children's books, began making up her own stories and poems when she was six years old. She says that her taste for stories came from her mother, who recited poetry, sang folk songs, and read aloud.

Mrs. Clymer was born and brought up in New York City. In high school she wrote and edited the school magazine, and in college she studied story writing. Later, after she married and had a child, she began to write children's books.

Mrs. Clymer has written stories based on the everyday life of children she has known. In recent years, she has been able to travel and to write about what she has seen. Her interest in archaeology led her to visit ancient ruins and to write the story *The Spider, the Cave, and the Pottery Bowl*. This book received an award for its true picture of the Southwest.

The Fast Sooner Hound

by ARNA BONTEMPS and JACK CONROY

A railroad man was walking down the street with his hands in his overall pockets. A long-legged, lop-eared hound trotted behind him. The man was smoking a pipe. After a while he stopped walking, took the pipe out of his mouth, and turned to the hound.

"Well, Sooner," he said, "here's the place."

They had come to a small building near the railroad tracks. Over the front door was a sign that said "Roadmaster." The dog didn't seem to pay much attention to the man's words. But when the man opened the door, the hound followed him inside.

The man in the office looked up from his desk. "What do you want?" he asked.

"I'm a Boomer fireman," the railroad man said. "And I'm looking for a job."

"So you're a Boomer! Well, I know what that means. You go from one railroad to another."

"That's right," the man in overalls answered proudly. "Last year I shoveled coal on the Katy. Before that I worked for the Frisco line. Before that it was the Wabash. I travel light. I travel far. And I don't let any grass grow under my feet."

"We might be able to use you on one of our trains," said the Roadmaster. "Have you got some place you can leave the dog?"

"Leave my dog!" cried the Boomer, knocking the ashes out of his pipe. "Listen here, Mr. Roadmaster, that Sooner always goes along with me."

"He does, eh? And why do you call him a Sooner?"

"He'd sooner run than eat — that's why. I raised him from a pup. And he ain't ever spent a night or a day or even an hour away from me. He'd cry fit to break his heart if we weren't together. He'd cry so loud you couldn't hear yourself think."

"I don't see how I can give you a job with the hound," the Roadmaster said. "It's against the rules of the railroad to allow a passenger in the cab. Makes no difference if it's person or beast. Nobody is allowed to ride with the fireman and the engineer in the cab. Nobody is allowed in the caboose. That's Rule Number One on this road. It's never been broken yet. What's more, it never will be broken as long as I'm Roadmaster. So it looks as if that Sooner is going to spoil things for you."

"Why, he ain't no trouble," said the Boomer. "He don't have to ride in the cab. He just runs alongside the train. When I'm on a freight train, he chases around a little in the fields to pass the time away. Sometimes he scares up a rabbit — just to play with when things get dull. But he ain't no trouble to nobody. He never rides in the cab *or* the caboose."

"You mean that old hungry-looking hound can outrun a freight train?" The Roadmaster laughed. "You can't make me believe that!"

"Shucks — he'll do it without half trying," said the Boomer proudly.

"Matter of fact, it will be a little bit tiresome on him having to travel so slow. Even so, that Sooner will put up with anything just to stay close by me. He loves me that much."

"Oh, come now," said the Roadmaster. "The dog isn't born that can outrun one of our freight trains. We run the fastest freights from coast to coast. That's why we get so much business. I'm sorry we can't give you a job. You look like a man that could keep a boiler popping off on an uphill grade. But I just don't see how we can work it with the hound."

"Listen," said the Boomer. "I'll lay my first pay check against a dollar bill that my Sooner will run circles around your freight train. What's more, he'll be as fresh as a daisy when we pull into the junction. His tongue won't even be hanging out. Of course, he'll want to trot around the station about a hundred times before we start — just to limber up, you know."

"It's a bet," said the Roadmaster. "You can have the job. I'm not a mean man, you know, but Rule One has got to stick."

So the Boomer fireman climbed into a cab beside the engineer and began to shovel coal for all he was worth. The freight train pulled out of the station and started to pick up speed. The Sooner loped along beside it. In no time at all, he had left the freight train far behind. Sometimes he would pop out of sight in the underbrush along the tracks in search of rabbits or squirrels. But before long he could be seen up ahead, waiting for the train to catch up. Once the Boomer looked out of the cab and saw a strange look on the hound's face. The Engineer noticed it too.

"What's the matter with your Sooner?" the Engineer asked. "He looks worried."

"That's right," the Boomer said. "He's worried about

the hog law. That's the law that says we can't work more than sixteen hours on this run. If that happens, we'll have to stop this train in the middle of the fields and wait for a fresh crew to take our places. I reckon that Sooner thinks we're going to get in trouble running so slow."

"Why, this ain't slow!" exclaimed the Engineer. "This engine is doing all it can. The boiler is hot enough to pop."

"Well, it ain't no speed for my Sooner." The Boomer laughed.

The freight train made its run and then returned. The Sooner led it all the way. And when the dog trotted into the Roadmaster's office a mile ahead of the train, the Roadmaster got angry. He knew right away that he had

257

lost his bet, but he didn't mind that. What he minded was what people would say about a freight train that couldn't keep up with a long-legged, lop-eared Sooner hound. They would say the train wasn't any good. The Roadmaster couldn't put up with such talk as that. No, sir. His freight trains must keep the name of being the fastest in the country.

"Look here, Boomer," he said, as the fireman climbed down from the cab. "You won the bet. That Sooner outran the freight train, but I'm going to transfer you to a local passenger run. What do you think about that?"

"Suits me," said the Boomer. "Me and my Sooner ain't choicy. We take the jobs we get, and we always stay together."

"You think the hound can keep up with our passenger train?"

"He'll do it easy," said the Boomer. "No trouble at all."

"If he beats our local, there'll be two dollars waiting for you when you get back. That Sooner is faster than he looks, but I don't believe he can beat a passenger train."

So the race was on again. The Sooner speeded up to a trot as they pulled out of the station. It seemed for a while that the passenger train might get ahead of him. But just as the race was getting exciting, the local train had to stop to pick up passengers. The Sooner had to run around in the fields so he wouldn't get too far ahead of the engine. Even so, he won the race. He came into the station ten minutes ahead of the passenger train.

The Roadmaster thought that maybe the stops were to blame for the local not keeping up with the Sooner

hound. The next time he put the Boomer in the cab of a limited passenger train that didn't make any stops till it got to the end of the line. So another race was on.

By that time, people who lived along the railroad tracks were getting interested in the races. They came out of their houses to see the old mangy, no-good Sooner hound that could outrun the trains and still come into the station without his tongue hanging out an inch and without panting the least bit. They began to think that something was surely wrong with the trains. But the trains were really right on schedule. They were keeping up their best speed. The trouble was with that old Sooner. He ran so fast he made the trains seem slow. He did it so easily you wouldn't think he was getting anywhere until you saw him pull away from the trains. But you couldn't tell that to the country people. They felt sure the trains were slowing down. They began to talk about not riding on them any more.

"Why," they said, "passengers might just as well walk. They could get there just as fast. Those trains are too slow to talk about. If you shipped a yearling calf to market on one of them, he'd be a grown-up beef by the time he got there."

When the Roadmaster heard that kind of talk, he got mad enough to bite the heads off nails. It would have to stop. Why, that old lop-eared Sooner was spoiling everything for the railroad. The people wouldn't ride the trains, and they were sending all their freight by trucks. The Roadmaster had half a mind to fire the Boomer and tell him to take his hound and go somewhere else. He hated to own he was licked, though. He was a stubborn man, and he didn't want to admit that the Sooner was just too fast for his trains.

"Hey, Boomer," he said one day, as the fireman climbed down from the cab at the end of a run. "That Sooner of yours is causing this road a lot of trouble. That no-good hound makes our trains look like snails."

"It ain't my Sooner that causes the trouble," said the Boomer. "It's that Rule Number One. My dog don't aim to give the road a black eye by outrunning the trains. He just aims to stay near me, that's all. Do away with the rule and let him ride with me in the cab, and everything will be okay."

"Not on your life. That's the oldest rule on this road, and I don't plan to change it on account of an old, mangy, lop-eared Sooner hound."

The Boomer shrugged his shoulders as he turned to walk away. "It's your railroad, Mr. Roadmaster," he said. Then he reached down and patted the Sooner's head. "Don't look ashamed, Sooner," he told his hound. "It ain't your fault at all."

Before the Boomer and the hound were out of sight, the Roadmaster had a fine idea. "I'll fix that Sooner," he said, snapping his fingers. "I've got what it takes to beat him. I'll put the Boomer in the cab of our Cannon Ball. That's the fastest thing on wheels. The Sooner hound is about the fastest thing on four legs. Now, if the fastest thing on four legs can beat the fastest thing on wheels, I'll admire to see it. That Sooner will be left so far behind, it'll take a dollar to send him a postcard."

"You're going to a lot of trouble," the Boomer said to the Roadmaster, when he heard the plan. "There's no use for all this fuss. Just let my dog ride in the cab with me. That's all *he* wants. It's all *I* want."

But the Roadmaster wouldn't change his plan. He was so sure the Cannon Ball would leave the Sooner far behind that he smiled from ear to ear.

"I aim to see this race from the cab myself," he said, "but if that Sooner beats the Cannon Ball, I'll walk back, and he can have my seat."

Word got around that the Sooner was going to try to keep up with the Cannon Ball. Farmers left off plowing, hitched up, and drove to the railroad crossings to see the sight. The children were dismissed from school. So many men left the towns to see the race, the factories had to close down. It was like circus day or the county fair.

Just before the starting whistle blew, the Roadmaster climbed into the cab of the Cannon Ball with the Boomer and the Engineer. He wanted to be sure that the Boomer shoveled plenty of coal and that the Engineer kept the fast train moving at top speed. He also wanted to be close at hand to laugh at the Boomer when the Cannon Ball pulled away from the old lop-eared Sooner.

A clear track for a hundred miles was ordered for the Cannon Ball, and all the switches were spiked down.

The train pulled out of the station like a streak of lightning. It took three men to see the Cannon Ball pass on that run: one to say, "There it comes," one to say, "Here it is," and another to say, "There it goes." You couldn't see a thing for steam, cinders, and smoke. The rails sang like a violin for half an hour after the train had passed into the next county.

Every valve was popping off. The wheels rose three feet in the air above the roadbed. The Boomer shoveled coal for all he was worth, but he worked with a smile on his face. He knew his hound, and he didn't mind giving the dog a good run. He worked so hard he wore the hinges off the fire door. He wore the shovel down to a nub. He sweated so hard his socks got soaking wet in his shoes.

The Roadmaster stuck his head out of the cab window. *Whoosh!* Off went his hat — and he nearly lost his head too. Gravel pinged against his goggles like hailstones. He peered through the smoke and steam. Where was the Sooner? The Roadmaster couldn't see hide nor hair of him anywhere. He let out a whoop of joy.

"The SOONER! The SOONER!" he yelled. "He's *nowhere* in sight! This is the time we outran that old lop-eared hound."

"I can't understand that," the Boomer said. "That Sooner ain't never failed me before. It just ain't like him to lay down on me. Let me take a look."

He dropped his shovel and poked his head out of the

window. He looked far and wide. The Roadmaster was right. The Sooner was nowhere to be seen. Where could he be?

The Roadmaster kept poking fun at the Boomer and laughing all the rest of the way to the station. But the Boomer didn't answer. Every moment or two he'd glance out of the window. Surely something was wrong. What had become of his Sooner?

Presently the station came into sight. The Cannon Ball began to slow down.

A moment later the Boomer saw a great crowd of people around the station. He supposed they were waiting to greet the Cannon Ball and to give it a cheer for making such a fast run. But no, they weren't even looking down the tracks. They were all watching something else.

"Those people aren't even noticing us," the Roadmaster said to the Engineer. "Blow the whistle."

The Engineer blew the whistle just before he brought the Cannon Ball to a stop. Still nobody paid any attention. The people were all looking the other way and laughing. The Boomer and the Roadmaster and the Engineer were all puzzled. They climbed down out of the cab.

"Well, here we are!" the Roadmaster cried, trying to get some attention. Nobody gave him any, so he pushed his way through the crowd. "What's going on here?" he insisted. "Didn't you people come down here to see the Cannon Ball?"

"Take it away," somebody answered. "It's too slow to catch cold. The Sooner's been here ten minutes and more."

The Boomer's heart gave a big jump when he heard that news. It seemed too good to be true. But a minute later he saw with his own eyes. Around the corner of the station came the old lop-eared hound, chasing a rabbit that he had rounded up along the way. He was having so much fun playing with the little creature and making the people laugh, that he had plumb forgot about the Cannon Ball.

"He's here!" the Boomer shouted. "He's here! My Sooner's true blue, and he's won again!"

The Roadmaster was overcome. "P-p-put him in the cab," he sputtered. "P-p-put him in the cab and get going."

"But where will *you* sit?" the Boomer asked with a grin.

"I'll walk," the Roadmaster answered. "Anything to stop that hound from outrunning our trains."

A few moments later the Boomer was back in the cab, his hound beside him. The big crowd of people let out a great cheer as the Cannon Ball pulled out of the station for the home trip. The Sooner seemed to know whom the cheer was for. There was an unmistakable smile on his face. As the train gathered speed, his long ears flapped gaily in the breeze.

Just before the station went out of sight, the three in the cab of the Cannon Ball saw a man leave the crowd and begin to walk down the tracks. It was the Roadmaster starting for home.

AUTHOR

Arna Bontemps was one of America's most distinguished writers. In his lifetime, he was a librarian, a high-school teacher, a college professor, a poet, and a writer of plays, biographies, and fiction on black life for both children and adults. He was the winner of many awards, including the Jane Addams Children's Book Award for furthering the cause of peace and justice.

Born in Alexandria, Louisiana, he grew up in Los Angeles, California, and lived in New York, Alabama, Illinois, and Connecticut. He had married, had had six children, and had visited most parts of the world before his death in 1973 at his home in Nashville, Tennessee.

When he was asked why he decided to write for children, Mr. Bontemps replied, "For two reasons. As a child, I read a great deal and never forgot the books I had enjoyed most, and secondly, by the time I started writing as a man, I had children of my own and wanted them to read *my* books — as well as other people's, of course." He said that he never had to worry about ideas for books but that he had trouble finding enough time to write them all down.

The other author of *The Fast Sooner Hound,* the story you have just read, is Jack Conroy, who sometimes worked with Arna Bontemps. Mr. Conroy also writes on his own and has been a folk-lorist, a literary critic, and an editor.

Starting from Scratch

One of the most fascinating things about our language is that common words can be used in so many special ways. Sometimes a phrase of two or more words can mean something completely different from what the words would mean if they were not used together. "The Fast Sooner Hound" has some examples of this special way of using words.

In telling the Roadmaster why he wanted the dog to stay with him, the Boomer said the dog would cry fit *"to break his heart* if we weren't together." Does that mean that the dog's heart would actually break into pieces? *To break one's heart* means "to cause disappointment, sorrow, or grief." The Boomer simply meant that his dog would be very disappointed and sad if they had to be separated.

Do you remember reading how the Boomer shoveled coal *for all he was worth?* The author was not talking about how much money the Boomer had. *For all one's worth* means "to the most of one's powers or abilities." The Boomer was shoveling coal as well as he possibly could.

You probably use special phrases every day. Do you ever say something like, "I'll *stick up for you* because you're my friend"? You don't mean that you'll use a stick for anything. *To stick up for someone* is "to defend or support that person, usually by saying or doing something kind about or for the person."

Did you ever tell anyone that you made something *from scratch? From scratch* means "beginning from the start." If you make a cake *from scratch,* for example, you don't begin with a prepared mix. You get the shortening, the flour, the eggs, and whatever else you need and mix them yourself from the very beginning.

You read the phrase *break his heart* in "The Fast Sooner Hound." Can you think of other phrases with the word *heart* in them? Can you think of any phrases with the word *head* in them? If you need to, look up the words *heart* and *head* in your dictionary. You'll probably find some common phrases there.

Books to Enjoy

And It Is Still That Way by Byrd Baylor

The author has collected favorite legends retold by Papago, Hopi, Apache, and other Native American children from Arizona.

Paddington on Top by Michael Bond

Paddington the bear always comes out on top in each of these funny, mixed-up adventures.

Jane Goodall by Eleanor Coerr

This is the life story of a scientist who is famous for studying chimpanzees in Tanzania, Africa.

The Skates of Uncle Richard by Carol Fenner

Marsha dreams of becoming a champion figure skater, but with the ugly old skates that were Uncle Richard's, how can she?

Can't You Make Them Behave, King George?
by Jean Fritz

This humorous biography tells of the troubles that King George III of England had with the colonists during the American Revolution.

What Can She Be? A Geologist
by Gloria and Esther Goldreich

Many good photographs help to show the real-life career of a geologist, a person who studies rocks, mountains, rivers, oceans, caves, and other parts of the earth.

Gateways

MAGAZINE THREE

Contents

The Mysterious House

by HANS JÜRGEN PRESS

At 49 Canal Street was the headquarters of the Handprint Club, a group of children who were very clever in tracking down criminals. They used the top room, called the Airport, just under the pigeon loft on the roof. The Club met there regularly after school. Frank, who played the trumpet, was the leader. Then there were Ralph and quick-witted Angela. And lastly, there was Keith W.S., who had a pet squirrel with him all the time. (W.S. stands for "With Squirrel.")

This story tells how the Handprint Club solved one case. It will also let you, the reader, try your skill at discovering the clues. You can follow the trail by looking carefully at the pictures.

The Handprint Club had been quietly sitting up in the Airport for an hour while they did their homework. Ralph chewed his pen and stared out of the dirty window. Keith W.S. cracked a nut for his squirrel and put the shell into an empty jam jar. Ralph frowned.

"Hey, what's that? No, there can't be!" Ralph scrubbed at the dirt on the window.

"What can't there be?" asked Frank.

From the book THE ADVENTURES OF THE BLACK HAND GANG by Hans Jürgen Press. © 1965 by Otto Maier Verlag Ravensburg. English translation © 1976 by Methuen Children's Books Ltd. Published by Prentice-Hall, Inc., Englewood Cliffs, New Jersey 07632

"Anyone living in that house over there," Ralph answered.
"It's been empty for three years."

They all crowded around the window.

"We all know that only a few rats live there," said Keith
W.S. "Look, the doors and windows are all barred shut."

"Let me have a look," said Angela, putting her nose right
on the pane. After a few seconds she said, "I think Ralph's
right. There really is someone in the house."

How did she guess there was someone living in the house?

It was clear to Angela and Ralph that there was someone living in the house. The smoking chimney gave it away.

They kept watching the house. Five days later, they were rewarded. While Angela was on guard one evening, she saw the figure of a man climbing over the wall near where the boats were tied up on the canal.

The next day the Handprint Club met before school to look closely at the wall.

"Look there!" called Keith W.S. suddenly.

"I can't see anything," Frank said.

Keith W.S. took the squirrel from his shoulder and placed it on the wall. It ran down a vine and in a flash had grabbed something round.

"Look at that!" Ralph shouted. "It's the heel of someone's shoe."

"Listen, all of you," said Frank. "We must look for a man with a heel off his shoe."

They started looking on their way to school. Angela walked along slowly, swinging her bag. Suddenly she said out loud, "Hey, there he is! That's him."

Later that day she described him to the rest of the Club and said, "We'll know him by his pants."

What sort of pants was the man without a heel on his shoe wearing?

The Club sat up in the Airport listening closely to Angela.

"Well, now we know that the man without a heel wears checked pants," Frank said.

"But no one's seen his face yet," Ralph pointed out.

"We'll get a chance as soon as we see him go into that house. Each of us must cover an entrance."

Three minutes later they were all at their posts. Frank was watching the front door. Ralph watched the gate by the canal. Angela stood by the garden gate watching the side road through two holes she had cut in her newspaper. Keith W.S., disguised as a garden statue, stood without moving in a bed of prickly plants. Suddenly he saw something. A trap door opened and then shut quickly. The Handprint Club hurried over to it.

"Lift up the trap door," said Angela. "I'm going in. I want to know where it leads."

"What if something happens to you?" asked Keith W.S.

Angela showed them her bag. "I brought Isobel 13 with me — just in case. . . ."

Isobel 13 was the best carrier pigeon the Club owned.

Angela made her way down the hole. She crawled quietly along the tunnel and came out through a small door into a dark room. She began to look around, but before she could see what was there, she heard a noise. Quickly she wrote on a piece of paper: *Inside house. Going to hide in chest. Love, Angela.* Then she sent Isobel 13 off up the chimney with the message.

"Where on earth is Angela?" said Frank, looking at his watch. "She's been down there eleven minutes. I hope she's all right."

Ralph said, "Let's go up to the pigeon loft and see if she sent any message."

They ran off and climbed up to the loft. Frank said, "There's Isobel 13, back already."

How did Frank recognize Isobel 13?

When Frank had read Angela's message, Ralph said that they should clean the soot off Isobel 13. Her flight up the chimney had made her black all over.

"No," Frank said. "She'll clean herself."

"I wonder what Angela is doing now," said Ralph.

Angela was still inside the house. Raising the lid of the chest in which she had hidden, she peeped out. Everything was quiet. Suddenly she noticed the door. A thin ray of light shone through the keyhole. In a flash she was across the room to the door, her eye against the keyhole. Mr. X sat only a few feet away, his back to her. He was bent over something on the table in front of him, examining it closely.

A few minutes later the door to the Airport burst open. The Handprint Club jumped up, shouting, "Thank goodness you're safe, Angela!"

"I'm all right," she said. "I've found out what Mr. X is up to. I saw him looking at postage stamps. And I've brought you something else." She opened an old cough-drop tin.

"Where did you find that old cigar stub?" asked Ralph.

"I picked it up in the secret tunnel," Angela said proudly. "It's a Don Carlos cigar. We must find out where Mr. X bought it."

The Handprint Club spent the whole afternoon looking for a shop that sold Don Carlos cigars, but without luck. The following day they kept looking. Suddenly they heard Frank's trumpet. He always used it to signal the Club.

The Handprint Club crowded around him and Frank whispered, "I've found out where you can buy Don Carlos cigars."

Which shop sold Don Carlos cigars?

DON CARLOS SOLD ONLY BY OTTO PROUD was the advertisement Frank had seen on a passing truck.

That afternoon the Handprint Club settled down in the Airport with a telephone book to look up the address. There were a great many Prouds listed.

"Here it is," cried Frank. "Otto Proud, tobacconist, 12 Frederick Street."

"Let's go," said Ralph.

"Wait a minute." Angela shook her head. "What are we going to do when we get there?"

"Look for a clue," said Frank.

"But we already know that Mr. X smokes Don Carlos cigars," Angela said. "Is there anything strange about that?"

"Well, we know that Mr. X also likes stamps," Frank answered. "Perhaps Otto Proud is interested in stamps."

Half an hour later they all stood outside Otto Proud's shop. Hundreds of different cigars were shown in his window, but there were no stamps.

"Just a minute," said Keith W.S. "Look, there's a stamp!"

The lone 50 Rupee Zanzibar stamp puzzled the Handprint Club for a long time.

"Why has Otto Proud only one stamp for sale?" Ralph wondered. "Perhaps he bought up a whole batch cheaply. Is that possible?"

At noon the next day, Angela raced into the Airport.

"Look, it's impossible for anyone to have lots of 50 Rupee Zanzibars," cried Angela. "They're rare."

"Who says so?" asked Frank.

"My father," Angela answered. "He saves stamps, and he knows all about them."

"She's right," said Ralph, who had just come in, waving a newspaper. "Here, read this."

The Club read: "Stamp forgers operating in Newtown."

Seconds later the Handprint Club stood outside Mr. X's house. Smoke was pouring out of the chimney, and they noticed bits of burned paper whirling about in the air. Keith W.S. picked up one of the bits. It was partly burned, but it was clearly a 50 Rupee Zanzibar.

"Just a minute," said Angela, pulling a catalog out of her bag. "There's a picture of it in here."

Keith W.S. compared the picture to the burned stamp.

"Ours is different. It's a forgery!" Ralph cried.

What was missing on the forged stamp?

"But if the flag's missing, he can't sell it," said Frank.

"Of course he can't," Angela said. "That's why he's burning them. They're poor copies. He'll keep the good ones and get out of here."

"We must stop him," said Ralph.

The Handprint Club took up their posts all around the house and watched the exits. The minutes went slowly by, but nothing happened.

Suddenly they heard Frank's trumpet. Angela, Ralph, and Keith W.S. rushed to the bridge.

"He's off!" shouted Frank. "He came out of the cellar with a metal case and ran off down the canal bank. I see he's had a heel put on his shoe."

Angela thought quickly. "He's planning to leave the country," she said. "Let's go to the harbor."

Frank blew a battle cry on his trumpet, and they gave chase. They charged along the harbor wall and over the bridge to the other side of the canal. Mr. X was running at top speed around the corner. Ralph saw him dart into a building site on Bridge Street and then lost sight of him.

The Handprint Club climbed up a heap of sand.

"Even if we've lost him, we can tell the police what he looks like," said Keith W.S.

Angela saw something, gasped, then whispered quickly, "Ralph, dash off to a pay phone and call the police — Emergency, 911."

"911," Ralph repeated. "All right, but why?"

"Because we've got Mr. X in a trap. Hurry up!"

What did Angela see that told her where Mr. X was?

STORAGE

OFFICE

CEMENT

NUTS

CONSTRUCTION
KEEP OUT

287

If the police sirens hadn't made such a row, perhaps Mr. X would have stayed hidden in the cement mixer. As it was, though, the Handprint Club saw the striped tie, with Mr. X attached and still holding his metal case, shoot out of the mixer and fly head first over the wall.

"He'll kill himself!" Angela shouted.

But Mr. X didn't hurt himself at all. He landed in a pile of hay in a farmyard.

Three police cars came to a halt in the farmyard. Police Sergeant Shorthouse arrested Mr. X.

"It's not against the law to jump into a pile of hay," cried Mr. X. "If I want to, that's my business. Let me go at once."

"You are a forger! Where are the stamps you've printed? Show us where they're hidden."

The man said nothing.

The police searched all over without success. They were just about to let Mr. X go when the Handprint Club jumped down from the wall.

"Who are you?" asked Sergeant Shorthouse angrily.

"We are the Handprint Club," Frank said, politely. "May we show you where he's hidden the metal case with the forged stamps?"

Frank felt the metal case had to be in a bucket at the bottom of the well. During the chase, Frank had seen this farmyard and had noticed the well. The rope on it had been rolled up with a water bucket hooked onto the end of it. Look at the well now.

AUTHOR

Hans Jürgen Press was born and grew up in a small town in Germany. His parents kept an inn, where young Hans enjoyed watching the guests. Interested in nature too, he liked exploring the countryside. He even set up a small "zoo" in the back yard. At the age of five, he started to draw, and he always put lots of people and animals in his pictures. When he grew up, he went on drawing — cartoons for the children's page of newspapers as well as illustrations for magazines both in Germany and abroad. He also wrote books, which have been published in many countries.

Mr. Press lives in Hamburg, Germany, and he is still getting new ideas from the world around him. He says, "I draw and write the way I would like to see things if I were still a child myself."

Wagon Wheels

by BARBARA BRENNER

"There it is, boys," Daddy said. "Across this river is Nicodemus, Kansas. That's where we're going to build our house. There's free land for everyone here in the West. All we have to do is go and get it."

We had come a long way to get to Kansas — all the way from Kentucky. It had been a hard trip and a sad one. Mama died on the way.

Now there were just the four of us — Daddy, Willie, Little Brother, and me.

"Come on, boys," Daddy called. "Let's put our feet on free dirt."

We crossed the river, wagon and all. A man was waiting for us on the other side. "I'm Sam Hickman," he said. "Welcome to the town of Nicodemus."

"Why, thank you, Brother," Daddy said. "But where *is* your town?"

"Right here," Mr. Hickman said.

We didn't see any houses, but we saw smoke coming out of holes in the prairie. "Shucks!" my Daddy said. "Holes in the ground are for rabbits and snakes, not for free black people. I'm a carpenter.

I can build fine wood houses for this town."

"No time to build wood houses now," Mr. Hickman told my Daddy. "Winter is coming, and winter in Kansas is *mean*. Better get yourself a dugout before the ground freezes."

Daddy knew Sam Hickman was right. We got our shovels and we dug us a dugout. It wasn't much of a place — dirt floor, dirt walls, no windows, and the roof was just grass and branches. But we were glad to have that dugout when the wind began to whistle across the prairie.

Every night Willie lit the lamp and made a fire. I cooked a rabbit stew or fried a pan of fish fresh from the river. After supper Daddy would always say, "How about a song or two?" He would take out his banjo and Plink-a-plunk! Plink-a-plunk! Pretty soon that dugout felt like home.

Winter came. And that Kansas winter *was* mean. It snowed day after day. We couldn't hunt or fish. We had no more rabbit stew. We had no more fish fresh from the river. All we had was cornmeal mush to eat.

Then one day there was no more cornmeal. There was not a lick of food in the whole town of Nicodemus. And there was nothing left to burn for firewood. Little Brother was so cold and hungry that he cried all the time.

Daddy wrapped blankets around Little Brother. "Hush, baby son," he said to him. "Try to sleep. Supply train will be coming soon."

But the supply train did not come — not that day nor the next.

On the third day, we heard the sound of horses. Daddy looked out to see who it was. "Indians," he said. "I wonder why they're here? What are they going to do?"

We watched from the dugout. First the Indians made a circle. Each man took something from his saddlebag and dropped it on the ground. Then they all turned and rode away.

Then everyone ran out into the snow to see what the Indians had left. It was FOOD!

"Look!"

"Fresh deer meat!"

"Fish!"

"Dried beans and squash!"

"Bundles of sticks to keep our fires burning!"

Everyone was talking at once.

There was a feast in Nicodemus that night, but before we ate, Daddy spoke to us. "Johnny, Willie, Little Brother," he said, "I want you to remember this day. I want you to remember that the Osage Indians saved our lives in Nicodemus."

When spring came, Daddy said, "Boys, this prairie is too flat for me. I want to find land with trees and hills. I'm going to move on."

"I'll start loading the wagon," I said.

"Hold on, now," said Daddy. "I want you boys to stay. You have shelter and friends here. I'll go alone, and I'll send for you when I find a place."

I was scared to stay alone — so was Willie. Poor Little Brother was trying to understand what Daddy was saying.

We all listened as Daddy continued. "I'll leave you cornmeal for
your bread, salt for your meat, and
some molasses for a sweet. You be
good boys, you hear? Take care of
Little Brother. Never let him out of
your sight."

There were tears in Daddy's eyes
when he said good-by to us.

Mrs. Sadler and Mrs. Hickman
said, "Ed Muldie must be off his
head to leave you poor babies all
alone."

"I'm no baby," I told them. "I'm
eleven. And Willie is eight. We
can take care of ourselves. Little
Brother is only three, but we can
take care of him too."

We did what our Daddy told us
to do. We hunted and fished and
cooked and swept the dugout clean.
We even baked our own cornbread.
And we never did let Little Brother
out of our sight.

We made a wagon out of an old
box. Mrs. Sadler gave us wheels
for it. When we put Little Brother
in the wagon and pulled him along,
you could hear the wheels squeak a
mile away. When the people of

Nicodemus heard that sound, they always said, "There go the Muldie boys."

One day we were picking berries near the river. "Johnny, I smell smoke," said Willie. We looked up. The whole sky was orange!

Someone shouted, "Prairie fire!" The fire was behind us and it was coming fast!

"We'll be burned up," Willie cried. "There's no place to run!"

Then I saw a deer running toward the river. "Quick!" I said to Willie. "Run to the river!"

We ran, pulling the wagon behind us. People from Nicodemus were running with us now. When we got to the water, I told Willie to jump in. "You hold the wagon," I said to him. "I'll hold Little Brother."

Everyone was jumping in around us. Mr. Hickman helped me hold Little Brother, and Mr. Hill helped Willie with the wagon.

There was fire and smoke all around, but the water kept the fire from us. We stayed there for a long time. When the fire died out, we all walked home.

April went by — and May and June. We hunted and fished and waited for a letter from Daddy. Nothing came. Then in July the post rider came with a letter for us.

It said:

Dear boys,

I have found fine free land near Solomon City. There's wood here to build a house and good black dirt for growing corn and beans.

There's a map with this letter. It shows where I am and where you are. Follow the map. Stay close to the Solomon River until you come to the deer trail. You will find me. I know you can do it because you are my fine big boys.

Love to you all,

Daddy

We started out the next day. We piled cornbread and blankets into Little Brother's wagon until there was no room for Little Brother.

"Can you walk like a big boy?" I asked him. He nodded.

All of Nicodemus came out to say good-by — the Hills, the Hickmans, the Sadlers. . . . "Poor babies," they said, "going a hundred fifty miles all by themselves." But we knew we could do it. Our Daddy had told us so.

We went to the river, and we followed the map. We walked all day, and when Little Brother got tired, I carried him. At night we stopped and made a fire. "We'll take turns," I said to Willie. "First I'll watch the fire and you'll sleep. We'll fire the gun sometimes. It will scare the wild animals away." There were plenty of wild animals on the prairie — wolves, panthers, coyotes. Each night our fire and the sound of the gun kept them away.

But one night I heard Willie call to me. "Johnny," he said, "wake up but don't move." I opened my eyes. There on the ground next to me was a big prairie rattlesnake warming itself by the fire. I didn't move, I didn't breathe, for fear it would bite me.

"What shall we do?" Willie whispered. I tried to think of what Daddy would do. Then I remembered something. Daddy once told me that snakes like warm places.

I said to Willie, "Let the fire go out." It seemed like we were there for hours staying so still. At last the fire went out. The night air got chilly, and the snake moved away into the darkness.

For twenty-two days we followed the river. Then one day we came to a deer trail. It led away from the river, just as the map showed. "This way," I said to my brothers.

We walked along the trail. Then, on the side of the hill, we saw a little house with a garden in front. Corn was growing. A man came out of the house, and when he saw us, he began to run toward us.

"Daddy!"

"Willie! Johnny! Little Brother!"

Then there was such hugging and kissing and talking and crying and laughing and singing that I'll bet they heard us all the way back in Nicodemus! And old Mrs. Sadler must have said, "Sounds like the Muldie boys have found their Daddy!"

AUTHOR

Barbara Brenner has been interested in writing since she was ten years old, when one of her teachers told her that she wrote well. She later worked at many kinds of jobs and was married and the mother of two before she began to make a career of writing books. Her sons often gave her ideas for her stories, and many of the family activities have appeared in her books.

Mrs. Brenner writes nature and folktale books as well as stories based on real events, such as the one you have just read. She is married to an illustrator, who has drawn the pictures for some of her books. Several of her science books have appeared on lists of outstanding science books for children.

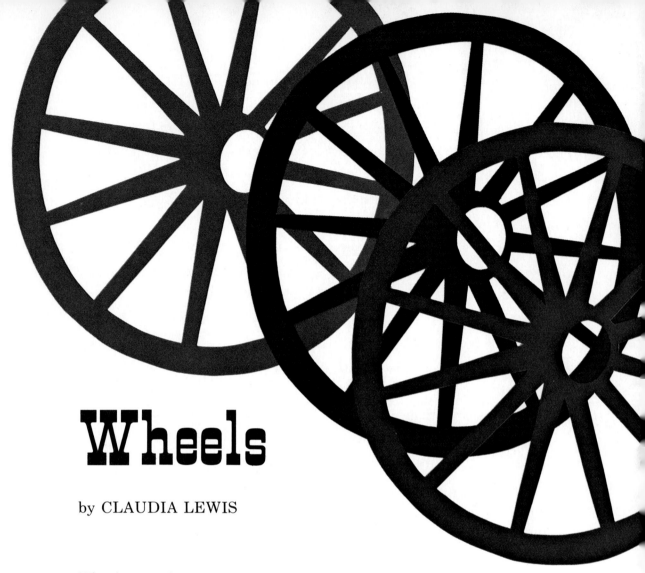

Wheels

by CLAUDIA LEWIS

Wheels over the mountains
Wheels over the plains —
Covered-wagon wheels
In the winds and the rains

Marked the path
Of the pioneers
Across our land
In the early years.

Straight through the wilderness
Westward bound
The wagons moved on,
Breaking new ground.

And now, far above
That ancient trail
Carved by the wheels
The jet planes sail.

From the eastern shore
To the west they flow
And they skim in half a day
All the continent below.

And where are their wheels?
Tucked inside,
With nothing to do
But ride and ride

Across those miles
That were hard and slow
For the covered wagons
Of long ago.

SKILL

Encyclopedia

You have learned how to get information from a dictionary. It helps you to check the spelling, pronunciation, and meaning of any word you are not sure about. Because a dictionary gives this kind of information about thousands of words, there is no room for additional information. For more information, you should use an encyclopedia.

What can you find in an encyclopedia?

Suppose you have been asked to report to your class about an important crop grown in this country, and you have chosen corn. You already know most of what you would find in a dictionary if you looked up the word *corn.* You know how to spell and pronounce the word. You know that corn is a tall plant with large ears having kernels that are used chiefly for food. However, to find out how and where corn is raised, what products are made from it, and other interesting facts about it, you should turn to an **encyclopedia.**

A dictionary explains in only a few words what an airplane, a horse, or an ocean is. However, an encyclopedia may give you ten or twenty pages of detailed information about each of these topics. An encyclopedia helps answer questions like these: *What causes lightning? When was baseball first played? Where was Abraham Lincoln born? What is the tallest mountain in South America?*

Because an encyclopedia is usually made up of a set of

books, each of which is called a **volume,** it has enough space for long articles on many of its subjects, or **main topics.** It also has maps, charts, graphs, photographs, and other useful drawings. These help you understand the written material and sometimes give additional information. Look at the picture of marbles in the article from an encyclopedia on page 302 of this lesson. In addition to reading the article about the different kinds of marbles, you could study the pictures and read the captions, or titles, to get a clearer picture of what each kind of marble looks like.

How are guide letters useful?

The main topics in most encyclopedias are arranged in alphabetical order. In the picture below, notice the letter or letters at the top of each volume. They are called **guide letters,** and they tell you the beginning letters of all the main topics listed in that volume.

MARBLES

MARBLES is a children's game played with little balls of many colors. It is a very old game. Egyptian and Roman children played with marbles before Christ was born. In the United States, the neighborhood marbles game is a sign of spring. The game is so popular that many cities and states have marble tournaments.

How to Play Marbles. Most American children play a game called *ringer*. Two to six children can play. A circle 10 feet (3 meters) across is marked on the ground. When two or more are playing, 13 marbles are placed on a cross marked at the center of the ring. Two lines, each about 9 inches (23 centimeters) long, form the cross. One marble is placed at the center and three each on the four parts of the cross. Each marble lies about 3 inches (8 centimeters) from the next one. Each player uses a larger marble, the shooter, to knock, or "shoot," the small marbles out of the ring. Some boys and girls call their shooters *taws*, *glassies*, or *monnies*. The marbles in the ring, or object marbles, are called *mibs*, *miggs*, *ducks*, *commies*, or *hoodles*. The player who shoots the most marbles out of the ring wins the game.

Players start the first game by *lagging* for turns. They toss or shoot their shooters from a *pitch line* drawn outside the circle, with its center touching the circle. On the opposite side of the circle, also with its center touching the circle, is a *lag line*. The player whose shooter comes closest to the lag line plays first, and others follow in order of the nearness of their shooters to the line. In the games that follow, the winner of the game before plays first, and all other players lag for their shooting turn.

WORLD BOOK photo

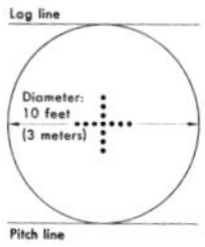
Lag line
Diameter:
10 feet
(3 meters)
Pitch line

Marble Players often play a game called *ringer, left*. The game is played in a ring 10 feet (3 meters) in diameter, *above*. The player who shoots the most marbles out of the ring wins the game. Most marbles are made of colored glass, but they differ in color and design, *below*.

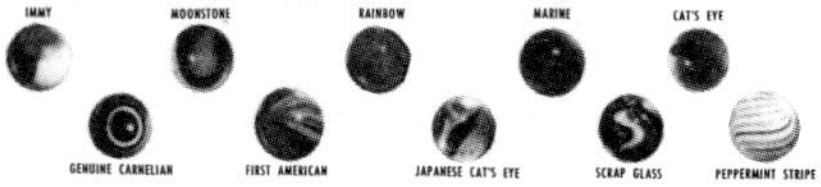
IMMY
MOONSTONE
RAINBOW
MARINE
CAT'S EYE
GENUINE CARNELIAN
FIRST AMERICAN
JAPANESE CAT'S EYE
SCRAP GLASS
PEPPERMINT STRIPE

TERMS USED WHEN TALKING ABOUT MARBLES

Bowling occurs when a player rolls a shot on the ground.

Edgers are marbles near the edge of the ring.

For Fair means playing for the fun of the game. After each game, the marbles are returned to their owners.

For Keeps occurs when each player keeps the marbles that he shoots out of the ring.

Histing occurs when a player raises his hand from the ground when shooting.

Hit occurs when a player knocks a marble out of the ring on a shot.

Hunching occurs when a player moves his hand forward across the ring line when shooting from the ring line, or when his hand advances from the spot where the shooter stopped, when shooting inside the ring.

Knuckling Down is a position in which one knuckle must touch the ground until the shooter has left the hand.

Lofting, a difficult shot, occurs when a player shoots in an arc through the air to hit a marble.

Marbles are the object marbles only. They can also be called *mibs*, *miggs*, *ducks*, *commies*, or *hoodles*.

Miss occurs when a player fails to knock a marble from the ring on a shot.

Roundsters, or *circling*, is the act of selecting the best location outside the ring for knuckling down.

Shooter is the attacking marble. It also can be called a *taw*, a *glassy*, or a *monny*.

Shot is the act of snapping the shooter at a marble by a quick extension of the thumb.

152

All shots except the lag are made in a position called *knuckling down*. One knuckle of the hand must touch the ground until the shooter marble has left the hand. *Histing* (raising the hand from the ground) and *hunching* (moving the hand forward) are forbidden. The player holds the shooter between his forefinger and thumb, and shoots it out with his thumb.

A player starts his turn from any spot outside of the ring. If he knocks an object marble out of the ring, he may shoot again from the spot where the shooter has come to rest. If the shooter also leaves the ring, the player takes *roundsters*. That is, he may shoot from any position on, or outside of, the ring line. In case the shooter slips from the player's hand and does not move more than 10 inches (25 centimeters), the player calls "slips." He may then shoot again. Each player's turn continues until he misses the marbles with his shooter. He then picks up his shooter and waits for his next turn. He starts every new turn by taking roundsters.

The player who first shoots seven marbles out of the ring wins. When the seventh marble is shot from the ring, the shooter marble must also leave the ring. If it does not, the object marble is put back on the cross lines for the next player. Histing, hunching, smoothing the ground, or removing pebbles and other obstacles are penalized by loss of one shot.

Any player who changes shooters during the game must leave the game. Any player who walks across the ring must give up one of the marbles he has won. A player who talks with a coach during play gives up all the marbles he has won up to that point. Marbles given up are put back on the cross lines. In case of a tie score, the winners play another game. Some players like to play marbles *for keeps*. Each keeps the marbles he shoots from the ring. But often the game is played *for fair*, and the marbles are returned to their owner.

Composition of Marbles. The ordinary marble is made of glass. A pigment is often inserted to color the marbles. Most of these marbles come from West Virginia, where a plant in Clarksburg manufactures millions every year. *Aggies*, marbles made of agate, a fine-grained variety of quartz, are made in Idar-Oberstein, Germany. Germany also supplies marbles made from limestone. At one time, many marbles in the United States were made of painted and glazed clay. Many people collect marbles. CARL A. TROESTER, JR.

MARBURY V. MADISON marked the first time the U.S. Supreme Court declared a federal law unconstitutional. This 1803 case is one of the most important decisions in history. It established the supremacy of the Constitution over laws passed by Congress and the right of the court to review the constitutionality of legislation.

In 1801, President John Adams appointed William Marbury justice of the peace in the District of Columbia. But Adams' term ended before Marbury took office, and James Madison, the new secretary of state, withheld the appointment. Marbury asked the Supreme

MARCH

Court, under Section 13 of the Judiciary Act of 1789, to force Madison to grant the appointment. But the court refused to rule on the appointment because Section 13 gave the Supreme Court powers not provided by the Constitution and, therefore, the court declared Section 13 unconstitutional. STANLEY I. KUTLER

See also JEFFERSON, THOMAS (The Courts).

MARCEL. See HAIRDRESSING.

MARCEL, GABRIEL (1889-1973), was a French philosopher. He was an unsystematic thinker who presented his philosophy for the most part in three philosophical diaries: *Metaphysical Journals* (1927), *Being and Having* (1935), and *Presence and Immortality* (1959). His philosophy consists of reflections on concrete human experiences such as love and fidelity. He believed that human experience can be understood only by directly participating in it. Therefore, he attempted not merely to observe, but to relive these experiences in the course of his reflections. Marcel's other works include *Homo Viator* (1944), an analysis of hope; and *Man Against Society* (1951), an examination of the effects of a technological society on the human personality.

Marcel was born in Paris. He became a Roman Catholic at 39. He is often classified as a Christian existentialist (see EXISTENTIALISM). IVAN SOLL

MARCELLUS is the name of two popes of the Roman Catholic Church whose reigns were brief.

Saint Marcellus I governed the church in 308 and 309. Little is known about his life, except that he divided the parishes of Rome into seven regions, each with its own burial places.

Marcellus II (1501-1555) governed the church until he died, 22 days after his election. As a cardinal, he served as one of the reform leaders in the court of Pope Paul III, who ruled from 1534 to 1549. He was one of Paul's three legates to the first session of the Council of Trent in 1545. Marcellus pledged himself to reconvene the Council of Trent to finish its work of reform and definition of doctrine, but he died before this could be done. THOMAS P. NEILL AND FULTON J. SHEEN

MARCH is a highly rhythmic piece of music first used by military bands to accompany marching. The march usually has one dominant tune repeated over and over with other tunes coming in between. The tempo of military marches varies with the occasion. In the U.S. Army, soldiers march about 120 steps a minute. This march is called *quick time*. A *double-time* march is about 180 steps a minute. In the British Army, soldiers march about 75 steps a minute to a slow march, and about 108 steps a minute to a quick march. People often call a quick march *quickstep*.

One of the most famous composers of march music was John Philip Sousa. His works include "The Stars and Stripes Forever," "The Washington Post," and "Semper Fidelis." Sir Edward Elgar wrote the well-known *Pomp and Circumstance*, a set of five military marches.

Composers have used the march as an art form in operas and oratorios. Famous marches occur in Verdi's opera *Aida* and Mozart's *The Marriage of Figaro*. The march from Handel's *Scipio* became the parade march of the British Grenadier Guards.

See also BAND; ELGAR, SIR EDWARD; SOUSA, JOHN P.

153

DISNEY, WALT

© Walt Disney Productions

Disneyland and Walt Disney World are spectacular amusement parks that feature exhibits, rides, and shows based on movies by Walt Disney. There, visitors meet such Disney characters as, *left to right*, Pluto, Goofy, and Mickey Mouse.

DISNEY, WALT (1901-1966), was one of the most famous motion-picture producers in history. Disney first became known in the 1920's and 1930's for creating such cartoon film characters as Mickey Mouse and Donald Duck. He later produced feature-length cartoon films, movies about wild animals in their natural surroundings, and films starring human actors. The Disney studio has won more than 45 Academy Awards for its movies and for scientific and technical contributions to film making.

Disney achieved one of his greatest successes in 1955, when he opened Disneyland, a spectacular amusement park in Anaheim, Calif. A similar park, Walt Disney World, opened near Orlando, Fla., in 1971, after Disney's death. Most of the exhibits, rides, and shows at both parks are based on characters from Disney movies.

© Walt Disney Productions

Cartoon Characters made Walt Disney famous throughout the world. Donald Duck first appeared in a short cartoon in 1934. In 1942, the full-length cartoon motion picture *Bambi* starred Flower, the skunk; Thumper, the rabbit; and Bambi, the deer.

Early Life. Walter Elias Disney was born in Chicago. His family moved to Missouri when he was a child, and Disney spent much of his boyhood on a farm near Marceline. At the age of 16, Disney studied art in Chicago. In 1920, he joined the Kansas City Film Ad Company, where he helped make crude cartoon advertisements to be shown in movie theaters.

The First Disney Cartoons. In 1923, Disney moved to Los Angeles with the goal of becoming an *animator*, an artist who draws movie cartoons. He set up his first studio in a garage. For several years, Disney struggled just to pay his expenses. He finally gained success in 1928, when he released the first short Mickey Mouse cartoons. Earlier film makers had found that animals were easier to animate than people. Mickey Mouse, drawn with a series of circles, proved ideal for animation.

In 1927, sound had been added to motion pictures, and a process for making movies in color was developed a few years later. Disney and his assistants made imaginative use of both sound and color, and Disney himself provided Mickey Mouse's voice. His cartoon *Flowers and Trees* (1932) was the first film that was made in full Technicolor.

From 1929 to 1939, Disney produced a cartoon series called *Silly Symphonies*. Mickey Mouse appeared in these and later cartoons, along with such characters as Donald Duck, Goofy, and Pluto. Throughout his career, Disney actually drew few cartoons. His genius lay in creating, organizing, and directing the films.

Full-Length Movies. In 1937, Disney issued the first full-length cartoon film ever made, *Snow White and the Seven Dwarfs*. It became one of the most popular movies in history. Disney's later full-length animated films included *Pinocchio* (1940), *Fantasia* (1940), *Dumbo* (1941), *Bambi* (1942), *Cinderella* (1950), *Lady and the Tramp* (1955), and *The Jungle Book*, which was issued in 1967, after his death.

During World War II (1939-1945), Disney's studio made educational films for the United States government. After the war, Disney created fewer animated movies. He concentrated on making films that starred real animals or human actors.

In 1949, Disney released *Seal Island*. This short movie was the first in a series of "True-Life Adventures" that show how animals live in nature. Disney released his first full-length nature film, *The Living Desert*, in 1953. All his nature movies include scenes of animal life rarely seen by human beings.

Disney released *Treasure Island*, his first full-length movie with human actors, in 1950. *Mary Poppins* (1964) probably ranks as the most successful of these Disney pictures.

After television became popular about 1950, many film makers either ignored TV or fought it as a threat to the movie industry. But Disney adjusted easily to the new form of entertainment. He produced a number of movies especially for television. Disney also served as the host of a weekly television show that presented Disney films. ROY PAUL NELSON

See also MOTION PICTURE (pictures: *Snow White and the Seven Dwarfs*; A Documentary Film).

192

© Walt Disney Productions

© Walt Disney Productions

© Walt Disney Productions

Disney Movies have featured both cartoon characters and human actors. Mickey Mouse starred in *Steamboat Willie, upper left*, the first cartoon to use sound. *Mary Poppins, left*, combines human actors with cartoon scenes. The film describes the adventures of a nursemaid who can fly. *Pinocchio, above*, is a full-length cartoon about a puppet named Pinocchio. Near the story's end, a whale swallows Pinocchio and Geppetto, the puppet's father. They escape from the whale's stomach on a raft.

DISNEY WORLD. See DISNEY, WALT; FLORIDA (Places to Visit); ORLANDO.

DISNEYLAND. See DISNEY, WALT; ANAHEIM; CALIFORNIA (Places to Visit; picture).

DISORDERLY CONDUCT. See BREACH OF THE PEACE.

DISPERSION. See LIGHT (Dispersion).

DISPLACED PERSON (DP) is a person who is forced to leave his country because of war or political, religious, or racial persecution. Nazi Germany moved millions of persons to slave-labor and concentration camps. Others fled their homes. Western Europe had more than 8 million DP's at the end of World War II in 1945. About 1 million Russians refused to return home. Boundary changes and escape from Communist terrorism swelled the number of DP's after the war.

On Dec. 15, 1946, the United Nations established the International Refugee Organization to care for and settle DP's. Between 1948 and 1952, more than 440,000 DP's entered the United States. Canada received over 160,000. After 1956, the United States admitted Hungarian and other Eastern European DP's. Many North Koreans, North Vietnamese, and Chinese who escaped Communist rule were accepted by free Asian countries and Hong Kong. Many Cuban DP's settled in the United States during the 1950's and 1960's. STEFAN T. POSSONY

DISPLACEMENT means putting an object out of place. Rock formations may be *displaced* by faulting (see FAULT). A ship or other floating object will *displace* an amount of water equal to its own weight (see GRAVITY, SPECIFIC; SHIP [table: Nautical Measurements]).

DISPLACEMENT BEHAVIOR includes a variety of animal or human activities. Such activities seem to be out of place in the situation in which they occur. For example, songbirds may pause during fights to feed, or smooth their feathers. Many mammals scratch themselves or groom their fur when faced with a decision of whether to fight or run away. An embarrassed man may adjust his tie. Much displacement behavior occurs during emotional conflict. But scientists do not know exactly why such behavior takes place. JOHN A. WIENS

DISRAELI, *dihz RAY lih*, **BENJAMIN** (1804-1881), EARL OF BEACONSFIELD, was the only man to be born a Jew who became prime minister of Great Britain. The eldest son of a noted Jewish author, he became a member of the Church of England in 1817. He gave up the study of law as a young man, and created a sensation by writing *Vivian Grey* and other novels. He tried several times to win a seat in the House of Commons before being elected as a Tory in 1837.

National Portrait Gallery, London

Benjamin Disraeli

His extreme clothes and exaggerated speech made him stand out in the House of Commons. After almost 10 years he became the champion of high tariffs. He opposed Sir Robert Peel's bill to repeal the Corn Laws (see CORN LAWS). Disraeli became Chancellor of the Exchequer in 1852, and held that office three more times.

Disraeli was largely responsible for the 1867 Parliamentary Reform Act. He served as prime minister for

193

All the main topics that start with the letter *A* come first, followed by those starting with *B,* and so on. Use the guide letters printed on the spines, the narrow back edges of the volumes, to quickly find the volume you need. The numbers on the spines make it easy for you to keep the volumes in alphabetical order or to speak about a volume by number.

In the encyclopedia shown, so many main topics start with the letters *C* and *S* that there are two volumes for each of those letters. To know whether you should look in volume 3 or in volume 4 for the main topic **COAL,** for example, you would have to think about the second letter of *coal.* Because *co* comes between the guide letters **CI** and **CZ** in alphabetical order, you would choose volume 4.

The guide letters on volume 11, **J-K,** tell you that you would find in it any main topic beginning with either the letter *J* or *K.*

Except for the names of people, main topics having more than one word are alphabetized by the first word. You would find **NEW MEXICO** under the guide letter **N, SPACE TRAVEL** under **S,** and **MOUNT WHITNEY** under **M.** But to locate information about a person, use the first letter of the person's last name. Look at the encyclopedia pages at the bottom of page 302. On the left page, page 192, information about Walt Disney is given under the main topic **DISNEY, WALT** and is found in the **D** volume.

How do you select a key word?

To find what you want to know in an encyclopedia, you must first decide on a key word to look for. Suppose you are trying to answer this question: *How did the invention of the automobile change our country?* You know that the words *invention* and *country* are probably too broad and general to be helpful to you. It is the automobile that you really want to know about. That is why *automobile* should be your key word. The key word, then, is the word that most exactly names the subject.

You have also learned that often it is important to use more than one key word. To learn all you could about the mining done in New Mexico, for instance, you should choose both *mining* and *New Mexico* as key words.

What are guide words?

A guide word or words, similar to those in a dictionary, appear on facing pages at the top of most encyclopedia pages, such as those shown on the top of page 302. Once you have decided on a key word to look for as a main topic and selected the correct volume, the guide words will help you to find that main topic quickly. If you open the **A** volume near the back to look for the guide word **AUTOMOBILE,** you may find many pages with guide words that begin with the letters **AU.** Use the third letter of *automobile* to narrow your search to the few pages that have guide words starting with the letters **AUT.**

Sometimes the title of an article, appearing in large type as the heading on a page, serves as the guide word or words. If you find that a picture takes the place of a guide word or words on an encyclopedia page, you have to use a main topic instead. For example, there are no guide words on encyclopedia page 193. You have to use the *last* main topic, **DISRAELI, BENJAMIN,** for your guide words.

REVIEW

Reread the headings of this lesson, and recite your answer to each question. Then review all your answers. Now you are ready to use an encyclopedia.

USING AN ENCYCLOPEDIA

Answer each of the following questions on a sheet of paper. Write the number and letter of each part of a question first, *1.a, 1.b,* and so on, and then your answer.

1. What is the number of the volume shown on page 301 in which you would look for each of the following topics?
   a. New York City
   b. silver
   c. Benjamin Banneker
   d. steamships
   e. Canary Islands
   f. Harriet Tubman
2. Which key word or key words would you use to find information to answer each of these questions?
   a. How do helicopters stay in the air?
   b. What section of the United States produces the most lumber?
   c. What is the size of a football field?
   d. What famous clipper ships did Donald McKay build?
3. What are the guide words on the encyclopedia pages shown in the picture at the top of page 302?
4. If you were trying to find the main topic **MOUNTAINS** in the **M** volume, would you look before or after the pages shown in the top illustration on page 302?

Eugenie Clark:
Shark Lady

by ANN McGOVERN

"Wake up, Genie," Mama called. "We have to go downtown soon."

Eugenie Clark sighed into her pillow. Who wants to go downtown on a Saturday? Saturdays were for climbing rocks and trees with Norma, her best friend. Saturdays were for digging up fat worms, bringing home bugs and snakes — making sure that Grandma didn't see them.

Those were the good Saturdays. But today was different. Her friend Norma had to go shopping with her mother. Grandma wasn't feeling well and needed to have peace and quiet. There was no place for nine-year-old Eugenie to be except with Mama at work.

Mama worked in a big building in downtown New York City. She sold newspapers at the stand in the lobby.

In the rumbling subway train speeding downtown, Mama looked at her daughter's sad face and wished there was something she could do to make Eugenie happier.

Eugenie's father had died when she was a baby. So Mama had to work extra hard to earn enough money to take care of the family. Working extra hard meant working Saturday mornings too.

The subway train pulled into their station and they got out. A sign at the top of the subway stairs said TO THE AQUARIUM.

"A good idea," Mama said. "I'll leave you at the aquarium, and I'll pick you up at noon. That will be more fun for you than sitting around the stand all morning."

Eugenie walked through the doors of the aquarium and into the world of fish.

She walked among the tanks filled with strange fish. Then she came to a big tank at the back. She stared at it for a long, long time. The green, misty water seemed to go on and on. She leaned over the rail, her face close to the glass, and made believe that she was walking on the bottom of the sea.

Eugenie went to the aquarium the next Saturday, and the next Saturday, and the Saturday after that. She went on all the cold Saturdays, the rainy and snowy Saturdays of autumn and winter. Sometimes her best friend, Norma, went with her, but often she went alone to be with the fish.

Eugenie read about fish too. She read about a scientist who put a diving helmet on his head and went deep under the waves. He walked on the bottom of the sea with the fish swimming around him.

"One day I'll walk with the fish too," she said.

In the summer, Mama took her to the beach. Mama had taught Eugenie to swim before she was two years old.

When Mama came out of the water, her long black hair streamed down her back. Eugenie thought Mama looked like pictures she had seen of beautiful pearl divers of the Orient. Mama was Japanese.

Mama was a good swimmer, and Eugenie loved to watch her swim with long, graceful strokes.

Now, in the autumn and in the winter, Eugenie watched the very best swimmers — the fish in the aquarium. She found all the fish exciting — the smallest fish glowing like tiny stars and the fish with fluttering fins that looked like fairy wings. But it was the biggest fish in the aquarium that she came back to again and again.

She watched the big shark swimming, turning, swimming, turning, never resting its long, graceful body. She watched it and lost track of time.

"Mighty shark," she thought. "One day I'll swim with sharks."

Eugenie kept visiting the aquarium and studying the fish there. Soon she convinced her mother that she could study fish better if she had an aquarium at home too. Her mother agreed. Throughout ele-

mentary and high school, Eugenie collected and studied all kinds of fish. By the time she began to think about college, she knew that she would become an ichthyologist — a person who studies and works with fish. She went on to college and graduate school, earning high honors in her chosen field.

Now she was Dr. Eugenie Clark. She had won scholarships to study fish in many parts of the world. She had married a doctor and they had Hera, a baby girl. She had also found time to write a book about her adventures. The book was titled *Lady with a Spear.*

In her book, she had written about a marine laboratory on the Red Sea where she had studied and worked for a year.

Thousands of people read her book. Anne and William Vanderbilt of Florida read it too.

There was no marine laboratory in the western part of Florida where the Vanderbilts lived. They called Eugenie and invited her to meet with them.

"It would be great if we had a marine lab here like the one you described in your book," Mr. Vanderbilt said to her. "What do you think? Would you like to start one?"

Her own lab! It was a great thought.

Six months later, in early January, 1955, Dr. Eugenie Clark opened the doors of a small wooden building. A sign over the door said *Cape Haze Marine Laboratory*. Nearby were beaches, bays, islands, and the Gulf of Mexico. And the sea was right outside the door!

Eugenie couldn't wait to see what treasures were in those waters. That very afternoon, she and Beryl Chadwick, a fisher who lived nearby, netted many fish. They even found some sea horses. Eugenie was eager to start the job of finding out about all the fish. Beryl said he would help her.

Eugenie also wanted to study sharks in captivity. The lab needed a place to keep sharks alive. So next to the lab's dock, a big pen was built for holding sharks and other large fish.

The lab grew. From the beginning, scientists came to it to work on their research projects. There was a library just for books and magazines about sea life. There were thirty tanks for fish and other sea creatures. New shark pens were always being built.

Every day, people brought in buckets filled with some swimming or creeping creatures of the sea. They brought in snakes and turtles. One man came in with an alligator almost as big as Eugenie. Beryl made a pond for it under the shade of a tree.

During the twelve exciting years she worked at the lab, Eugenie had more children. Now

Hera had a little sister, Aya, and two brothers, Tak and Niki.

"I was doing what I always wanted to do most," she wrote later. "I was studying sharks and other fish, with everything in one place. I had the collecting grounds, the lab, and my home and family."

Eugenie had traveled widely, exploring the underwater world beneath many seas. She was still learning and making important scientific discoveries.

One of those discoveries was made when Eugenie went to Israel to do research at the Marine Laboratory on the Red Sea. She was studying a little fish called the Moses sole.

The first time she caught the Moses sole in her net, she was surprised to see a bit of white milk-like fluid coming out along its fins. She reached out and touched the fins. The white stuff felt slippery. Her fingers felt tight and tingly. That white fluid might be full of poison!

Eugenie made tests in the lab.

Then she began experiments in the sea. She put the Moses sole in a large plastic bag that fit over a branch of coral where many little fish lived. Next she squeezed the Moses sole through the plastic bag. She squeezed until a few drops of milk came out. In minutes, every small fish that had been swimming in the bag was dead, killed by the poison of the Moses sole.

"What would happen to bigger, more dangerous fish?" she wondered. She began testing the Moses sole with sharks in the lab. She tied the little fish to a line in the shark tank.

First the sharks swam toward the Moses sole with their mouths open, ready to gobble the little fish. Then, with their jaws still wide open, the sharks jerked away. They leaped about the tank, shaking their heads wildly from side to side. All the while, the Moses sole kept swimming, as if nothing were happening.

Next, Eugenie put other live fish right next to the Moses sole

on the line. The sharks kept away from those fish too.

For the next test, Eugenie washed the skin of a Moses sole with alcohol. She dropped the fish into the shark tank. The little fish was swallowed by the shark in no time! Washing the fish with alcohol had removed its poison.

What was this powerful poison? The little Moses sole didn't look very special. It looked like any flat fish you might see in a fish store, but it certainly kept away sharks in the tanks. Now Eugenie wanted to find out what would happen when it came in contact with big sharks in the sea.

Eugenie and her helpers set out a shark line in the sea, far from shore. They put different kinds of fish on the line, some alive and some dead. All along the line, in between the other fish — but not too close — they hung the Moses sole.

They set the line during the day. Nothing happened as long as it was light. Then the sun began to set and the sea grew dark.

Eugenie and the others put on scuba gear and slipped into the water to watch.

The sea was calm and as smooth as glass. Suddenly the water moved over the shark line. One dark shadow, then another, drifted up from the deep. From the dark depths of the sea, sharks were swimming up. Silently, swiftly, they swam to the little fish wriggling on the line.

The sharks ate up all the fish one by one — all but the Moses sole!

Day after day Eugenie repeated the test. She noticed that the sharks came to the line most often just after sunset and again the next morning before the sun rose. Each time, they avoided the Moses sole!

Naftali Primor, one of Eugenie's students in Israel, also studied the Moses sole. She found that the poison from this little fish was better as a shark repellent than any other chemical. A very small amount of it could keep hungry sharks away for many hours — eighteen hours in one of the tests. It didn't wash away in the water as other chemicals did.

Eugenie is glad that a useful shark repellent might come from the little fish. But she doesn't think that the Moses sole should be used only for that. She says that sharks aren't as dangerous to swimmers and divers as most people think. There is another useful chemical in the milk-like fluid of the Moses sole. It can stop the action of the poison in some snake bites, scorpion bites, and bee stings. Eugenie Clark thinks that if research companies become willing to spend the time and money, they might find a way to make this chemical. Then the lives of many people who have been bitten by animals and insects could be saved.

So many dreams have come true for Eugenie Clark. When she was a little girl, she dreamed of walking on the bottom of the sea with fish. She dreamed of swimming with sharks. She dreamed of becoming a teacher. Later she dreamed of working at her own marine lab. She has done all these things.

People ask her what she wants to do when she gets old. "I want to keep on diving," Eugenie says. "I hope I will still be diving when I'm ninety!"

AUTHOR

Ann McGovern says that she was a shy, stuttering child who expressed herself by writing. In high school, she wrote many stories and poems with the help of one of her teachers. When she began working, she wrote at night or whenever she could find the time. For a number of years, she has worked in the publishing field. During that time, she has written over thirty children's books, has founded a children's book club, and has reviewed children's books.

Ann McGovern and her husband enjoy scuba diving and underwater photography. Their hobby often takes them and their children to coral reefs in faraway places. Ms. McGovern's books *Sharks, The Underwater World of the Coral Reef,* and *Shark Lady,* a part of which you have just read, show her love of these subjects.

Grayback's Baby

by ALICE E. GOUDEY

Small waves go quietly across the blue-green water of
the ocean.

The air is clear. The first rays of morning sunlight
dance on the waves like a million little lights.

Three kittiwakes fly above the water. "Kittiwake!
Kittiwake! Kittiwake!" they call. It's as if they're glad
to be alive on such a wonderful day.

Suddenly a dolphin leaps from the quiet of the water. Then another one leaps into the air. Soon, all about, dolphins are leaping high in the air.

Young, happy-looking dolphins of different sizes chase one another and then leap upward.

Mother dolphins join the young ones.

Even Old Scarsides, who is almost twelve feet long, leaps out. There are scars of many battles on his thick gray skin.

But one dolphin, Grayback, does not join the others in their play. She stays quietly by herself a little way off.

Two others stay with Grayback. They swim slowly around her. Now and then they touch her with their noses. It is as if they are worried about her safety.

It is almost noon before the dolphin herd leaves the open water and starts swimming toward the bay. With strong downward movements of their flat tails, or flukes, they send their bodies through the water.

Up and down, up and down, their dark gray backs move through the water.

When they enter the bay, the gulls see the dolphins. "Keeow! Keeow! Keeow!" The gulls scream their noisy greeting.

Grayback is the last to enter the bay. Her companions swim close beside her.

Not far away, two long, gray, shadowy forms circle slowly about.

Old Scarsides makes a clapping sound with his powerful jaws when he sees them — two hungry tiger sharks!

But he will leave them alone as long as they do not bother any member of the herd.

The dolphins are hungry now. They have not eaten since early morning.

Just ahead of them they hear a school of little mullets.

Flip! Flip! Splash! The little fish flop in and out of the water.

The dolphins dash in among them and snap them up as they jump above the water.

The hungry dolphins swallow the mullets whole. Even though they have almost a hundred teeth in their jaws, they don't often use them for chewing. They use their teeth for catching and holding their kill or for biting one another and their enemies.

The laughing gulls swoop down. They, too, gobble up the little fish when they flop out of the water.

It is almost sundown when the gulls look down into the clear water of the bay and see a little dolphin by Grayback's side.

Grayback's first baby has been born!

"Keeow! Keeow! Keeow!" the gulls scream.

We might think that the gulls are saying, "Just another big fish. Just another big fish in the ocean. Too big for us to swallow. *Much* too big for us to swallow."

It is true that Grayback's baby looks like a big fish. But the baby dolphin does not belong to the fish family. It belongs to the great family of mammals. It cannot get oxygen from the air *in* water as the fishes do. It must get its oxygen from the air *above* the water as mammals do.

Now the gulls see the baby dolphin swim quickly toward the surface of the water. Grayback swims just below the baby. She is ready to push it up if it needs her help. If it does not get air quickly, it cannot live.

The gulls see the baby's small, rounded head come above the water. At last the baby is breathing!

It draws fresh air in through a hole on the top of its head. This hole is called a *spiracle*.

When the baby dolphin has filled its lungs with air, it

closes its spiracle. Then it goes beneath the water again
to rest quietly at its mother's side.

If the baby didn't close its spiracle, water would run
into its lungs. It would drown.

But it doesn't rest for long. In about thirty seconds, it
rises to the surface again.

Woo-oof! Woo-oof! It blows the old air out with a
rushing sound. Now it draws in fresh, clean air again.

Like all dolphins, the baby *could* stay under the water for about six minutes, but it usually comes up for air two or three times each minute.

Grayback and her companions stay close beside the baby. It is well that they do because, as night comes on, the two tiger sharks circle closer and closer to them.

The sharks are not alone. Little pilot fish swim close to them. The pilot fish are waiting to gobble up bits of food that the sharks drop while they eat.

Also, two shark suckers cling to the sides of the sharks and get a free ride. They hold onto the sharks' rough skin with little suction discs on the tops of their heads. They, too, snap up bits of food that the sharks drop.

A baby dolphin would make a good meal for the sharks, the pilot fish, and the shark suckers!

The sharks make quick turns and swim in figure eights. They turn this way and that way, as if hunting for something.

They cannot see very well, but their sense of smell leads them toward Grayback and her baby.

Grayback and her companions form a ring around the baby dolphin. Old Scarsides whistles sharply as the sharks dart toward them.

Then the whole herd of dolphins shoots through the water. They are upon the sharks in an instant. They ram them with their hard snouts and slam them with their tails. Water flies in all directions! The dolphins whistle sharply. Old Scarsides snaps his powerful jaws again and again as he rushes forward for another poke with his snout.

The noise of the battle can be heard across the bay.

A night heron, flying across the bay, hears it. "Quok! Quok!" it cries.

The gulls, rocking on the water, hear it. They fly up, circle about, and sound their alarm cry.

The fish under the water dart away to a safer place.

One of the sharks sinks its teeth into the side of a dolphin. Blood flows from the wound and stains the water.

The taste and smell of the blood make the sharks fight more wildly than ever.

At last Old Scarsides gives one of the sharks a hard blow behind one of its gills. The shark sinks to the bottom of the bay.

When this happens, the other shark whirls quickly and heads out toward the open water.

Grayback's baby is safe at last.

AUTHOR

When Alice E. Goudey was seventeen, she began teaching in a one-room country school in Kansas. Because there were so few books for the children to read, she herself began to write. She says that these early efforts were not good writing and that later she took writing courses in New York at Columbia University and New York University.

Mrs. Goudey has long been interested in ecology, and she is best known for her nature and animal books. The story that you have just read is from *Here Come the Dolphins,* one of the books in her "Here Come" series. Others are *Here Come the Bears* and *Here Come the Beavers.*

Mrs. Goudey says that her aim in writing is to give young people a sense of the wonder and beauty in the world around us.

Three Strong Women

by CLAUS STAMM

Long ago in Japan, there lived a famous wrestler. He was on his way to the capital city to wrestle before the Emperor.

He strode down the road on legs thick as the trunks of small trees. He had been walking for seven hours and could walk for seven more without getting tired.

The time was autumn. The sky was a cold blue, the air chilly. In the small bright sun, the trees along the roadside glowed red and orange.

The wrestler hummed to himself in time with the long swing of his legs. Wind blew through his thin brown robe, and he wore no sword at his side. He felt proud that he needed no sword, even in the darkest and loneliest places. The icy air on his body only reminded him that few tailors would have been able to make warm clothes for a man so broad and tall. He felt much as a wrestler should — strong, healthy, and rather conceited.

A soft roar of fast-moving water beyond the trees told him that he was passing above a river bank. He hummed louder; he loved the sound of his voice and wanted it to sound clearly above the rushing water.

He thought, "They call me Forever-Mountain because I am such a good, strong wrestler — big, too. I'm a fine, brave man and far too modest ever to say so...."

Just then he saw a girl who must have come up from the river, for she carried a bucket on her head.

Her hands on the bucket were small. There was a dimple on each thumb, just below the knuckle. She was a round little girl with red cheeks and a nose like a friendly button. Her eyes looked as though she were thinking of ten thousand funny stories at once. She climbed up onto the road and walked ahead of the wrestler, jolly and bouncy.

"If I don't tickle that girl, I shall be sorry all my life," said the wrestler under his breath. "She's sure to go 'squeak,' and I shall laugh and laugh. If she drops her bucket, that will be even funnier — and I can always run and fill it again and even carry it home for her."

He tiptoed up and poked her lightly in the ribs with one huge finger.

The girl gave a squeal, laughed, and brought one arm down so that the wrestler's hand was caught between it and her body.

"Ho-ho-ho! You've caught me! I can't move at all!" said the wrestler, laughing.

"I know," said the jolly girl.

He felt that it was very good of her to take a joke so well, and he started to pull his hand free. Somehow, he could not.

He tried again, using a little more strength. "Now, now — let me go, little girl," he said. "I am a very powerful man. If I pull too hard, I might hurt you."

"Pull," said the girl. "You won't hurt me."

She began to walk, and though the wrestler tugged and pulled until his feet dug great furrows in the ground, he had to follow.

Ten minutes later, still tugging while following helplessly after her, he was glad that the road was lonely and that no one was there to see.

"Please let me go," he begged. "I am the famous wrestler Forever-Mountain. I must go and show my strength before the Emperor." (He burst out weeping from shame.) "And you're hurting my hand!"

The girl steadied the bucket on her head with her free hand and looked over her shoulder. "You poor, sweet little Forever-Mountain," she said. "Are you tired? Shall I carry you? I can leave the water here and come back for it later."

"I do not want you to carry me. I want you to let me go, and then I want to forget I ever saw you. What do you want with me?" moaned the wrestler.

"I only want to help you," said the girl, now pulling him up and up a narrow mountain path. "Oh, I am sure you'll have no more trouble than anyone else when you come up against the other wrestlers. You'll win, or else you'll lose. And you won't be too badly hurt either way. But aren't you afraid you might meet a really *strong* man one day?"

Forever-Mountain turned white. He stumbled. He was imagining being laughed at throughout Japan as "Hardly-Ever-Mountain."

Maru-me glanced back.

"You see? Tired already," she said. "I'll walk more slowly. Why don't you come along to my mother's house and let us make a strong man of you? The wrestling in the capital isn't due to begin for three months."

"All right. Three months. I'll come along," said the wrestler.

"Fine," she said happily. "We are almost there."

She freed his hand. "But if you break your promise and run off, I shall have to chase you and carry you back."

Soon they arrived in a small valley. A simple house stood in the middle.

"Grandmother is at home, but she is an old lady and she's probably sleeping." The girl shaded her eyes with one hand. "But Mother should be bringing our cow back from the field. Oh, here comes Mother now!"

She waved. The woman coming around the corner of the house put down the cow she was carrying and waved back. She smiled and came across the grass, walking with a lively bounce like her daughter's.

"Excuse me," she said, brushing some cow hair from her dress. "These mountain paths are full of stones. They hurt the cow's feet. And who is the nice young man you've brought, Maru-me?"

The girl explained. "And we have only three months!" she finished.

"Well, it's not long enough to do much, but it's not so short a time that we can't do something," said her mother, looking thoughtful. "But he does look very weak. He'll need a lot of good things to eat. Maybe when he gets stronger, he can help Grandmother with some of the easy work about the house."

"That will be fine!" said the girl, and she called her grand-mother — loudly, for the old woman was a little deaf.

"I'm coming!" came a creaky voice from inside the house. A little old woman leaning on a stick and looking very sleepy tottered out the door. As she came toward them, she tripped over the roots of a great oak tree.

"Heh! My eyes aren't what they used to be. That's the fourth time this month I've tripped over that tree," she said. Wrapping skinny arms about its trunk, she pulled it out of the ground.

"Oh, Grandmother! You should have let me pull it up for you," said Maru-me.

"Hm. I hope I didn't hurt my poor old back," said the old lady. She called out, "Daughter! Throw that tree away so no one will fall over it. But please make sure it doesn't hit anybody."

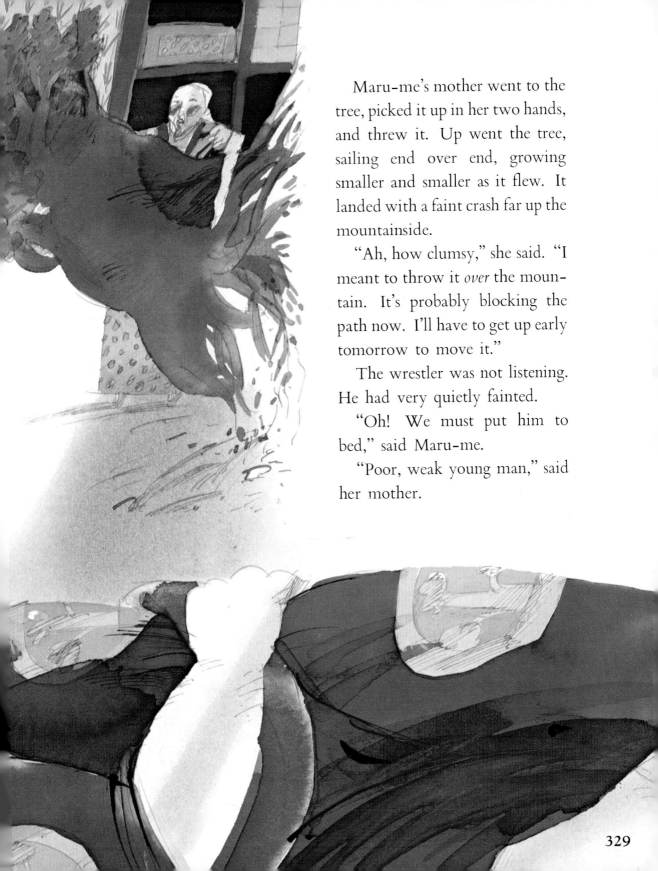

Maru-me's mother went to the tree, picked it up in her two hands, and threw it. Up went the tree, sailing end over end, growing smaller and smaller as it flew. It landed with a faint crash far up the mountainside.

"Ah, how clumsy," she said. "I meant to throw it *over* the mountain. It's probably blocking the path now. I'll have to get up early tomorrow to move it."

The wrestler was not listening. He had very quietly fainted.

"Oh! We must put him to bed," said Maru-me.

"Poor, weak young man," said her mother.

"I hope we can do something for him. Here, let me carry him; he's light," said the grandmother. She threw him over her shoulder and carried him into the house, creaking along with her cane.

The next day they began the work of making Forever-Mountain over into what they thought a strong man should be. They gave him the simplest food to eat — and the toughest. Day by day they prepared his rice with less and less water, until no ordinary man could have chewed it.

Every day he was made to do the work of five men. Every evening he wrestled with Grandmother. Maru-me and her mother agreed that Grandmother, being old and feeble, was the least likely to hurt him.

He grew stronger and stronger but hardly knew it. Grandmother could still throw him easily into the air — and catch him again — without ever changing her sweet old smile.

He quite forgot that outside this valley he was one of the greatest wrestlers in Japan and was called Forever-Mountain. His legs had been like logs. Now they were like pillars. His big hands were hard as stones. When he cracked his knuckles, the sound was like trees splitting on a cold night.

Sometimes he did an exercise that wrestlers do in Japan. He would raise one foot high above the ground and bring it down with a crash. Then people in nearby villages looked up at the winter sky and told one another that it was very late in the year for thunder.

Soon he could pull up a tree as well as the grandmother could. He could even throw one — but only a short way. One evening, near the end of his third month, he wrestled with Grandmother and won.

"Heh-heh!" she laughed. "I would never have believed it!"
Maru-me squealed with joy.

"Very good, very good! What a strong man," said her
mother, who had just come home from the fields, carrying, as
usual, the cow. She put the cow down and patted the wrestler
on the back.

They agreed that he was now ready to show some *real*
strength before the Emperor.

The next morning, Forever-Mountain tied his hair up in
the topknot that all Japanese wrestlers wear and got ready to

leave. He thanked Maru-me and her mother and bowed very low to the grandmother, since she was the oldest and had been a fine wrestling partner.

When Forever-Mountain reached the palace grounds, many of the other wrestlers were already there. They sat about eating great bowls of rice, comparing one another's weight, and telling stories. They paid little attention to Forever-Mountain, except to wonder why he had arrived so late this year. Some of them noticed that he had grown very quiet and that he took no part at all in their boasting.

All the ladies and gentlemen of the court were waiting in a special courtyard for the wrestling to begin. Behind a screen sat the Emperor — by himself. He was too noble for ordinary people to look at.

The first two wrestlers chosen to fight were Forever-Mountain and a wrestler who was said to have the biggest

stomach in the country. He and Forever-Mountain both threw some salt into the ring. It was understood that this drove away evil spirits.

Then the other wrestler, moving his stomach somewhat out of the way, raised his foot and brought it down with a fearful stamp. He glared at Forever-Mountain as if to say, "Now *you* stamp, you poor frightened man!"

Forever-Mountain raised his foot. He brought it down.

There was a sound like thunder. The earth shook, and the other wrestler bounced into the air and out of the ring, as gracefully as any soap bubble.

He picked himself up and bowed to the Emperor's screen.

"The earth-god is angry. Perhaps there is something the matter with the salt," he said. "I do not think I shall wrestle this season." And he walked out, looking over one shoulder at Forever-Mountain.

Five other wrestlers then and there decided that they were not wrestling this season either. They all looked angry with Forever-Mountain.

From then on, Forever-Mountain brought his foot down lightly. As each wrestler came into the ring, Forever-Mountain picked him up very gently, carried him out, and placed him before the Emperor's screen, bowing most politely every time.

The court ladies and gentlemen looked troubled and a little afraid. They loved to see fierce, strong men tugging and grunting at each other, but Forever-Mountain was a little too much for them. Only the Emperor was happy behind his screen. He ordered all the prize money handed over to Forever-Mountain. "But," he said, "you had better not wrestle anymore."

Forever-Mountain promised not to wrestle again. Everybody looked happier.

"I think I shall become a farmer," Forever-Mountain said, and he left at once to go back to Maru-me.

When Maru-me saw him coming, she ran down the mountain, picked him up, together with the heavy bags of prize money, and carried him halfway up the side of the mountain. Then she put him down. The rest of the way he carried her.

Forever-Mountain kept his promise to the Emperor and never fought in public again. But up in the mountains, sometimes, the earth shakes and rumbles, and they say then that Forever-Mountain and Maru-me's grandmother are practicing wrestling in the hidden valley.

AUTHOR

Claus Stamm has lived in Japan, where he found the ideas for stories he has written. The story you have just read is a tall tale that Mr. Stamm heard in Japan. He liked the story so much that he decided to re-tell it in English.

What Are Pockets For?

by DAVID McCORD

What are pockets for?
An old piece of sash cord,
a knob from a door;
a small U magnet,
if you can find it;
a sprung clock spring,
with the key to wind it;
oodles of marbles,
a twist of copper wire;
a baseball calendar,
a flint for fire;
one soiled Jack of Hearts
or the five of Spades;
that unshown copy of
your last month's grades;
two colored pebbles,

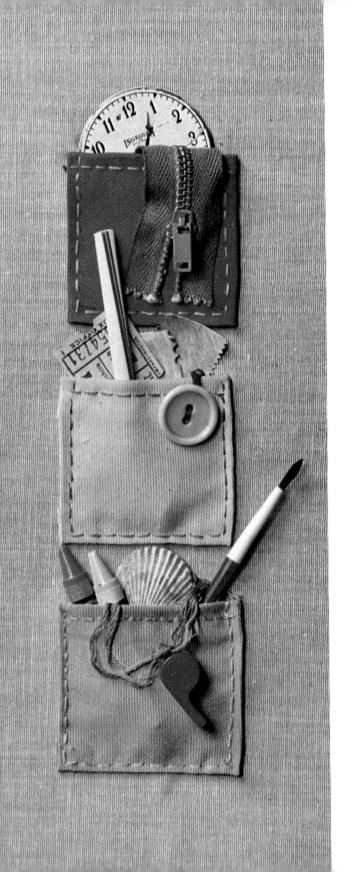

one hickory nut;
a shell, some fish line
with three feet of gut;
a cog out of something
which never did run;
a cellophane of candy —
I'll give you one;
your first circus ticket-stub,
the snap you took
of the clown on the slack
wire before it shook;
a flashlight bulb,
a dirty green stamp;
the long-missing part of
your bicycle lamp;
one thin pair of pliers
to ply or to nip;
one old zipper fastener
with nothing to zip;
that half-busted harness-
bell you found inside
the barn on the farm,
and the buckle too wide
for its three-inch strap;
and a whole lot more
of stuff. Did you say,
What are pockets for?

A Lick Is a Lick Is a...

Have you ever seen a rose? A yellow one? An orange one? A pink one? An almost black one? A big one? A small one? A poet once wrote "a rose is a rose is a rose." She may have meant that no matter what color, no matter what size, or no matter what you might call it, a rose is still a rose. That may be true of the flower, but it's not true of the word. The word *rose* has several meanings.

Rose is a color. A *rose* is a flower. A certain kind of nozzle for spraying water is called a *rose*. A diamond cut in a certain way is called a *rose*. There are thousands of words in the English language that, like *rose*, have many different meanings.

In the story "Wagon Wheels," do you remember that the father talked about finding *free* land? In the early 1900's — the time in which this story took place — land was given to people who wanted it. It didn't cost anything. "Costing nothing" is one meaning of *free.*

At another point in "Wagon Wheels," the father talked about himself and his family as *"free* black people." Here *free* means "not held captive in slavery." Does *free* have that meaning when we speak of a *free* country? A *free* country is one in which the people have a say in their government.

Now, think about the word *lick.* The father said, "There was not a *lick* of food in the whole town of Nicodemus." When you read that, you decided that *a lick* meant "a bit," didn't you? But you know that there are other meanings for the word *lick.*

How many times have you *licked* an ice-cream cone? Have you ever been on a team that *licked* another team?

One meaning that you may not know for *lick* is "a deposit of natural salt that is licked by passing animals." Is it true that a lick is a lick is a lick?

People who speak another language and who try to learn English say that it is quite hard to do. Perhaps it is because a single word can have so many meanings. Do you think someone who didn't know English well would have trouble figuring out the meanings of *collar* in the following part of a story?

My shirt *collar* was tight and I was uncomfortable. Even so, I had to *collar* the thief who had stolen the *collar* right off my dog's neck!

The Train in the Sky

by VIC HERMAN

Many years ago, in Mexico, steam trains made the exciting trip over the high mountain range between Los Mochis and Chihuahua. One day, the engineer on a train called the Anita allowed his young son, Juanito, and Conchos, a Tarahumara Indian boy, to ride in his cab and help run the train. As they passed through the villages, they let off and picked up passengers, each time loading the woodcar and checking the steam pressure of the locomotive. In a small village named Temoris, after new passengers had boarded and the conductor, Don Carlos, had raised his lantern for the train to start, an old man on a burro pushed through the crowd.

"Wait! Hold the train! I am Tomás Francisco! Wait for me!" he called.

The old man rode up to Don Carlos. He searched his pocket, then pulled out a ticket. "Here it is," he said. "Here is the ticket. It is for my burro Pepe and me."

"*Bueno,*" the conductor said. "Get yourself and your burro aboard *muy pronto.* We must leave right away."

Tomás Francisco led the burro to the steps of the last coach. Then he and Don Carlos tried to push the animal through the narrow entrance.

But Pepe was a large burro. Try as they might, they could not get him through.

Juanito's father finally went back to see if he could help. They tried again but had to give up.

"It is no use," Don Carlos said. "The animal is too big. We must leave without you."

The old man turned to the engineer. "Please, *señor* engineer," he cried, "Please take us. We must get to San Rafael to

341

pick up wood to haul to the marketplace at Creel. The climb ahead is too steep for Pepe and me."

"But you see for yourself that the burro will not fit through the door opening," the engineer said. "I am very sorry, but it is as Don Carlos says. We must leave without you."

Juanito, who had joined the group, pulled at his father's sleeve. *"Papacito,* Pepe could ride in the cab of the Anita," he said.

"No, Juanito. Not in my cab." He looked at his watch. "There is no more time for talk. Come, we must go."

The old man followed Juanito and his father to the locomotive. "Please, *señor* engineer. Pepe is very gentle. We would be no trouble."

"Not in my cab would I have a burro!" the engineer said.

"But *señor.* I am Tomás Francisco, the cousin of your fireman, Alfredo Gonzales.

Alfredo says you are the finest engineer in all of Mexico. He says you are kind too. He says that you would never be unkind to anyone."

Juanito's father stopped, his foot on the step of the cab. "Alfredo said that?" He looked at the burro for a moment. Then he reached down and patted Pepe's head. "He is not so big a burro after all. Come, let us see if we can get him into the cab."

Conchos came to the door to help. With all of them pushing and Conchos pulling, the burro was soon inside.

The old man smiled happily. "I am small. I can ride on top of this pile of wood to make more room in the cab."

"I too will ride on the wood-pile," said Conchos.

Once again Don Carlos raised his lantern. Juanito pulled the whistle cord, and his father opened the throttle.

As the great iron wheels began to turn, the burro suddenly placed his front feet on the fireman's seat. Then he put his head out the window. The Anita sounded its horn and pulled out of Temoris with the engineer at one window and Pepe at the other.

Just past Temoris, the road rose steeply. The locomotive slowed down.

"Put more wood on the fire, *muchachos*," the engineer said.

"We must keep the steam high so that the engine does not stall."

The train kept climbing into the rough mountain country, passing the villages of Cerocahui and Parajes. Juanito looked out the window. The high mountain peaks, covered with snow, were very close. They were now above the timberline, leaving the green trees behind.

Still climbing, the train passed through tunnels and over bridges. The fire had to be fed often now, and the woodpile was getting low. But Juanito was not worried. He knew that they would soon be coming to the village of Bahuichivo, where they would stop and take on more wood.

He glanced over at Pepe. The burro had grown tired of looking out the window and was sleeping. "Rest up, my little friend," Juanito said. "Soon you will have a heavy load to carry."

When they reached Bahuichivo, they worked swiftly to load the woodcar from a shed. Juanito's father had set up many along the route.

Juanito brought out the pots of hot food they had with them. Don Carlos joined them, and they shared the food.

The burro woke up and rubbed up against Tomás Francisco. "Pepe sees me eating, and he wants some food too," the old man said. He fed the burro hay from his sack.

As they ate, they watched the long line of people waiting to buy tickets. "We are going to be crowded again," Juanito's father said. "Never before have we had so many passengers from this town."

Don Carlos nodded. "I have heard that last night there was a big wedding and fiesta here. Now the wedding guests are returning home to their villages."

When the passengers were

aboard, the train started up again. With so many people in its coaches, it gathered speed very slowly.

"Keep a close check on the steam! The longest climb of all is just ahead," his father said to Juanito.

The tracks curved back and forth and still they went up and up. Conchos and the old man helped Juanito stir up the fire until it blazed brightly. But when Juanito checked the gauge, he saw that the steam pressure was falling. Soon the locomotive's great wheels began to turn more and more slowly.

"What is happening to the steam?" the engineer called back.

"Papa, the boiler will not hold any more wood, but still the pressure keeps dropping. I do not understand."

"It is because of the many passengers and the long climb. Well, keep trying. San Rafael is only a short distance away."

The locomotive crept up the mountain, but soon it was only inching along. Then the engine shook and stopped dead. The wheels spun against the rails, shooting sparks.

Quickly the engineer put on the brakes, locking the wheels to the rails. The little train was alone in the sky, on the edge of the mighty mountains. All around were steep canyon walls.

The engineer sat quietly thinking.

Juanito said, "Papa, we can let the engine rest a little while and build the steam pressure all the way up. Then we can start again."

His father shook his head. "It is not so easy as that, my son," he said. "Once the train has stopped on such a grade as this, steam pressure alone is not enough. You see, the engine cannot start and climb at the same time. The wheels would spin on the tracks, but the train would not move."

Don Carlos, who had joined them, said, "Perhaps the passengers could get off the train. Then it would be light enough to start."

"*Muy bien*," said Juanito's father. "That would indeed help. But even so, I cannot chance it. I must take off the brakes when I open the throttle. If the engine does not drive the train forward, the train may begin to slide backward. On this incline, it would reach a terrible speed in no time. Then the brakes would not hold. No, it's too dangerous to do."

Juanito thought. Then he had an idea.

"Papa, we could put gravel on the tracks so that the wheels would not slip so much. I could get up the steam, and Don Carlos could ask the passengers to push the train when you tell them that we are ready to start."

The engineer looked at his son. Then a slow smile spread across his face. "That is a good plan, Juanito. We will try it."

Tomás Francisco said, "Don't forget Pepe! He is a strong burro. I will tie a rope to the frame in front of the locomotive, and he can pull the engine."

Juanito's father helped the old man get Pepe out of the cab. The burro seemed happy to be on the ground again. He let them lead him to the front of the locomotive.

Juanito threw wood on the fire. Conchos spread gravel on the rails. Don Carlos ran to talk to the passengers.

The engineer joined Juanito in the cab. He looked at the steam pressure. "It is almost enough," he said, as he made the fire a little higher. Then he went to the engineer's seat.

"We are ready!" he shouted back to Don Carlos. The passengers were at their places, ready to push. Tomás Francisco said that he was ready too.

"Blow the whistle, my son."

Juanito pulled the cord twice. Bit by bit his father opened the throttle, then took off the brakes. The passengers pushed. Pepe pulled.

For a moment, nothing happened. Then slowly, inch by inch, the train began to move. Juanito held his breath.

The wheels began to turn a little faster, gripping the tracks firmly now. The engineer turned to wink at his son. The plan had worked!

Juanito's father let up on the throttle. "I think maybe we can make it on the engine alone," he said. "But I don't want to take any chances. We are going slowly enough for the passengers to be able to walk as they push the train. It is not far. San Rafael is just around the next bend."

The people waiting at the station couldn't believe the sight of a burro pulling the locomotive while passengers pushed the train from behind.

When they found out what had happened, they cheered.

Tomás Francisco and Pepe took their bows along with the other passengers. Then Tomás came to the cab to say good-by to the engineer and the others.

"Thank you, great conqueror of the Sierra Madre, for getting my friend and me to San Rafael."

The engineer smiled. "Well, almost to San Rafael," he said. "*Muchas gracias* to you, and to your strong burro."

AUTHOR

The story you have just read was taken from the book *Juanito's Railroad in the Sky*. The author, Vic Herman, has written over fifty books for children, all of them about Mexicans or Mexican Americans.

Mr. Herman grew up in Los Angeles, California, where he learned to speak Spanish and gained an interest in and love for his Mexican-American neighbors and their culture. He studied art in New York City, and later his work as an artist took him to Mexico. There, he did a group of paintings, "Many Faces of Mexico," that brought him great honor: They were shown in the cities of both Mexico and the United States. In fact, he was given a medal for furthering good relations between the two countries.

The Hermans live in California.

Subway Ride

by LEE BENNETT HOPKINS

On the subway I can read the ads, count the stops,
  study faces —
    white faces, pink faces,
    brown faces, black faces,
    old faces, new faces,
    and my own face's face in the train window.

I can be a conductor (if I'm in the first car
  or the last) and look out the window at
  the darkness whizzing by.

I can think thoughts — my very own secret
  subway-ride thoughts.
And I ride and ride
Until it's my turn to get off.
Then I leave it all to someone else.

SKILL

A Street Map

As you know, a map is a drawing of the earth's surface. It may show all the earth's surface, as a round globe map of the world that you see in many classrooms does. It may show only part of the earth's surface, as a map of a city that you see in a social studies book does. There are many kinds of maps, and different ones are used for different reasons. Every map helps you understand some part of the world. Maps can help you learn about places you have never been. They can help you learn about the place where you live.

What is a street map?

One kind of map, called a **street map,** helps you to find your way around in a city or town. You can see where the streets and roads are. You can see in which direction you must go to get from one place to another. A street map of an area shows each street as though you were above the area looking straight down on it. A street map also shows such things as parks, lakes, ponds, and important buildings.

How do you read a street map?

Look at the map on page 351 that shows the downtown part of an imaginary city called Cummins. Cummins is a fairly large city that has an underground subway system. You can read this map by looking at the streets and by understanding how to use the legend and the compass rose.

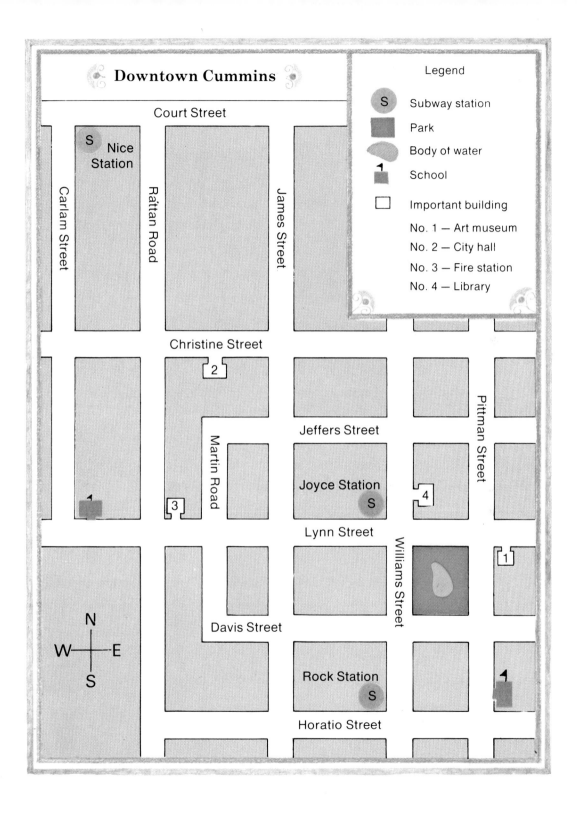

Downtown Cummins

Court Street

Carlam Street

Rattan Road

James Street

S Nice Station

Christine Street

Martin Road

2

Jeffers Street

Joyce Station S

3

1

Lynn Street

4

Pittman Street

Williams Street

1

Davis Street

N
W — E
S

Rock Station S

4

Horatio Street

Legend

S Subway station

Park

Body of water

School

Important building

No. 1 — Art museum

No. 2 — City hall

No. 3 — Fire station

No. 4 — Library

You can see that the names of the streets are printed on the map. You can also see that some streets cross other streets at certain points. Sometimes it is important to know where streets meet. If you were looking for the school on the corner of Lynn and Carlam streets, for example, you would have to find the place where Lynn and Carlam streets meet. To do this, put one finger of your right hand on Lynn Street and one finger of your left hand on Carlam Street. Move your fingers along the streets until you come to the place where Lynn and Carlam streets meet. There you will find the school.

What is a legend?

A **legend,** or key, tells you what each symbol on the map stands for. Look at the legend in the upper-right corner of the map on page 351. You see a symbol for a subway station, a park, a body of water, a school, and an important building. A subway station is shown as an **s** in a circle. A school is shown as a square with a flag on top. Each important building is shown by a square and is numbered. When you find a square with a number in it, you must use the legend to see which building the number represents. The park is colored green, and the body of water is colored blue. Use the legend to find the following places: the subway station that is in the upper-left corner of the map, the name of the important building on Christine Street, and the park.

What is a compass rose?

A **compass rose** tells you direction. Direction is very important in reading a street map. If you are told that some place or some street is north of where you are, for example, you have to know which direction is north. Look at the compass rose in the lower-left corner of the map on page 351. The letters *N, S, E,* and *W* on the compass rose stand for *north, south, east,* and *west.* Pretend that you want to walk to important building No. 1, the art museum, and that you are at the Joyce subway station. Find both places. Now look at the compass rose. The compass rose tells you that you would have to walk east on Lynn Street until you came to Pittman Street. The art museum is at the corner of Lynn and Pittman streets.

REVIEW

Reread the headings of this lesson, and think about the answer to each heading question. Recite the answer to yourself. Then review all your answers. You should now be ready to read a street map by yourself.

READING A STREET MAP

Use the street map of downtown Lynn on page 355 to answer each of the following questions. Copy the number of each question on a sheet of paper. Then write your answer.

1. What is the public building on the corner of Garfield Street and Fourth Avenue?
2. At the corner of which streets is the hospital on the east side of downtown Lynn?
3. What kind of building is located at the corner of Fourth Avenue and Adams Street?
4. If you were in the library on Second Avenue, in which direction would you walk on Second Avenue to get to Lincoln Street?
5. In which direction would the fire engines leave the fire station if a fire broke out in the school on First Avenue?
6. Pretend that you got off a bus at the corner of Fourth Avenue and Adams Street and wanted to go to the school near the corner of Garfield Street and Kennedy Avenue. In which direction would you walk on Fourth Avenue? In which direction would you then walk on Garfield Street?

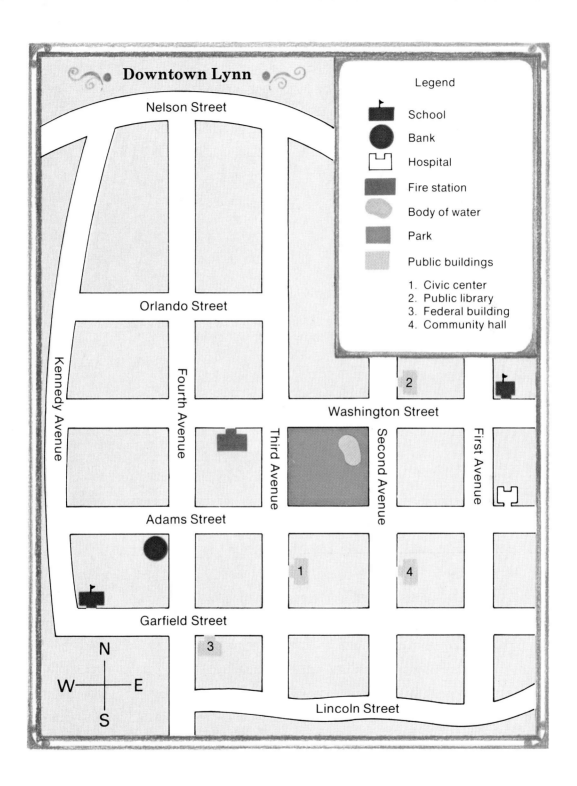

Downtown Lynn

Nelson Street

Orlando Street

Kennedy Avenue

Fourth Avenue

Third Avenue

Second Avenue

First Avenue

Washington Street

Adams Street

Garfield Street

Lincoln Street

2

1

4

3

N
W E
S

Legend

School

Bank

Hospital

Fire station

Body of water

Park

Public buildings

1. Civic center
2. Public library
3. Federal building
4. Community hall

Are Your Arms a Hundred Years Old?

by SHARON BELL MATHIS

Michael's great-great-aunt, Dewbet Thomas, has come to live with Michael and his parents. "Aunt Dew" has a precious old wooden box — her hundred penny box. The importance of this box is not understood by Michael's mother, but Michael feels that the box is *very* important. He knows how much it means to Aunt Dew. As this part of the story opens, Michael has just told Aunt Dew that he is going to hide the box to keep it safe.

"No, don't hide my hundred penny box!" Aunt Dew said out loud. "Leave my hundred penny box right alone. Anybody takes my hundred penny box takes me!"

"Just in case," Michael said impatiently and wished his great-great-aunt would sit back down in her chair so he could talk to her.

"What your momma name?"

"Oh, no," Michael said. "You keep *on* forgetting Momma's name!" That was the only thing bad about being a hundred years old like Aunt Dew — you kept *on* forgetting things that were important.

"Hush, John-boy," Aunt Dew said and stopped dancing and humming and sat back down in the chair and put the quilt back over her legs.

"You keep on forgetting."

"I don't."

"You do, you keep on forgetting!"

"Do I forget to play with you when you worry me to death to play?"

Michael didn't answer.

"Do I forget to play when you want?"

"No."

"Okay. What your momma name? Who's that in my kitchen?"

"Momma's name is Ruth, but this isn't your house. Your house is in Atlanta. We went to get you and now you live with us."

"Ruth."

Michael saw Aunt Dew staring at him again. Whenever she stared at him like that, he never knew what she'd say next. Sometimes it had nothing to do with what they had been talking about.

"You John's baby," she said, still staring at him. "Look like John just spit you out."

"That's my father."

"My great-nephew," Aunt Dew said. "Only one ever care about me." Aunt Dew rocked hard in her chair then and Michael watched her. He got off the bed and turned off the record player and put the record back into the bottom drawer. Then he sat down on the hundred penny box.

"See that tree out there?" Aunt Dew said and pointed

her finger straight toward the window with the large tree pressed up against it. Michael knew exactly what she'd say.

"Didn't have no puny-looking trees like that near my house," she said. "Dewbet Thomas, that's me, and Henry Thomas, that was my late husband, had the biggest, tallest, prettiest trees and the widest yard in all Atlanta.

"And John, that was your daddy, liked it most because he was city and my five sons, Henry, Jr., and Truke and Latt and the twins — Booker and Jay — well, it didn't make them no never mind because it was always there.

"But when my oldest niece Junie and her husband — we called him Big John — brought your daddy down to visit every summer, they couldn't get the suitcase in the house good before he was climbing up and falling out the trees. We almost had to feed him up them trees!"

"Aunt Dew, we have to hide the box."

"Junie and Big John went out on that water and I was feeling funny all day. Didn't know what. Just feeling funny.

"I told Big John, I said, 'Big John, that boat old. Nothing but a piece a junk.' But he fooled around and said, 'We taking it out.'

"I looked and saw him and Junie on that water. Then it wasn't nothing. Both gone. And the boat turned over, going downstream.

"Your daddy, brand-new little britches on, just standing there looking, wasn't saying nothing. No hollering. I try to give him a big hunk of potato pie. But he just looking at me, just looking and standing. Wouldn't eat none of that pie. Then I said, 'Run get Henry Thomas and the boys.' He looked at me, and then he looked at that water.

He turned round real slow and walked toward the west field. He never run. All you could see was them stiff little britches — red they was —moving through the corn. Bare-waisted, he was. When we found the boat later, he took it clean apart — what was left of it — every plank, and pushed it back in that water. I watched him. Wasn't a piece left of that boat. Not a splinter."

"Aunt Dew, where can we hide the box?"

"What box?"

"The hundred penny box."

"We can't hide the hundred penny box and if she got to take my hundred penny box — she might as well take me!"

"We have to hide it!"

"No — we don't. It's *my* box!"

"It's *my* house. And I said we have to hide it!"

"How you going to hide a house, John?"

"Not the house! Our hundred penny box!"

"It's *my* box!"

Michael was beginning to feel desperate. "Suppose Momma takes it when you go to sleep?"

Aunt Dew stopped rocking and stared at him again. "Like John just spit you out," she said. "Go on count them pennies, boy. 'Less you worry me in my grave if you don't. Dewbet Thomas's hundred penny box. Dewbet Thomas a hundred years old and I got a penny to prove it — each year!"

Michael got off the hundred penny box and sat on the floor by his great-great-aunt's skinny feet stuck down inside his father's old slippers. He pulled the big wooden box toward him and lifted the lid and reached in and took out the small cloth roseprint sack filled with pennies. He dumped the pennies out into the box.

He was about to pick up one penny and put it in the sack, the way they played, and say "One," when his great-great-aunt spoke.

"Why you want to hide my hundred penny box?"

"To play," Michael said, after he thought for a moment.

"Play now," she said. "Don't hide my hundred penny box. I got to keep looking at my box and when I don't see my box, I won't see me neither."

"One!" Michael said and dropped the penny back into the old print sack.

"18 and 74," Aunt Dew said. "Year I was born. Slavery over! Black men in Congress running things. They was in charge. It was the Reconstruction."

Michael counted twenty-seven pennies back into the old print sack before she stopped talking about Reconstruction. "19 and 01," Aunt Dew said. "I was twenty-seven years. Birthed my twin boys. Hattie said, 'Dewbet, you got two babies.' I asked Henry Thomas. I said, 'Henry Thomas, what them boys look like?'"

By the time Michael had counted fifty-six pennies, his mother was standing at the door.

"19 and 30," Aunt Dew said. "Depression. Henry Thomas, that was my late husband, died. Died after he put the fifty-six penny in my box. He had the double pneumonia and no decent shoes, and he worked too hard. Said he was going to sweat the trouble out his lungs. Couldn't do it. Same year I sewed that fancy dress for Rena Coles. She want a hundred bows all over that dress. I was sewing bows and tying bows and twisting bows. Henry the one started that box, you know. Put the first thirty-one pennies in it for me and it was my birthday. After fifty-six, I put them all in myself."

"Aunt Dew, time to go to bed," his mother said, standing at the door.

"Now, I'm not sleepy," Aunt Dew said. "John-boy and me just talking. Why you don't call him John? Look like John just spit him out. Why you got to call that boy something different from his daddy?"

Michael watched his mother walk over and open the window wide. "We'll get some fresh air in here," she said. "And then, Aunt Dew, you can take your nap better and feel good when you wake up." Michael wouldn't let his mother take the sack of pennies out of his hand. He held tight and then she let go.

"I'm not sleepy," Aunt Dew said again. "This child and me just talking."

"I know," his mother said, pointing her finger at him a little. "But we're just going to take our nap anyway."

"I got a long time to sleep and I ain't ready now. Just leave me sit here in this little narrow piece a room. I'm not bothering nobody."

"Nobody said you're bothering anyone, but as soon as I start making that meat loaf, you're going to go to sleep in your chair and fall out again and hurt yourself. And John'll wonder where I was and say I was on the telephone, and that'll be something all over again."

"Well, I'll sit on the floor and if I fall, I'll be there already, and it won't be nobody's business but my own."

"Michael," his mother said and took the sack of pennies out of his hand and laid it on the dresser. Then she reached down and closed the lid of the hundred penny box and pushed it against the wall. "Go out the room, honey, and let Momma help Aunt Dew into bed."

"I been putting Dewbet Thomas to bed a long time and I can still do it," Aunt Dew said.

"I'll just help you a little," Michael heard his mother say through the closed door.

As soon as his mother left the room, he'd go in and sneak out the hundred penny box.

But where would he hide it?

Michael went into the bathroom to think, but his mother came in to get Aunt Dew's washcloth. "Why are you looking like that?" she asked. "If you want to play, go in my room. Play there, or in the living room. And don't go bothering Aunt Dew. She needs her rest."

Michael went into his father's and mother's room and lay down on the big king bed and tried to think of a place to hide the box.

He had an idea!

He'd hide it down in the furnace room and sneak Aunt Dew downstairs to see it so she'd know where it was. Then maybe they could sit on the basement steps inside and play with it sometimes. His mother would never know. And his father wouldn't care as long as Aunt Dew was happy. He could even show Aunt Dew the big pipes and the little pipes.

Michael heard his mother close his bedroom door and walk down the hall toward the kitchen.

He'd tell Aunt Dew right now that they had a good place
to hide the hundred penny box. The best place of all.

Michael got down from the huge bed and walked quietly
back down the hall to his door and knocked on it very
lightly — too lightly for his mother to hear.

Aunt Dew didn't answer.

"Aunt Dew," he whispered after he'd opened the door
and tiptoed up to the bed. "It's me. Michael."

Aunt Dew was crying.

Michael looked at his great-great-aunt and tried to say something, but she just kept crying. She looked extra small in his bed and the covers were too close about her neck. He moved them down a little and then her face didn't look so small. He waited to see if she'd stop crying but she didn't. He went out of the room and down the hall and stood near his mother. She was chopping up celery. "Aunt Dew's crying," he said.

"That's all right," his mother said. "Aunt Dew's all right."

"She's crying real hard."

"When you live long as Aunt Dew's lived, honey — sometimes you just cry. She'll be all right."

Michael tiptoed into his room. "Aunt Dew?"

"What you want, John-boy?"

"I'm sorry Momma's mean to you."

"Ain't nobody mean to Dewbet Thomas — cause Dewbet Thomas ain't mean to nobody," Aunt Dew said, and reached her hand out from under the cover and patted Michael's face. "Your Momma Ruth. She move around and do what she got to do. First time I see her — I say, 'John, she look frail but she ain't.' He said, 'No, she ain't frail.' I make out like I don't see her all the time," Aunt Dew said, and winked her eye. "But she know I see her. If she think I don't like her that ain't the truth. Dewbet Thomas like everybody. But me and her can't talk like me and John talk — 'cause she don't know all what me and John know."

"I closed the door," Michael said. "You don't have to sleep if you don't want to."

"I been sleep all day, John," Aunt Dew said.

Michael leaned over his bed and looked at his great-great-aunt. "You haven't been sleep all day," he said. "You've been sitting in your chair and talking to me and then you were dancing to your record and then we were counting pennies and we got to fifty-six and then Momma came."

"Where my hundred penny box?"

"I got it," Michael answered.

"Where you got it?"

"Right here by the bed."

"Watch out while I sleep."

He'd tell her about the good hiding place later. "Okay," he said.

Aunt Dew was staring at him. "Look like John just spit you out," she said.

Michael moved away from her. He turned his back and leaned against the bed and stared at the hundred penny box. All of a sudden it looked real *real* old and beat up.

"Turn round. Let me look at you."

Michael turned around slowly and looked at his great-great-aunt.

"John!"

"It's me," Michael said. "Michael."

He went and sat down on the hundred penny box.

"Come here so I can see you," Aunt Dew said.

Michael didn't move.

"Stubborn like your daddy. Don't pay your Aunt Dew no never mind!"

Michael still didn't get up.

"Go on back and do your counting out my pennies. Start

with fifty-seven — where you left off. 19 and 31. Latt married that schoolteacher. We roasted three pigs."

"First you know me, then you don't," Michael said.

"Michael John Jefferson what your name is," Aunt Dew said. "Should be plain John like your daddy and your daddy's daddy — 'stead of all this new stuff. Name John and everybody saying 'Michael.' " Aunt Dew was smiling. "Come here, boy," she said. "Come here close. Let me look at you. Got a head full of hair."

Michael got up from the hundred penny box and stood at the foot of the bed.

"Get closer," Aunt Dew said.

Michael did.

"Turn these covers back little more. This little narrow piece a room don't have the air the way my big house did."

"I took a picture of your house," Michael said and turned the covers back some more.

"My house bigger than your picture," Aunt Dew said. "Way bigger."

Michael leaned close to her on his bed and propped his elbows up on the large pillow under her small head. "Tell me about the barn again," he said.

"Dewbet and Henry Thomas had the biggest, reddest barn in all Atlanta, G-A!"

"And the swing Daddy broke?" Michael asked and put his head down on the covers. Her chest was so thin under the thick quilt that he hardly felt it. He reached up and pushed a few wispy strands of her hair away from her closed eyes.

"Did more pulling it down than he did swinging."

"Tell me about the swimming pool," Michael said. He touched Aunt Dew's chin and covered it up with only three fingers.

It was a long time before Aunt Dew answered. "Wasn't no swimming pool," she said. "I done told you was a creek. Plain old creek. And your daddy like to got bit by a cottonmouth."

"Don't go to sleep, Aunt Dew," Michael said. "Let's talk."

"I'm tired, John."

"I can count the pennies all the way to the end if you want me to."

"Go 'head and count."

"When your hundred and one birthday comes, I'm going to put in the new penny like you said."

"Yes, John."

Michael reached up and touched Aunt Dew's eyes. "I have a good place for the hundred penny box, Aunt Dew," he said quietly.

"Go 'way. Let me sleep," she said.

"You wish you were back in your own house, Aunt Dew?"

"I'm going back," Aunt Dew said.

"You sad?"

"Hush, boy!"

Michael climbed all the way up on the bed and put his whole self alongside his great-great-aunt. He touched her arms. "Are your arms a hundred years old?" he asked. It was their favorite question game.

"Um-hm," Aunt Dew murmured and turned a little away from him.

Michael touched her face. "Are your face and your eyes and fingers a hundred years old too?"

"John, I'm tired," Aunt Dew said. "Don't talk so."

"How do you get to be a hundred years old?" Michael asked and raised up from the bed on one elbow and waited for his great-great-aunt to answer.

"First you have to have a hundred penny box," his great-great-aunt finally said.

"Where you get it from?" Michael asked.

"Somebody special got to give it to you," Aunt Dew said. "And soon as they give it to you, you got to be careful 'less it disappear."

AUTHOR

The books of Sharon Bell Mathis have won many prizes. Her *Sidewalk Story* received an award from the Council on Interracial Books for Children. *Ray Charles* was given the Coretta Scott King Award. *The Hundred Penny Box,* part of which you have just read, was a *Boston Globe — Horn Book* Award Honor Book, a Newbery Medal Honor Book, and an American Library Association Notable Book.

Sharon Bell Mathis grew up in Brooklyn, New York, and then lived in Washington, D.C., where she was married, raised three daughters, and later went to graduate school. She has been a special-education teacher and a school librarian. She has also taught courses in writing.

About her books, Ms. Mathis says, "I know the strength and beauty that black children have, and I wish to salute it."

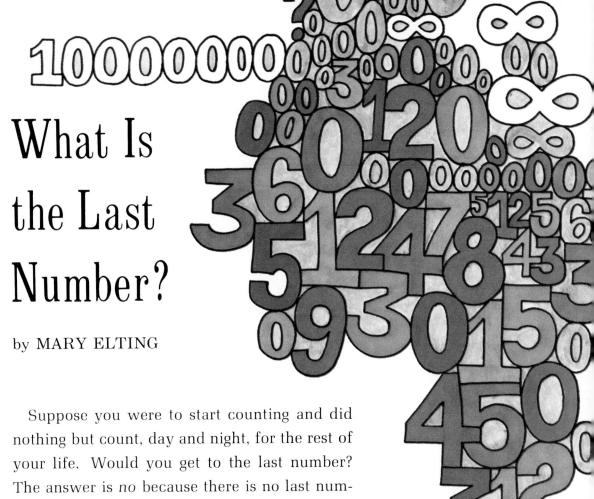

What Is the Last Number?

by MARY ELTING

Suppose you were to start counting and did nothing but count, day and night, for the rest of your life. Would you get to the last number? The answer is *no* because there is no last number. People who study mathematics tell us that we can never get to the end of numbers by counting. No matter how big a number we think of, there is always a bigger number. This idea is a very important one in science. It has a name — infinity. Scientists write infinity this way: ∞

A million is a large number. A billion is larger. From there on, we don't use names for numbers very often. Some of them don't even have names. One of the largest numbers that has a name is a *googol*. It is a 1 with 100 zeros after it.

The Tortoise Who Talked Too Much

Retold by NANCY DeROIN

Long ago, one of the kings of Benares was a chatterbox. He could *not* keep quiet. Once he started to talk, no one else could get a word in. All his counselors were worried, but none knew how to put a stop to his talking. It was not very safe to tell the king to shut up.

One day when this king and his counselors were walking in the palace courtyard, they found a tortoise lying on its back. The poor thing's shell was cracked, and he had died. The king wondered how this could have happened. The king's favorite counselor had been waiting for just such a chance. She told this story to the king:

> This tortoise used to live in a pond near the foot of the Himalayas. Two wild young geese, flying far from their home in search of food, landed on the pond. There they met the tortoise, and a friendship got started. By and by, the three creatures became the best of friends.
>
> The day came when the two geese felt ready to fly back home. Not wanting to leave their friend, they said, "We have a lovely home on Mount Cittakuta in

a cave of gold. Will you come home with us, friend?"

"Gladly," the tortoise said. "But how shall I ever get there? If I follow you, it will take forever!"

"Oh, it will be no problem to take you there. You just have to keep your mouth shut and not say a word on the way."

"That is easy enough," the tortoise said. "Take me with you."

So the two geese gave the tortoise a stick to hold between his teeth. Each goose took hold of one end of the stick and rose into the air, flying for home.

The tortoise held fast, his teeth fastened tightly on the stick.

As they flew above the town, some village children looked up and saw this strange sight in the air. They pointed, laughed, and jeered, saying, "Look at that, will you! Two geese carrying a tortoise on a stick!"

Just as the geese were flying over the palace of the king, the tortoise felt he had to answer the children. He was about to say, "Well, and what of it? If my friends carry me through the air, what is that to you, you good-for-nothings?" But the moment he opened his mouth to speak, the tortoise fell into the king's open courtyard and died.

The counselor stopped speaking. Then she added, "Whoever cannot keep from talking will come to trouble, sooner or later. . . .

"Although his life depended on
The stick he held between his teeth,
The tortoise could not hold his tongue;
He spoke — and here he lies beneath.
He spoke unwisely, out of season;
To his death the tortoise fell;
He talked too much — that is the reason."

"She is talking about me!" the king thought suddenly. And from that day on, the king understood that there were times to speak and times to hold his tongue. He became known as a man of few words.

AUTHOR

Born in Washington, D.C., Nancy DeRoin worked there as a reporter and an editor while studying at American University. After graduation, she moved to Chicago, Illinois, where she taught at the Buddhist Educational Center. In *Jataka Tales,* the book from which "The Tortoise Who Talked Too Much" was taken, she presents, in a modern way, Buddhist fables that are more than two thousand years old.

from

by E. B. WHITE

When Wilbur was born, he was a small, sickly pig who needed special care. Fern, his owner's eight-year-old daughter, took care of him until he was big enough to be sold to Mr. Zuckerman.

At Mr. Zuckerman's farm, Wilbur lived in a nice barn with many other animals for neighbors. Lurvy, the hired man, fed him regularly, and Fern came to visit him almost every day. Wilbur would have been really happy except for one thing — he didn't have a real friend among all his neighbors in the barn.

The following two chapters are only a small part of a complete story for children titled *Charlotte's Web,* by E. B. White, with illustrations by Garth Williams.

Loneliness

The next day was rainy and dark. Rain fell on the roof of the barn and dripped steadily from the eaves. Rain fell in the barnyard and ran in crooked courses down into the lane where thistles and pigweed grew. Rain spattered against the Zuckermans' kitchen windows and came gushing out of the downspouts. Rain fell on the backs of the sheep as they grazed in the meadow. When the sheep tired of standing in the rain, they walked slowly up the lane and into the fold.

Rain upset Wilbur's plans. Wilbur had planned to go out, this day, and dig a new hole in his yard. He had other plans, too. His plans for the day went something like this:

Breakfast at six-thirty. Skim milk, crusts, middlings, bits of doughnuts, wheat cakes with drops of maple syrup sticking to them, potato skins, leftover custard pudding with raisins, and bits of shredded wheat.

Breakfast would be finished at seven.

From seven to eight, Wilbur planned to have a talk with Templeton, the rat that lived under his trough. Talking with Templeton was not the most interesting occupation in the world but it was better than nothing.

From eight to nine, Wilbur planned to take a nap outdoors in the sun.

From nine to eleven, he planned to dig a hole, or trench, and possibly find something good to eat buried in the dirt.

From eleven to twelve, he planned to stand still and watch flies on the boards, watch bees in the clover, and watch swallows in the air.

Twelve o'clock — lunchtime. Middlings, warm water, apple parings, meat gravy, carrot scrapings, meat scraps, stale hominy, and the wrapper off a package of cheese. Lunch would be over at one.

From one to two, Wilbur planned to sleep.

From two to three, he planned to scratch itchy places by rubbing against the fence.

From three to four, he planned to stand perfectly still and think of what it was like to be alive, and to wait for Fern.

At four would come supper. Skim milk, provender, leftover sandwich from Lurvy's lunch box, prune skins, a morsel of this, a bit of that, fried potatoes, marmalade drippings, a little more of this, a little more of that, a piece of baked apple, a scrap of upside-down cake.

Wilbur had gone to sleep thinking about these plans. He awoke at six and saw the rain, and it seemed as though he couldn't bear it.

"I get everything all beautifully planned out and it has to go and rain," he said.

For a while he stood gloomily indoors. Then he walked to the door and looked out. Drops of rain struck his face. His yard was cold and wet. His trough had an inch of rainwater in it. Templeton was nowhere to be seen.

"Are you out there, Templeton?" called Wilbur. There was no answer. Suddenly Wilbur felt lonely and friendless.

"One day just like another," he groaned. "I'm very young, I have no real friend here in the barn, it's going to rain all morning and all afternoon, and Fern won't come in such bad weather. Oh, *honestly!*" And Wilbur was crying again, for the second time in two days.

At six-thirty Wilbur heard the banging of a pail. Lurvy was standing outside in the rain, stirring up breakfast.

"C'mon, pig!" said Lurvy.

Wilbur did not budge. Lurvy dumped the slops, scraped the pail, and walked away. He noticed that something was wrong with the pig.

Wilbur didn't want food, he wanted love. He wanted a friend — someone who would play with him. He mentioned this to the goose, who was sitting quietly in a corner of the sheepfold.

"Will you come over and play with me?" he asked.

"Sorry, sonny, sorry," said the goose. "I'm sitting-sitting on my eggs. Eight of them. Got to keep them toasty-oasty-oasty warm. I have to stay right here, I'm no flibberty-ibberty-gibbet. I do not play when there are eggs to hatch. I'm expecting goslings."

"Well, I didn't think you were expecting woodpeckers," said Wilbur, bitterly.

Wilbur next tried one of the lambs.

"Will you please play with me?" he asked.

"Certainly not," said the lamb. "In the first place, I cannot get into your pen, as I am not old enough to jump over the fence. In the second place, I am not interested in pigs. Pigs mean less than nothing to me."

"What do you mean, *less* than nothing?" replied Wilbur. "I don't think there is any such thing as *less* than nothing. Nothing is absolutely the limit of nothingness. It's the lowest you can go. It's the end of the line. How can something be less than nothing? If there were something that was less than nothing, then nothing would not be nothing, it would be something — even though it's just a very little bit of something. But if nothing is *nothing*, then nothing has nothing that is less than *it* is."

"Oh, be quiet!" said the lamb. "Go play by yourself! I don't play with pigs."

Sadly, Wilbur lay down and listened to the rain. Soon he saw the rat climbing down a slanting board that he used as a stairway.

"Will you play with me, Templeton?" asked Wilbur.

"Play?" said Templeton, twirling his whiskers. "Play? I hardly know the meaning of the word."

"Well," said Wilbur, "it means to have fun, to frolic, to run and skip and make merry."

"I never do those things if I can avoid them," replied the rat, sourly. "I prefer to spend my time eating, gnawing, spying, and hiding. I am a glutton but not a merrymaker. Right now I am on my way to your trough to eat your breakfast, since you haven't got sense enough to eat it yourself." And Templeton, the rat, crept stealthily along the wall and disappeared into a private tunnel that he had dug between the door and the trough in Wilbur's yard. Templeton was a crafty rat, and he had things pretty much his own way. The tunnel was an example of his skill and cunning. The tunnel enabled him to get from the barn to his hiding place under the pig trough without coming out into the open. He had tunnels and runways all over Mr. Zuckerman's farm and could get from one place to another without being seen. Usually he slept during the daytime and was abroad only after dark.

Wilbur watched him disappear into his tunnel. In a moment he saw the rat's sharp nose poke out from underneath the wooden trough. Cautiously Templeton pulled himself up over the edge of the trough. This was almost more than Wilbur could stand: on this dreary, rainy day to see his

breakfast being eaten by somebody else. He knew Templeton was getting soaked, out there in the pouring rain, but even that didn't comfort him. Friendless, dejected, and hungry, he threw himself down in the manure and sobbed.

Late that afternoon, Lurvy went to Mr. Zuckerman. "I think there's something wrong with that pig of yours. He hasn't touched his food."

"Give him two spoonfuls of sulphur and a little molasses," said Mr. Zuckerman.

Wilbur couldn't believe what was happening to him when Lurvy caught him and forced the medicine down his throat. This was certainly the worst day of his life. He didn't know whether he could endure the awful loneliness any more.

Darkness settled over everything. Soon there were only shadows and the noises of the sheep chewing their cuds, and occasionally the rattle of a cow chain up overhead. You can imagine Wilbur's surprise when, out of the darkness, came a small voice he had never heard before. It sounded rather thin, but pleasant. "Do you want a friend, Wilbur?" it said. "I'll be a friend to you. I've watched you all day and I like you."

"But I can't see you," said Wilbur, jumping to his feet. "Where are you? And *who* are you?"

"I'm right up here," said the voice. "Go to sleep. You'll see me in the morning."

Charlotte

The night seemed long. Wilbur's stomach was empty and his mind was full. And when your stomach is empty and your mind is full, it's always hard to sleep.

A dozen times during the night, Wilbur woke and stared into the blackness, listening to the sounds and trying to figure out what time it was. A barn is never perfectly quiet. Even at midnight there is usually something stirring.

The first time he woke, he heard Templeton gnawing a hole in the grain bin. Templeton's teeth scraped loudly against the wood and made quite a racket. "That crazy rat!" thought Wilbur. "Why does he have to stay up all night, grinding his clashers and destroying people's property? Why can't he go to sleep, like any decent animal?"

The second time Wilbur woke, he heard the goose turning on her nest and chuckling to herself.

"What time is it?" whispered Wilbur to the goose.

"Probably-obably-obably about half-past eleven," said the goose. "Why aren't you asleep, Wilbur?"

"Too many things on my mind," said Wilbur.

"Well," said the goose, "that's not *my* trouble. I have nothing at all on my mind, but I've too many things under my behind. Have you ever tried to sleep while sitting on eight eggs?"

"No," replied Wilbur. "I suppose it *is* uncomfortable. How long does it take a goose egg to hatch?"

"Approximately-oximately thirty days, all told," answered the goose. "But I cheat a little. On warm afternoons, I just pull a little straw over the eggs and go out for a walk."

Wilbur yawned and went back to sleep. In his dreams he heard again the voice saying, "I'll be a friend to you. Go to sleep — you'll see me in the morning."

About half an hour before dawn, Wilbur woke and listened. The barn was still dark. The sheep lay motionless. Even the goose was quiet. Overhead, on the main floor, nothing stirred: the cows were resting, the horses dozed. Templeton had quit work and gone off somewhere on an errand. The only sound was a slight scraping noise from the rooftop, where the weather vane swung back and forth. Wilbur loved the barn when it was like this — calm and quiet, waiting for light.

"Day is almost here," he thought.

Through a small window, a faint gleam appeared. One by one the stars went out. Wilbur could see the goose a few feet away. She sat with head tucked under a wing. Then he could see the sheep and the lambs. The sky lightened.

"Oh, beautiful day, it is here at last! Today I shall find my friend."

Wilbur looked everywhere. He searched his pen thoroughly. He examined the window ledge, stared up at the ceiling. But he saw nothing new. Finally he decided he would have to speak up. He hated to break the lovely stillness of dawn by using his voice, but he couldn't think of any other way to locate the mysterious new friend who was nowhere to be seen. So Wilbur cleared his throat.

"Attention, please!" he said in a loud, firm voice. "Will the party who addressed me at bedtime last night kindly make himself or herself known by giving an appropriate sign or signal!"

Wilbur paused and listened. All the other animals lifted their heads and stared at him. Wilbur blushed. But he was determined to get in touch with his unknown friend.

"Attention, please!" he said. "I will repeat the message. Will the party who addressed me at bedtime last night kindly speak up. Please tell me where you are, if you are my friend!"

The sheep looked at each other in disgust.

"Stop your nonsense, Wilbur!" said the oldest sheep. "If you have a new friend here, you are probably disturbing his rest; and the quickest way to spoil a friendship is to wake somebody up in the morning before he is ready. How can you be sure your friend is an early riser?"

"I beg everyone's pardon," whispered Wilbur. "I didn't mean to be objectionable."

He lay down meekly in the manure, facing the door. He did not know it, but his friend was very near. And the old sheep was right — the friend was still asleep.

Soon Lurvy appeared with slops for breakfast. Wilbur rushed out, ate everything in a hurry, and licked the trough. The sheep moved off down the lane, the gander waddled along behind them, pulling grass. And then, just as Wilbur was settling down for his morning nap, he heard again the thin voice that had addressed him the night before.

"Salutations!" said the voice.

Wilbur jumped to his feet. "Salu-*what?*" he cried.

"Salutations!" repeated the voice.

"What are *they*, and where are *you?*" screamed Wilbur. "Please, *please*, tell me where you are. And what are salutations?"

"Salutations are greetings," said the voice. "When I say 'salutations,' it's just my fancy way of saying hello or good morning. Actually, it's a silly expression, and I am surprised that I used it at all. As for my whereabouts, that's easy. Look up here in the corner of the doorway! Here I am. Look, I'm waving!"

At last Wilbur saw the creature that had spoken to him in such a kindly way. Stretched across the upper part of the doorway was a big spider web, and hanging from the top of the web, head down, was a large grey spider. She was about the size of a gumdrop. She had eight legs, and she was waving one of them at Wilbur in friendly greeting. "See me now?" she asked.

"Oh, yes indeed," said Wilbur. "Yes indeed! How are you? Good morning! Salutations! Very pleased to meet you. What is your name, please? May I have your name?"

"My name," said the spider, "is Charlotte."

"Charlotte what?" asked Wilbur, eagerly.

"Charlotte A. Cavatica. But just call me Charlotte."

"I think you're beautiful," said Wilbur.

"Well, I *am* pretty," replied Charlotte. "There's no denying that. Almost all spiders are rather nice-looking. I'm not as flashy as some, but I'll do. I wish I could see you, Wilbur, as clearly as you can see me."

"Why can't you?" asked the pig. "I'm right here."

'Yes, but I'm nearsighted," replied Charlotte. "I've always been dreadfully nearsighted. It's good in some ways, not so good in others. Watch me wrap up this fly."

A fly that had been crawling along Wilbur's trough had flown up and blundered into the lower part of Charlotte's web and was tangled in the sticky threads. The fly was beating its wings furiously, trying to break loose and free itself.

"First," said Charlotte, "I dive at him." She plunged head-first toward the fly. As she dropped, a tiny silken thread unwound from her rear end.

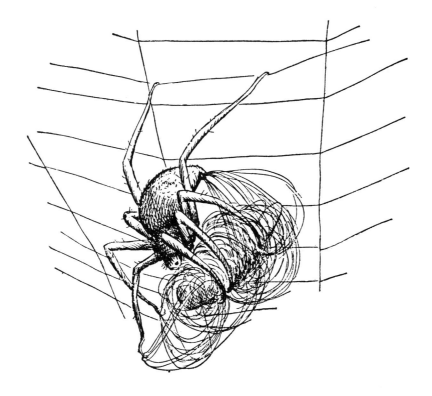

"Next, I wrap him up." She grabbed the fly, threw a few jets of silk around it, and rolled it over and over, wrapping it so that it couldn't move. Wilbur watched in horror. He could hardly believe what he was seeing, and although he detested flies, he was sorry for this one.

"There!" said Charlotte. "Now I knock him out, so he'll be more comfortable." She bit the fly. "He can't feel a thing now," she remarked. "He'll make a perfect breakfast for me."

"You mean you *eat* flies?" gasped Wilbur.

"Certainly. Flies, bugs, grasshoppers, choice beetles, moths, butterflies, tasty cockroaches, gnats, midges, daddy longlegs, centipedes, mosquitoes, crickets — anything that is careless enough to get caught in my web. I have to live, don't I?"

"Why, yes, of course," said Wilbur. "Do they taste good?"

"Delicious. Of course, I don't really eat them. I drink them — drink their blood. I love blood," said Charlotte, and her pleasant, thin voice grew even thinner and more pleasant.

"Don't say that!" groaned Wilbur. "Please don't say things like that!"

"Why not? It's true, and I have to say what is true. I am not entirely happy about my diet of flies and bugs, but it's the way I'm made. A spider has to pick up a living somehow or other, and I happen to be a trapper. I just naturally build a web and trap flies and other insects. My mother was a trapper before me. Her mother was a trapper before her. All our family have been trappers. Way back for thousands and thousands of years, we spiders have been laying for flies and bugs."

"It's a miserable inheritance," said Wilbur gloomily. He was sad because his new friend was so bloodthirsty.

"Yes, it is," agreed Charlotte. "But I can't help it. I don't know how the first spider in the early days of the world happened to think up this fancy idea of spinning a web, but she did, and it was clever of her, too. And since then, all of us spiders have had to work the same trick. It's not a bad pitch, on the whole."

"It's cruel," replied Wilbur, who did not intend to be argued out of his position.

"Well, *you* can't talk," said Charlotte. "*You* have your meals brought to you in a pail. Nobody feeds me. I have to get my own living. I live by my wits. I have to be sharp and clever, lest I go hungry. I have to think things out, catch what I can, take what comes. And it just so happens, my friend, that what comes is flies and insects and bugs. And *further*more," said Charlotte, shaking one of her legs, "do you realize that if I didn't catch bugs and eat them, bugs would increase and multiply and get so numerous that they'd destroy the earth, wipe out everything?"

"Really?" said Wilbur. "I wouldn't want *that* to happen. Perhaps your web is a good thing after all."

The goose had been listening to this conversation and chuckling to herself. "There are a lot of things Wilbur doesn't know about life," she thought. "He's really a very innocent little pig. He doesn't even know what's going to happen to him around Christmastime; he has no idea that Mr. Zuckerman and Lurvy are plotting to kill him." And the goose raised herself a bit and poked her eggs a little further under her so that they would receive the full heat from her warm body and soft feathers.

Charlotte stood quietly over the fly, preparing to eat it. Wilbur lay down and closed his eyes. He was tired from his wakeful night and from the excitement of meeting someone for the first time. A breeze brought him the smell of clover — the sweet-smelling world beyond his fence. "Well," he thought, "I've got a new friend, all right. But what a gamble friendship is! Charlotte is fierce, brutal, scheming, bloodthirsty — everything I don't like. How can I learn to like her, even though she is pretty and, of course, clever?"

Wilbur was merely suffering the doubts and fears that often go with finding a new friend. In good time he was to discover that he was mistaken about Charlotte. Underneath her rather bold and cruel exterior, she had a kind heart, and she was to prove loyal and true to the very end.

Wilbur and Charlotte become very good friends and live happily together in Mr. Zuckerman's barn. The day comes when Charlotte becomes a true "life-saver" to Wilbur. The whole story is told in the book **Charlotte's Web.**

AUTHOR

For over fifty years, E. B. White has been an editor and a writer for a well-known magazine. He is the author of many books, and his three for children are regarded as classics. One is *Charlotte's Web,* part of which you have just read. Another is *Stuart Little,* a story about a boy only two inches tall who looks like a mouse. The last is *The Trumpet of the Swan,* the funny adventures of a swan who plays the trumpet.

Mr. White, who has lived on a farm in Maine for many years, tells how he got the idea for *Charlotte's Web:* "I like animals, and my barn is a very pleasant place to be, at all hours. One day when I was on my way to feed the pig, I began feeling sorry for the pig because, like most pigs, he was doomed to die. This made me sad. So I started thinking of ways to save a pig's life. I had been watching a big grey spider at her work and was impressed by how clever she was at weaving. Gradually I worked the spider into the story, a story of friendship and salvation on a farm."

When Mr. White was asked whether his stories are true, he said, "I like to think that there is some truth in them — truth about the way people and animals feel and think and act."

Listing all the honors and awards Mr. White's books have received would fill several pages. *Charlotte's Web* was a Newbery Honor Book and also won a Lewis Carroll Shelf Award as a book worthy to sit on the shelf with *Alice in Wonderland.* Mr. White himself was honored with the Laura Ingalls Wilder Award — for having made a lasting contribution to children's literature over a period of years.

Painting Portraits

When an author writes a story, he or she wants you, the reader, to really get to know the characters. There are many ways to help you do this. One of them is to paint a portrait of a character — with words!

In *Charlotte's Web,* when the author wrote, "Suddenly Wilbur felt lonely and friendless," he told you that Wilbur was most unhappy. If he hadn't told you any more about Wilbur, that one statement wouldn't really help you to know Wilbur very well.

Look at some of the other things the author wrote about Wilbur: First, "For a while he [Wilbur] stood *gloomily* indoors." *Gloomily* sounds like what it means. It certainly isn't a word that has a cheerful sound, is it? Then, "'One day just like another,' he [Wilbur] *groaned*." *Groaned* is another word that sounds like what it means. It has a long, drawn out, sad sound.

Later in the story, you read that Wilbur tried to be friendly with the goose, who wanted nothing to do with him. The author said that Wilbur answered the goose *bitterly*. To feel *bitter* is to feel angry as well as unhappy.

When the lamb told Wilbur that he didn't play with pigs, the author wrote, "Sadly, Wilbur lay down and listened to the rain." To complete that portrait of Wilbur, the author told how Wilbur felt as Templeton the rat ate Wilbur's breakfast: "This was almost more than Wilbur could stand. . . . *Friendless, dejected*, and *hungry*, he threw himself down in the manure and *sobbed*."

You can see how the author has used several different words to paint Wilbur's portrait. They built up to show clearly that Wilbur was a very unhappy pig. They helped you to know Wilbur.

You know from your reading that Wilbur did not remain an unhappy pig. Think about how he was feeling at the end of the story. You might want to make up a list of words or phrases that paint a picture of this very changed pig.

Books to Enjoy

A Game of Catch by Helen Cresswell

During a visit to England, a girl of today meets two children of the past, who step out of a castle painting to play with her.

Daniel Inouye by Jane Goodsell

Daniel Inouye of Hawaii, who lost an arm during World War II and so gave up his hopes of becoming a surgeon, became a United States senator.

The Mystery of Pony Hollow by Lynn Hall

Sarah discovers a mystery when she hears the sounds of a horse coming from an old shed in the woods.

Biography of a Whooping Crane by Lorle Harris

This is an account of the dangerous first year in the life of a whooping crane, a rare kind of bird that nearly became extinct but is now slowly increasing in number.

The Easy Hockey Book by Jonah Kalb

Here is good advice about everything beginners need to know in order to play better hockey.

Mr. Yowder and the Giant Bull Snake
by Glen Rounds

Mr. Yowder not only likes snakes but also speaks their language in this funny tall tale of the West.

Gateways

MAGAZINE FOUR

Contents

Pepe Goes North

by DORIS TROUTMAN PLENN

On the warm, sunny island of Puerto Rico, there live the tiny green tree frogs known as coquis (koh'kees). Each evening just after the sun goes down, the coquis begin to work. They call their work the Green Work, and to them it is the most important work in the whole world. Their work is singing the Green Song. It is the Green Song, they believe, that holds the stars in place and makes the moon shine.

The best singer and the smallest of the coquis was Pepe (peh'peh) Coqui. He lived in a sugar-cane field and often talked to the People who came there to work. One day Pepe was told that his field was not the whole world, and he heard about a wonderful city called New York, where many of the People from the Island had gone to live.

Pepe could hardly believe what he had heard, and he decided to see the world for himself. Of course, Pepe would have to learn many new words as he traveled, but he did not worry about that as he set out to find an airplane going to New York.

Pepe was happy. He waved back once to Coco, a friend of his, and set off briskly. By and by he came to the airport. He found the little window where a man was selling tickets. Suitcases and boxes were piled up like steps on one side of it. Pepe climbed and hopped up over these until he reached the counter in front of the window. "I want to buy a ticket; I am going to New York," he said. "Now just what *is* a ticket?" he asked the man.

The ticket seller pushed his glasses up on his forehead and looked at Pepe carefully. "A ticket," he said, "is a piece of paper that shows you have bought a seat on the plane."

"What can I do with the seat after I buy it?"

"You can sit on it."

"Oh, you mean a chair!" Pepe said. "How big is this chair?"

"It's a seat, and it's that big." The ticket seller pointed to a chair in the office.

"That chair is too big for me," said Pepe.

"Who cares?" The ticket seller began to shout.

Pepe was astonished. "Why, *I* do! What if I fell off? And then there is the matter of the cost."

"The cost is the same for every seat."

"Even if one sat only on a corner of it?"

"Nobody sits on a corner of it! A seat is for one person! It fits one person!"

"It doesn't fit *me*. Look!"

Pepe hopped down from the counter and sat on the seat inside the office. The ticket man had to put his spectacles back on to see him because he was so small and the chair was so big. The ticket man scratched his head. "How could we strap you in it?"

"Strap me?"

"Everyone must be strapped in for safety when the plane flies off the ground."

"In that case, I most certainly require a seat my size," Pepe told him with dignity.

"Just a minute," the ticket man said. "You wait here, and I will come back." He went out of his office, holding his head in his hands. He went to the office of his chief and threw himself into a chair. "I have a coqui in my office," he told the chief.

"Oh, that's all right," the chief answered. "They don't bite, you know, or sting, or anything ugly like that."

"But this one wants to buy a ticket to New York."

"Well, sell him one."

"He won't buy a regular one. He says the seat is too big."

"Hmmmmm," said the chief. "I'd better look into this. This is the first time a coqui has asked for a ticket. We'd better take good care of him."

The two went back to the ticket seller's office, where Pepe was waiting. He was still sitting in the middle of the big seat. "How do you do, sir?" the chief said.

"Very well, I thank you," Pepe replied. "Except in the matter of a seat for my visit to the world."

"Hmmm," said the chief. "It *is* a little roomy, isn't it? Let's see what we can do about the proper seat for you."

The chief called his chief, and this chief called the first vice president, who called two more vice presidents, who decided it

was a matter for the traffic manager. The traffic manager thought it should be taken care of by the captain and officers of the plane. They talked a while and then the engineer said, "I think I will be able to fix it. Yes, indeed. How big is he?"

"He's not very big," the ticket seller said. "About this big." He measured a space in the air with his hands.

"Oh, no," said his chief. "He's *this* big." And he, too, measured the air with his hands.

"I will have to measure him myself," said the engineer. He took a ruler and went in where

Pepe was still waiting. "Would you be good enough to sit on this ruler, please?"

"Why?"

"To see what your size is."

"I am the smallest of the coquis."

"But I must know your size exactly."

By now Pepe was expecting things to be strange, so although no one had ever before asked him to sit on a ruler, he hopped over and tried to sit on this one. It was not an easy thing to do because the ruler was made of shiny wood and was not only hard but slippery as well. Pepe slid down from it a few times, but finally he got a good grip on it with his feet and sat down. "Well, now, let me see," said the engineer. "It seems that you are almost an inch in size."

"I am?" Pepe was pleased. "That's a very fine size, I suppose?" he said.

"Oh, yes, indeed. I think that now we can fix a seat that will be just right. Now, if you will excuse me," said the engineer, and he ran out of the office.

The ticket seller came back.

"Well, now that everything is settled, please make yourself comfortable. Your seat will be ready for the next plane, and they are having a talk about the price of your ticket."

"Will the price be according to size?" Pepe asked him.

"Well, yes."

"In that case," Pepe told him, "the price will be almost an inch."

"Almost an inch of what?"

"That is my size. I am almost an inch. I sat on the ruler."

"We don't sell tickets like that!"

"Like what?"

"By the inch!" the ticket seller shouted.

"You said it was according to size."

"It is — but not like that! Money doesn't come by inches!"

"Well, you said the ticket would be by size," Pepe said firmly, "and as I told you, *that* is almost an inch. Then I will measure the money to that."

Once again the ticket seller ran out of his office, holding his head in his hands. He went into the room where the two chiefs and the three vice presidents were holding their meeting. They looked at him, surprised.

"There is no reason for any of you to think about this problem any longer," he told them. "He" — and the ticket seller pointed to his office — "has got it all settled."

"Why, that's fine," said the first vice president.

"Just a minute. Who has got it all settled?" asked the second one, who had been dozing.

"The coqui! The one in my office! The ticket is to be according to size — his size — which, he says over and over, is almost an inch!"

"It may be the right answer, and again it may not be," said the first vice president. "Let's go in and talk to him."

When they went into the office, Pepe greeted them politely. "What can I do for you?" he asked.

"Well, it's about this ticket," the first vice president began.

"Didn't the ticket seller explain to you?" Pepe asked in surprise.

"Yes, but how, exactly, would it work?"

"That is what I would like to know," said Pepe. "Here is the ruler. Now you measure a ticket almost an inch in size."

The vice presidents nodded to the ticket seller. His hands trembled as he put the ticket on the ruler. "I never thought I would be doing anything like this," he said. "Here, this is almost an inch."

"Well, cut that off," Pepe explained patiently.

The ticket seller cut off the ticket and gave it to Pepe. Pepe held up a dollar bill. He measured the bill to the ticket. "Almost an inch is not quite a quarter of a dollar," he said in a pleasant voice.

The ticket seller jumped. "It is not enough money!"

"It's according to size," Pepe told them all.

"I think," said the first vice president, "we had better let it go for the moment. Later, we can have many talks and decide about the regular price of coqui tickets."

The others thought the first vice president's words were very wise. They nodded to each other, and the ticket seller gave the ticket to Pepe. Pepe gave him the money. Then each of them bowed to Pepe.

In the plane, the carpenters worked on Pepe's seat. When it was finished, the engineer went to the ticket office to tell Pepe that his plane was ready to go.

But just as he started to tell him, Pepe felt it in his bones that the sun had gone down some time ago and that it was time to begin the Green Work. So he raised his head and lifted his voice in the Green Song. Outside the ticket office Pepe could hear the other coquis singing.

Then, as suddenly as he had begun, Pepe stopped singing. He put his head on one side and listened. He heard the other coquis stop one by one. Everything was safe in the skies for the night, and he felt contented. He hopped up on the counter where the ticket seller was writing out tickets. "Well, I'm ready," he said. "The Green Song is over for tonight. I will go now. Good-by."

Pepe went through a big gate and hopped up the steps into the plane. All the other passengers were already seated, and the motors were humming.

"Here is your seat, sir," the flight attendant said to Pepe. He saw his seat near the window.

Pepe hopped up and sat down.

"Adjust your belt, please."

"Do what to my belt?"

"Tighten it. We are taking off."

"Tighten it, or take it off — which do you mean?"

"Excuse me, sir," said the attendant. She leaned over and quickly bound the safety belt around Pepe.

"It's tight," he told her.

"It's supposed to be tight," she answered.

"I feel a little stuffed," Pepe told the attendant.

"You can unbuckle it as soon as we get aloft."

"As soon as we get where?" Pepe asked.

"As soon as we get up in the air. The plane is still climbing."

"It is? I am climbing with it. I am going on a visit to the world." Then he turned and looked out the window.

He was up among the stars. They were very close to him. They blinked at him as the plane sailed by to show that they were his friends. "Hello, stars!" he called out.

The attendant came back quickly. "You mustn't talk to the stars," she said in a low voice.

"I mustn't?"

"No. It's late, and the passengers are trying to sleep." Then she went away.

"Are you trying to sleep?" Pepe asked his neighbor.

"Not very hard," the neighbor said, smiling.

"I am Pepe. Who are you?"

"I'm Alberto. I'm happy to know you."

"I am a coqui. I sing the Green Song."

"Yes, I know. I am a poet."

The attendant came with a little light and shone it on their faces. "Gentlemen," she said firmly, "your whispering is disturbing the other passengers. I must ask you to allow them to sleep." Then she went away.

Alberto nodded and shrugged his shoulders. Then he and Pepe both sighed.

"Good night, Alberto," said Pepe.

"Good night, Pepe," Alberto answered.

When Pepe and Alberto awoke, it was morning.

Soon the motors stopped roaring and became quieter and quieter until at last they were still. The plane had landed.

"Is New York out there all around us?" Pepe asked.

"No. We must take a bus into New York. Why don't you get up on my shoulder, and I'll give you a lift?" Pepe hopped from his seat up to Alberto's shoulder.

Alberto got up and walked toward the door of the plane. Suddenly he stopped. Then he stepped out of the aisle and sat down again on a seat.

"Pepe," he said, "there is something I must tell you. Right outside the door, Pepe, there is a new word. It's a falling kind of word. It's white."

"What is white?"

"White is the color of the new word. And it is cold, Pepe. Look out the window."

Pepe did. Snow was blowing everywhere. There was nothing else to see but snow. He trembled and moved closer to Alberto's collar.

"Did you bring an overcoat, Pepe?"

"An overcoat?"

"A coat to put on to keep you warm."

"No."

"Well, let me see what I have." Alberto went through all his pockets. He took out a handker-

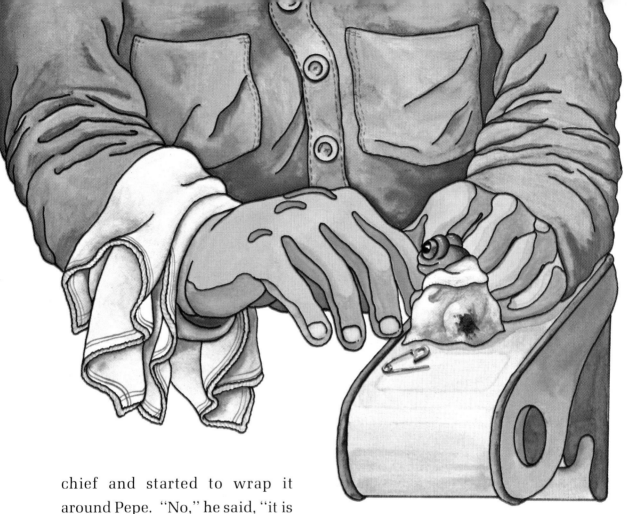

chief and started to wrap it around Pepe. "No," he said, "it is not warm enough. Also, it is too big." Then he went through his pockets again and found a pen-wiper. "Now, this is what I use to keep my pens clean. It has a spot of ink on it, but it is a very little spot. The important thing is that it is made of wool and will be warm."

"Yes," Pepe agreed. Alberto wrapped it around him.

"It looks fine," Alberto said. "Here, just let me fold back a collar for you and pin it all together. Now we can go."

They started to walk to the door. At that moment the attendant came into the plane with two big men. She pointed to Alberto. "There he is. He's the one you were asking about."

"Oh, no," said Alberto softly.

The big men stood on either side of Alberto. "The city's glad to see you. Let's go now," one of them said.

When they left the plane, the two big men walked very fast across the airfield. "Where are we going, Alberto?" cried Pepe. But Alberto only shook his head dismally. They came to a large automobile, and Alberto and Pepe got into the back seat. The two men sat in the front and drove the car away through the thick, falling snow. The car roared through the streets, going straight to the heart of the city.

Pepe shivered a little in his new overcoat.

"Are you cold, Pepe?"

"No. It's another kind of shivering. I don't know what it is."

"I do," Alberto told him. "It's because you feel that I am troubled. And you feel that we are together. Look now, Pepe. We are in New York."

Suddenly more People were around them than Pepe had ever seen. The car stopped, and one of the men opened the door. "Here you are," he said. "Right this way." He took Alberto's arm and led him through all the People. Pepe held on tightly. They walked up many wooden steps and came to a wide place. There were only a few People here. Pepe looked around and saw that the great crowd of People was now below them. They were all looking up at the platform on which he was standing with Alberto. A man who had been talking to the People below came toward them. "Here he is, Your Honor," said the big man, leading Alberto forward. The new man now took Alberto's arm and began walking him to the front toward the People.

"You're just in time," he said. "We are ready for you. Stand right here beside me. I am the mayor. I'm delighted to know you."

"I am happy to know you," Alberto said, bowing gracefully.

The mayor turned and began

talking to the People below. "And now," he said, "on this day, which has been set aside and called 'The Day of the Island,' we meet to celebrate the deeds of those of the Island's People who have come to live among us. On this day it gives me the greatest joy to tell you that the most distinguished Islander of them all, the Islander whose poems and songs are known the world over —"

"Pepe," Alberto whispered, "this is good. But I feel awful."

"Is the mayor talking about you, Alberto?"

Alberto tried to answer, but he choked. So he just nodded yes.

Pepe looked down and saw, beyond the whirling snow, hundreds and hundreds of faces that were like the faces of the People he knew on the Island. The mayor talked on.

"What does he want you to do, Alberto? What does he want you to do?"

"My throat won't work, Pepe," Alberto whispered.

"Does he want you to sing to the People?"

"In a manner of speaking, yes."

"Your throat must work to sing."

"You understand so well, Pepe. I always choke at times like this."

"Perhaps I could sing for you."

"Oh, Pepe! Would you? But it's not your time to sing! It's not evening, and it's cold! Do you think it might be wrong for you to try?"

"I don't think so. Of course, I could do only a little piece of the Green Song, not the real thing, you know."

They heard the mayor's voice: "Here he is! The poet whose songs are like a call from the Island itself! The man whose name the world honors!"

"Go ahead, Pepe," Alberto said with a choke in his voice.

Pepe hopped down on the table and opened his mouth. Snow fell into it. "Coqui, coqui," he sang. But he had swallowed the snow, and his notes went down his throat with it. The only

sound Pepe made was a strange
chirp.

"My word!" said the mayor.
"A cricket!"

Pepe drew himself up proudly.
"I am a coqui!" he announced in
a strong voice that went straight
into the microphone. When he
said it, there was a great roar
from the People below.

"A coqui!" they shouted.

"A coqui in New York!"

"Long live the coquis!"

They waved their handker-
chiefs and laughed and clapped.

"Chirp some more, little cricket," the mayor told Pepe kindly.

Pepe opened his mouth again, and the snow fell in, but this time he swallowed it before his notes leaped out. "Coqui, Coqui," he sang. Then he swallowed more snow and began again, singing part of the Green Song clearly and in tune. The People below were enchanted. They laughed and shouted and cried with joy.

But no coquis answered Pepe as he sang; only his own voice,

made enormous by the microphone, came booming to his ears. It frightened Pepe, and he stopped. "Alberto!" he called.

But Alberto was nowhere to be seen. He had disappeared.

"That will do, friend," said the mayor. "We thank you. And now, my friends — " he began.

But the crowd shouted, "Long live the coquis! We want the coqui!" over and over.

The mayor waved his arms up and down, and finally they were quiet. He looked at his watch. "We have only a few moments left in which to present the key to the city to — " He turned to the man beside him. "What *is* the name of that poet?"

"He's gone," the man answered in a sad voice. "Someone came up and pulled him down into the crowd."

"But what will I do with the key to the city?" the mayor cried. These words went into the microphone, and all the People heard them.

"Alberto!" Pepe yelled into the microphone.

It seemed to him that he heard a small voice, far below, coming from somewhere in the heart of the crowd. It said, "Here I am, Pepe! I am coming!"

But the crowd began roaring, "Give it to the coqui!" so loudly that Pepe could hear nothing else.

"And so," said the mayor, wiping his brow, "in token of our appreciation of your great gift of song, of the honor you have paid us all by coming here today, I wish to present to you — to you, that is, on behalf of the People — the key to the city of New York! I thank you one and all." The mayor put the key down beside Pepe and said to the gloomy man, "Come on, we must hurry. I never thought I'd live to see the day — giving the key to a cricket!"

The crowd clapped and hurrahed. They were still surprised by Pepe's visit and were happy that a coqui had been honored.

Pepe has just begun to see the whole world in New York. As he journeys on through the city, looking for Alberto, he has many exciting adventures. You can read about them in Doris Troutman Plenn's book **The Green Song,** *from which the story you have just read was taken.*

AUTHOR

Doris Troutman Plenn was born in North Carolina. She traveled a great deal in Europe and the United States and then decided to make her home in Puerto Rico.

Soon after moving to Puerto Rico, she became ill. While she was getting well, she looked forward to the evening and the chirping of the tree frogs, the *coquis*. She imagined that they were welcoming her to the island and telling her to get well and come out to see what was going on. Wanting to thank the *coquis* for the pleasure they had given her, she later put them in a book she wrote in honor of the birth of her newest niece. She said, "They were very little, and so was she, and the two seemed to suit each other." She called the book *The Green Song*.

A traveler once...

by CHARLES INGE

A traveler once, to his sorrow,
Desired a ticket to Morro;
But they said, "Go away,
You can't book today
For a journey you're taking tomorrow."

Arthur Mitchell: Dancer

by TOBI TOBIAS

Whenever company came to Arthur Mitchell's house, the young boy ran behind a curtain and called, "Watch me, everyone." Then he'd come out dancing and singing.

"Arthur, you stop showing off," his mother would warn. But she was proud of the lively, happy way he moved. It made her feel good just to look at him.

Everybody else would laugh and clap. "You watch that boy," they'd say. "He'll be a dancer one day."

At the beginning, though, there wasn't much dancing in Arthur's life. In fact, there wasn't much of anything except hard work — and the warm love of a close family. Arthur was born on March 27, 1934, in Harlem, a large black community in New York City. Like many people in the neighborhood, Arthur's parents were poor, even though both of them were working as hard as they could.

Arthur's mother, Mrs. Willie Mae Mitchell, kept house and took care of the large family. (Besides Arthur, there were Charles, Laura, Herbert, Shirley, and Mr. Arthur Mitchell, Sr.) She also took care of other people's children, along with her own, to get a little extra money.

Arthur's father was superintendent of the apartment house where the family lived. Mr. Mitchell could do anything he set his hand to, and he did. His pay was low, but the job gave them their few small rooms rent-free.

Arthur's father expected his boys to help him with the heavy work. They stoked coal for the furnace and kept the sidewalks clean. They hauled huge bundles of trash away and shoveled snow in winter. Arthur hated it. He hated always being dirty and tired. He also hated the fact that his father had hardly any time to have fun with him. Sometimes it seemed the only thing they did together was work.

But soon Arthur figured something out. If a job had to be done, it didn't do him any good to be sad or angry about it. So he turned it into what he liked best — a performance. Instead of walking when he worked, he danced. He got his work done fast, and he made it look like fun.

The best times in the Mitchell home were Sunday mornings. Arthur's father would get up early and cook. Good smells filled the crowded apartment. Everyone sat around the kitchen table, talking and laughing together. Those were the times Arthur could really feel the love in his family.

After Sunday breakfast, Mrs. Mitchell and her children would go off to church. Mr. Mitchell refused to go with them. It was hard for him to believe in the goodness they talked about in church when all he knew was a load of work and bad times. He could see no chance that things would change. For Arthur's mother and many of her friends, though, the church was the center of the neighborhood. There they came together and shared their thoughts, their troubles, their plans and hopes and dreams. Arthur sang in the church choir with people he had known all his life.

He went to school in the same community. Learning was easy for him, and he enjoyed it. He made many friends. People liked him because he was lively and full of new ideas. He was the leader of any group he joined. He also spent some time by himself every day, reading and thinking.

During these quiet hours, Arthur came to know that he wanted something more than what he and the people close to him had now. He wanted better food, better clothes, better things to do, a better way of living. He knew he'd have to work for these things, and he was willing to work. He was used to it. Arthur Mitchell was sure he could do anything that had to be done to get ahead.

He had jobs of his own as soon as he was old enough. He ran errands for people in the neighborhood who gave him a nickel or a dime. He washed windows. He worked as a delivery boy. Later he had a newspaper route.

Still, there was room for good times. One night, at a junior high school party, his teacher saw him dancing. It wasn't just Arthur's feet that were dancing, but his eyes and his smile and every part of his body. It was as good as any performance she had ever seen on the stage.

She told Arthur he ought to go to the High School of Performing Arts, a special school for young people with talent for dancing

and acting. He would have to show a group of judges what he could do. Many of the young people trying out would be able to show off years of dancing and acting lessons, but Arthur had never had the chance for this kind of training.

The next summer he went to a man who was once in show business. From him, Arthur learned an old-time song-and-dance act. He went to the tryouts in a rented evening suit and a top hat. There he did an easy-moving, soft-shoe dance. The judges were delighted.

Arthur was accepted at the High School of Performing Arts,

but his first year there was very hard. The two forms of dance that the school taught — ballet and modern dance — were new to him.

His body was stiff and tight. Though he pulled and pushed and sweated, he couldn't make it do what he wanted it to do.

Finally, the head of the school said he'd never become a dancer. "Try something else," he said.

That made Arthur very, very angry. He ran off to class and tried so hard to stretch his body that he hurt himself terribly. But Arthur's mind was made up. No matter what it took, he was going to be a dancer. From then on, he began to improve.

Whenever people asked Arthur to dance, he would, even if they couldn't pay him. As he heard about dance parts in shows, he tried out for them. But many times when he tried out for a part in a show, he didn't get it — even though he was the best dancer there.

He saw that the good parts went to white dancers. He couldn't understand why, and it hurt him. He promised himself he was going to make some changes.

When he was eighteen, Arthur graduated from the High School of Performing Arts. He won the school's highest dance award and a scholarship to go on with his training in modern dance at Bennington College. But a man named Lincoln Kirstein offered him something even better. Kirstein invited Arthur to study classical dance at the School of American Ballet. There he would have a chance to study with the famous choreographer, George Balanchine.

In 1952 there were not many black people in ballet. It was still a white person's art. In his blunt, honest way, Kirstein told Arthur that a black dancer would have to be twice as good as a white one. White people, he said, wouldn't be interested in watching Arthur Mitchell perform unless he could offer them something special. It wasn't fair, and it didn't make sense, but it was true.

Arthur liked the challenge. He believed that as a black dancer, he had special qualities. He had an ability to make his body express something when he moved. He had a sense of style and freedom. And now he also had the form and elegance of a classical dancer. If he could put those things together, Arthur thought, there would be no one like him. He'd be so different and so good that when he tried out for a part, they'd have to take him. His answer to Kirstein was yes.

For the next three years, Arthur did the same thing day in and day out. He got up early to do two hours of exercises by himself, just to prepare his body for class. He took three ballet classes a day. In addition to those lessons, he studied with the fine ballet teacher Karel Shook, who became his close friend. The only time Arthur wasn't dancing was when he was eating, sleeping, or working for his family.

Ballet training was long, hard, often discouraging, but very exciting. Most of the time, Arthur's muscles were aching with strain. He was always dripping with sweat, always fighting being tired. But for a few minutes each day, as he stretched and leaped and jumped and turned, he felt like the king of his own body. Dancing might be one of the hardest careers in the world, but he couldn't imagine doing anything else.

Still he wondered — bitterly sometimes — if a black dancer could ever succeed in an important American ballet company. He thought perhaps he should go back to modern dance, where black people were welcome. Night after night, he sat in the theater, watching white dancers perform ballets. He knew this was the kind of dancing he wanted to do. "Don't be a fool," his friends said. "They'll never take you." Just when Arthur was ready to give up hoping, he was asked to join the New York City

Ballet. The first time he danced with them, he heard a woman in the audience cry out. "Look, they've got a black man in the company! I didn't know they let blacks dance in this company!"

Arthur went on dancing. He wasn't going to let any person's cruel words stop him. The steps he had to do were fast and tricky, but he made them look easy. "You know," he heard the same voice say, "he's good." Arthur knew he was good. He was glad this woman was finding it out.

That night, and in the ten years that followed, Arthur proved that a black dancer should be judged by his dancing, nothing else.

After years of training, his body was strong. He could make it move almost any way he wanted to. He used every inch of his body when he danced. Smiling and sure of himself, he made everything he did look right, even when he made a mistake.

Slowly he was given parts in many different kinds of ballets. Each one was a chance for Arthur to learn something new.

The greatest honor came when a part in a ballet was made just for him. In 1957, George Balanchine created *Agon* for Arthur Mitchell.

Arthur became a top star in the New York City Ballet. But he was still the only black dancer in the company. He realized it was not enough to make his own success in the world. He wanted to help other black people.

Arthur Mitchell's new work began in the spring of 1968. He had an idea for an all-black classical ballet company. It would have a school for training its own dancers.

Arthur and his old friend Karel Shook started that school in an empty Harlem garage. They had thirty students and four professional dancers. Classes were given morning, afternoon, and night. They were trying to train dancers faster than anyone ever had done before.

"Now!" Arthur would shout at the students as they worked harder and harder. "Stronger! Clearer! You know you're beautiful. Now *show me* that you're beautiful."

Arthur's energy and faith and drive to succeed spread like a fire through his young dancers. They improved more quickly than anyone believed was possible. Arthur began to make short ballets for them. He used a platform built in the garage for a stage.

People in the neighborhood stopped to watch through the open doors. They were fascinated by the beauty of the dancing. Everyone wanted to share in what was happening. The young people asked, "Can we join?" They joined and they danced. Older people sewed costumes, brought food, and offered what little money they had to buy dancing shoes and practice clothes. Black dancers from all

over the country heard about
what Arthur was doing and
wanted to be part of it. By the
end of the summer, there were
four hundred students. A small
group of them were ready to perform for the public. It was the
beginning of a professional company — the Dance Theatre of
Harlem.

All — white, black, young, old,
talented or not — were welcome
in the school. Even if they could
only pay a few cents for the lessons, as long as they wanted to
learn, there was a place for them.

The best of the young dancers
were chosen for the company,
which was growing quickly. Now
Arthur was able to make more
difficult and interesting ballets
for them. He liked to use African
dance. Its powerful, rhythmic
movements were made close to
the ground, to the beat of drums.
He combined African dance with
the smooth steps and airy lifts of
ballet to make a special style for
the Dance Theatre of Harlem.
Other fine choreographers —
white and black — came to work
with these eager, gifted dancers.

All this time, the school and the company were getting larger and doing more work. By 1971 they needed more working space. Finally they found an old warehouse near the street on which Arthur grew up. It was run-down, but large and filled with light. The dancers raised enough money to change the junk-filled warehouse into rooms fitted out for work in dancing, music, sewing, and stagecraft. In 1971 the Dance Theatre of Harlem moved into its new home.

The group's work keeps growing, and Arthur is always at the center of this work that never stops. He knows he must do more than anyone else. He is teacher, choreographer, director, business manager, and often like a father to the children of the school and the young people in the company. He does not perform now. He has given up his own dancing career to help hundreds of other people dance.

"I am a fighter," Arthur Mitchell says, "and I fight with my art."

AUTHOR

Tobi Tobias was born, grew up, and still lives in New York City, where she and her husband have fixed up an old brownstone house. Her many books for children include the biographies *Maria Tallchief, Marian Anderson,* and *Isamu Noguchi: the Life of a Sculptor* as well as *Arthur Mitchell,* part of which you have just read. She says that she writes because she can't imagine doing anything else.

Besides being an author, Ms. Tobias is a well-known dance critic and an editor of *Dance Magazine.* She enjoys ballet, reading, paintings, and children, especially her own — John, who likes to know how things work, and Anne, who likes to dance.

SKILL

A Diagram

Sometimes when you are reading, you find that a special drawing has been included with the selection. This drawing may show how something works or how something is put together. Such a drawing is called a **diagram.**

How are diagrams marked?

Most diagrams have **captions,** or titles, that tell you what they are about. If a diagram has no caption, you should be able to learn what it is about by reading the material that goes with it. Read the caption of the diagram on page 431. The caption, "Outside and inside views of a flashlight," tells you that you are looking at a diagram of the outside and the inside of a flashlight.

The main parts of diagrams have labels. Lines are drawn from the labels to the parts they identify. Look at the labels of the flashlight. The words *Ring, Switch, Case, End seal, Glass lens, Bulb, Reflector, Switch, Batteries,* and *Spring* are the labels on this diagram.

Why are diagrams useful?

As you read a selection that has a diagram with it, you should refer to the diagram frequently. Sometimes the selection refers to things in the diagram. Sometimes the selection tells you something that is not easy to explain in words.

Then you need to refer to the diagram to help you understand better what you are reading. At still other times, a diagram may tell you more than the selection tells. Read the short article below.

A flashlight is a kind of electric light. Its electric power comes from batteries. A glass lens directs the light.

When the switch on a flashlight is closed, the electric current flows through the batteries to light the bulb. The flashlight is said to be "on." When the switch is open, the current cannot flow to the bulb. The flashlight is said to be "off." The dotted, red line on the diagram shows how the current flows to the bulb.

Outside and inside views of a flashlight

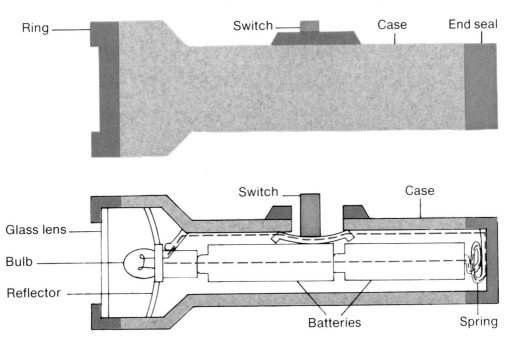

In the article, you read that the electric current flows through the batteries to light the bulb. You did not read anything about where the batteries are placed in the flashlight, did you? You can locate the batteries by looking for the label *Batteries* on the diagram that follows the article and then see where they are placed. The article gives you some information about batteries. The diagram tells you more about batteries.

The article does not tell you anything about what a flashlight looks like either. You can easily see what a flashlight looks like from the diagram. Here you have one example of a diagram giving you more information than is given in the written material.

REVIEW

Look over the headings of this lesson to review the answers to the questions they ask. Recite the answers to yourself. You are now ready to read a diagram on your own.

READING A DIAGRAM

Read the article on croquet that follows, and refer to the diagram on page 433 as you read it. Then answer each of the questions that follow the diagram.

Croquet is a game that is played outdoors, usually on smooth grass. The best court, or playing area, is sixty feet long and thirty feet wide, or eighteen by nine meters. Four players usually play the game. Each player has a mallet and ball that are the same color. The object of the game is to hit the ball through all the wickets from stake to stake and back again. The player who finishes first wins.

The diagram that follows shows how a croquet court is set up and the pieces in a croquet set.

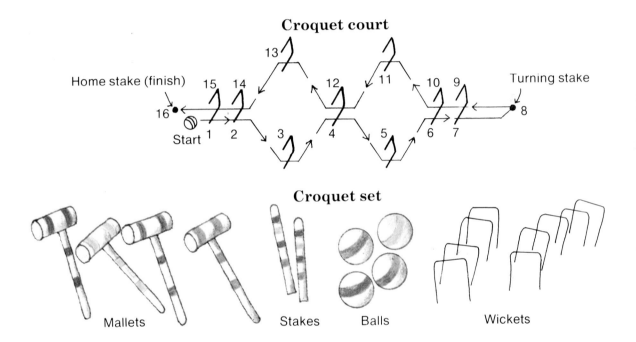

Croquet court

Home stake (finish)

Turning stake

Start

Croquet set

Mallets   Stakes   Balls   Wickets

On a separate piece of paper, write the number of each question and your answer to it.

1. How many wickets are used in the game of croquet?
2. How long and how wide is the best playing area?
3. On what kind of surface is the game usually played?
4. Where are the stakes placed on the court?
5. Do you start playing the game on the left or right end of the court?

The Angalao and the Three Friends

by G. AQUINO, B. CRISTOBAL,
and D. FRESNOSA

One fine summer day three friends — a monkey, a turtle, and a deer — went fishing in the sea. They had come down from the mountains where they lived as neighbors.

From the very start of their fishing, they were lucky. They fished the whole day; when night fell, their boat was full of fish. They barely had room to sit in it.

At supper the deer said, "We have been very lucky. But what shall we do with our catch so that it will not spoil?"

"We will dry the fish in the sun," the turtle said. "We do not have enough salt for all the fish we have caught."

"One of us will have to stay here to guard our catch," the deer said.

"That is true," the monkey said. "I have heard that there is an angalao (ahn-gah-lay'oh) in this part of the island who likes nothing better than to rob and kill those who fish here."

"What does it look like?" the turtle asked.

"It is a big, terrible-looking thing," the deer said.

"Then we should not have come here at all," the turtle said.

"It would have taken us days, even weeks perhaps, to catch the fish we caught today if we had gone somewhere else," the deer said.

435

"Let's draw lots to find out who will guard our catch tomorrow," the monkey said.

"Never mind," the deer said. "I'll do it."

"But the angalao will catch you and eat you," the monkey said. "You have a big family. Let me guard the fish. At least I do not have any wife or children."

"Thank you, friend, but I cannot let you do it. You are too small. I have my antlers to fight with."

And so the next day the deer stayed behind to guard their catch while the monkey and the turtle went back to fish.

The deer did not want to be caught off guard. He paced the length of the beach, looking and listening.

Finally the angalao came. "You dare fish in my place!" it shouted. Its voice was like thunder. "I will eat you and all your fish too."

The angalao ate up all the fish.

"I am very sorry for what happened," the deer said when his two friends returned that afternoon from their fishing.

"That's all right. We are glad you escaped," the turtle said.

"Let me guard our catch tomorrow," the monkey said. "Maybe the angalao will pity me because I am very small."

And so the next day the monkey stayed behind to guard their catch as it dried in the sun. The deer and the turtle went to catch some more fish.

Two hours passed. The monkey was beginning to feel safe. He thought, "Maybe the angalao will not come. Maybe it will not want to eat any more fish."

But in another moment, the monkey heard noises in the brush. It was as if water buffalo were rushing in.

It was the angalao again! After just one look at it, the monkey climbed to the topmost branch of the tree. He was lucky. The angalao had almost caught him by the tail.

"So, you also dared fish here?" it shouted. Then it ate up all the fish.

"I am very sorry," the monkey told his friends when they returned that afternoon, "but the angalao ate up all our fish."

"It's all right," said the turtle. "Anyway, we caught plenty of fish today."

"What's the use?" the deer said. "The angalao will come back tomorrow and eat it all up."

"Let me guard our catch tomorrow," the turtle said.

"The angalao will catch you for sure. You cannot run as fast as I can," the deer said.

"You cannot even climb a tree," the monkey said.

"Just you wait and see," the turtle said.

And so the next day the turtle stayed behind to guard their catch. The monkey and the deer went to fish in the sea.

After his friends left, the turtle went out and gathered plenty of rattan. Then he sat down to work splitting the rattan.

Soon after, he heard the angalao coming. The turtle trembled from his little head to his little tail, but he stayed and went on splitting rattan. The angalao was surprised to see the turtle. No one had ever waited for the angalao before. . . .

"Who are you?" it shouted. "What do you think you are doing here?"

"You can very well see what I am doing," the turtle said.

"But are you not afraid that I am going to eat you and all your fish?"

"Of course I am afraid of you."

"Why, then, don't you run away?"

"Well, if you kill me, that will be the end of me. I will not suffer any further. But if the typhoon catches up with me, it will be terrible," said the turtle.

"What typhoon are you talking about?"

"Haven't you heard? It is called bagyong ugis (bag-yohng you'jihs), and it is heading right for this island."

"So what? I am big and strong. I am not afraid of any-thing," said the angalao.

"Ha-ha-ha!" the turtle said. "That is what you think. When the bagyong ugis comes, it will blow you clear to the other side of the ocean."

"Is that so? Then why don't *you* run away?"

"I can't run fast enough. That's why I have thought of a plan to save myself," said the turtle.

"And what is your plan?"

"It is to tie myself to the biggest lauan (lah-oo-ahn) tree here. That's what these rattan splits are for. Then I will be lucky too. You are very strong. If you will please tie me to the biggest lauan tree, I will feel very safe."

"Wait a minute. Are you sure that even I cannot stand up to this bagyong ugis?" asked the angalao.

"I'm sure of it. Why, it can destroy a house as big as a mountain. It can toss the biggest ship into the air as if it were a ball of paper. Now will you please hurry and tie me up? There is no time to lose," said the turtle.

"Hold on for a moment," the angalao said. "I think I have a better idea. Why don't you let me borrow your rattan splits and let you tie me instead?"

"Then what happens to me?"

"Well, you will just have to take your chances. I am going to get your rattan and order you to tie me up. If you don't, I'll dig you out of your shell and slice you into tiny pieces."

The turtle pretended to hold out longer. He cried and asked for pity. But the angalao would not give in. So the turtle tied up the angalao to the biggest lauan tree that stood in the place. He tied the angalao so tight that it could not even wiggle its fingers and toes.

That night when the monkey and the deer came back, they were so surprised that they could not say a word for a long time. Not one single fish that they were drying had been touched.

"How did you do it?" they asked the turtle.

"It was not much, really," said the turtle — "just a little brain work."

AUTHORS

For many years, folktales such as the one you have just read could be heard only from the lips of story-tellers in the Philippine Islands. Then Guadencio Aquino, Bonifacio Cristobal, and Delfin Fresnosa decided to write some of the folktales down and publish them in a book for children to read.

Dr. Aquino and Mr. Fresnosa, a well-known short story writer, teach at universities in Manila in the Philippines, as did Mr. Cristobal before he died.

Look Who's Using a Tool

by MAUREEN McMAHON

It's a hot, dry day on the African plain. An elephant has an itchy back. It sees a fallen branch, half hidden in the tall grass. It curls its trunk around the branch and picks it up. Then it uses the branch to scratch its back.

Nearby, an elephant calf is into mischief. Its mama pulls up a small tree with her trunk. She spanks her naughty youngster with it.

These elephants are doing something only a few animals do. They are using tools.

Think about how tools make life easier for you and your family. You cut your meat with a knife. You eat with a fork or spoon. Perhaps you use a rake for leaves or a shovel for snow. Your parents pick up a hammer or screwdriver when something around the house needs fixing. Your parents use many cooking tools in the kitchen.

Certain mammals, birds, fish, and even insects also use tools in the same way. They use tools to catch or prepare food, to make life easier or to protect their families. And they use so many different kinds of tools!

In the Galapagos Islands, a tiny bird called the woodpecker finch uses a "poker." First the finch pecks a hole in a dead tree branch with its bill. Then it looks for a sharp thorn or stick. It chooses its tool carefully. The stick must be one to two inches (twenty-five to fifty millimeters) long and quite strong. Then, holding the tool in its bill, the bird pokes it into the hole. When a beetle grub comes out, the bird drops the tool and grabs the insect.

The female hunting wasp uses a "hammer" to build a snug home for her young. This tiny insect digs a tunnel in the sand and lays her eggs in it. Then she takes up an extra-large grain of sand. Holding it between her jaws, she pounds the loose sand to seal the tunnel opening.

A hungry chimpanzee may break off a twig or grass stem and poke it into a termite hole. As soon as the termites crawl onto this tool, the chimp pulls it out and licks off the tiny insects.

Gorillas use tools as weapons. Many have been seen throwing tree limbs and branches at their enemies to protect their homes and families.

A California sea otter likes to eat clams and other shellfish, but to get to its favorite meat, it must crack the clam's hard shell. For this it needs a tool.

When the otter dives to the ocean floor to pick up a clam, it also picks up a flat rock. Back at the surface, it floats on its

back, keeping the rock on its chest. Holding the clam in its front paws, the otter pounds it against the rock until the shell breaks.

When night falls, the sea otter uses another tool. It ties itself up with a "safety strap." Parents and young all wind and turn among long strands of seaweed until they are tied together. This keeps the sleeping family from drifting apart in fast-moving ocean currents.

The Egyptian vulture uses rocks too. It picks up a rock in its bill, stands over an ostrich egg and throws the rock down hard. The shell of the egg is very strong. But if the rock hits the egg often enough, the shell cracks and the vulture has its dinner.

Still another animal uses rocks to crack open its dinner. A sea gull will pick up a clam in its bill, fly high over land, then drop the clam to rocks or a road below.

The archerfish is a most interesting hunter. It uses water as its tool. This fish swims around until it sees an insect resting on a leaf near the surface of the water. Then it takes aim and squirts water out through its mouth! This stream of water knocks the insect off its leaf, and the archerfish gobbles up the insect.

These are some of the ways wild animals use tools. In captivity, they can be trained to do even more. Perhaps a certain dolphin deserves the top prize as a tool user. This dolphin was being tested by scientists. Again and again it failed to solve a very hard problem. Finally the dolphin became so angry that it grabbed a pipe in its jaws and used it to wreck the test equipment!

AUTHOR

Maureen McMahon (Mrs. Maureen Palmedo) is a writer who became interested in animal life while she was working for the National Wildlife Federation. Besides writing articles about nature and animals for several children's magazines, she enjoys writing about young people and their hobbies. Raised in New York City, she taught American history to junior high school students in Madison, Wisconsin. She and her family now live in Washington, D. C.

Opposites and Opposites

Do you remember the coqui in "Pepe Goes North"? Much of Pepe's worry came about because he was so *small* and the world around him was so *large*.

Small and *large* are opposites — words that mean completely different things. But *small* isn't the only word that is an opposite of *large*. *Large* isn't the only word that is an opposite of *small*.

Think about some of the words you know that are opposites of *large*. You could say, "My baby brother is *small*. My baby brother is *little*. My baby brother is *tiny*." Each sentence would have much the same meaning. The words *small, little,* and *tiny* are not exactly the same in meaning, but they are all opposites of *large*.

Can you think of words other than *large* that are opposites of *small*? Two words you might have thought of are *big* and *huge*. *Big* and *huge* may not have exactly the same meaning as *large*, but they are alike enough so that both are opposites of *small*.

Another word that has more than one opposite is *whisper*. Imagine a person whispering. Now imagine that person doing just the opposite. What word would you use to describe the opposite of whispering? *Shouting? Yelling? Screaming?*

Two words that are both opposites of one other word are not always so alike in meaning. *Easy* is an opposite of *hard*. *Soft* is an opposite of *hard* too. Does this mean that *easy* and *soft* mean the same thing? *Easy* means "not hard," but it can also mean "not worried." You might say, "Dad feels *easy* about leaving the kitten with my brother George." *Soft* means "not hard," but it also means "not loud." You might say, "His voice was so *soft* that it was like music floating on the wind." Although *soft* and *easy* are both opposites of *hard*, they are, in at least one way, quite different from each other.

Can you think of a word besides *hard* that is an opposite of *easy*? Can you think of a word besides *hard* that is an opposite of *soft*? That shouldn't be *hard* to do!

The Challenge

by JEAN LITTLE

In 1934, Ernst Solden, who taught English in Germany, decides to take his family out of Nazi Germany and make a new start in Canada, where he finds work as a storekeeper. Anna, the youngest of the five Solden children, has been teased by her brothers and sisters for as long as she can remember. She is awkward. She bumps into things. She is slow-moving. When the Solden children go to have medical examinations for school, the reason for Anna's problems is finally discovered.

Dr. Schumacher's waiting room was shabby and crowded.

"All right," Dr. Schumacher said, "Who's first?" Rudi stepped forward.

Papa went over and, taking Anna on his knee to make room, sat on the bench beside his wife.

"It will be fine," he told her. "Wait. You'll see."

"I don't trust these foreign doctors," Mama muttered.

"Klara, we're the foreigners here!" he reminded her, speaking quietly but not bothering to whisper. "Beside, Franz Schumacher is as German as you are."

Mama shook her head — but there stood Rudi, grinning.

"One healthy one!" Dr. Schumacher said. "You're next — Gretchen, is it?"

This time Mama sat still, although her eyes followed Gretchen every step of the way until the door closed behind her.

"Do you think she looked pale?" she asked Papa.

Ernst Solden laughed, a big laugh that filled the room. "Gret-chen — pale! She has cheeks like roses and you know it."

Gretchen came back, her cheeks as rosy as ever. Frieda went and returned. Fritz was a couple of minutes longer.

"Maybe something is wrong with Fritz . . ." Mama began, her eyes growing wide.

"He let me listen to my own heart," Fritz bragged, bouncing out into the waiting room.

"A fine family, you Soldens," Dr. Schumacher boomed, stretching out a broad hand to Anna. She slid off her father's knee at once and put her hand in the doctor's outstretched hand.

As they disappeared, Mama gave a deep sigh of relief.

"Didn't I tell you?" her husband teased.

She had to nod. Only Anna was left — and Anna had not been seriously ill in her entire life.

"Let me hear you read the letters on this card," Dr. Schumacher was saying to the youngest of the Soldens.

Anna froze. Reading! She couldn't. . . .

She looked where he was pointing. Why, there was only one letter there. That was easy! She did know the names of the letters now.

"E" she told him.

"And the next line down?" Dr. Schumacher asked.

Anna wrinkled up her forehead. Yes, there *were* other letters. She could see them now, when she squinted. They looked like little gray bugs, wiggling.

"They're too small to read," she said.

Ten minutes later, when he had made very sure, the doctor came out to the waiting room with the little girl.

"Did you know that this child can't see?" he asked sternly.

Ernst and Klara Solden's blank faces told him the answer. Feeling sorry then, he tried to soften his voice, although he was still angry on Anna's behalf.

"At least she can't see much," he corrected himself.

"Of course she can see!" Klara Solden gasped, turning away from the child to this "foreign" doctor whom she had not trusted from the beginning. "What do you mean? Don't be ridiculous!"

The doctor looked from one of Anna's parents to the other.

"She sees very poorly, very poorly indeed. She should be wearing glasses," he said. "She should have had them two or three years ago. But before we go any further, I want to have her examined by an eye doctor."

It was all like a nightmare to Anna. Once more, she had to read letters off a faraway card. Once again, she could see only the big E. The new doctor, Dr. Milton, looked into her eyes with a small bright light. He made her look through several lenses. All at once, other letters appeared.

"F . . . P," Anna read in a low voice. "T . . . O, I think . . . Z."

"Now these," Dr. Milton said, pointing to the next row of letters. But they were too small.

Dr. Milton clucked his tongue. Then he took Anna back to Dr. Schumacher's office and the two doctors talked. The Soldens waited anxiously. Anna was trying, inside, to pretend that she was not there. It was not helping.

Dr. Schumacher took her to yet another room where she sat on a chair and was fitted for frames.

"What a nice little girl," the technician said.

Anna glowered.

"Even with the glasses, she will not have normal vision," Franz Schumacher explained to Anna's parents when they were back in his office. "She'll have to go to a special class — a sight-saving class. Lessons are made easier there for children with poor eyesight."

"Not go to school with the others?" Mama questioned, hoping she was not understanding.

Dr. Schumacher spoke gently in German. "It is a nice place. She'll like it there. You will, Anna. You'll like it very much," he said.

From the beginning, he had been drawn to this little girl. Now, guessing at how hard life must have been for her since she started school, he wanted more than ever to be her friend.

All of this was in his voice as he spoke straight to her. He tried to reassure her about the special class. And he also said, without actually putting it into words, that he, Franz Schumacher, liked her, Anna Solden.

Anna did not look up or answer. He had become part of the bad dream in which she was caught. She hardly heard what he said. What she did hear, she did not believe. How could she like school?

Three days before school was to begin, Anna's new glasses arrived. Set on her nub of a nose, they looked like two round moons. She wanted to snatch them off and throw them into a far corner. Instead, she looked through them suspiciously.

For one startled moment, a new expression came over her small plain face, a look of deep surprise and wonder. She was seeing a world she had never guessed was there.

"Oh, Anna, you look just like an owl," Frieda said, laughing, but not meaning any harm.

The wonder left Anna's face instantly. She turned away from her family and stamped off up the stairs to her room where none of them could follow without permission. Papa, though, came up alone a minute or two later.

"Do you like them, Anna?" he asked quietly.

She almost told him then. She nearly said, "I never knew you had wrinkles around your eyes, Papa. I knew your eyes were blue but I didn't know they were so bright."

But she remembered Frieda's laughing words. How she hated being laughed at!

"Do I *have* to keep wearing them, Papa?" she asked suddenly.

Papa looked sorry for her but he nodded.

"You must wear them all the time and no nonsense," he said firmly.

Anna reddened slightly. It was not right, fooling Papa like this. But she was not ready to share what had happened to her. Even her father might not understand. She could hardly take it in herself.

"All right, Papa," she said, letting the words drag.

Wanting to comfort her, her father put his hand gently on top of her bent head. She squirmed. He let her go and started to leave. Then he turned back, stooped suddenly, and kissed her.

"Soon you'll get used to them, *Liebling,* (lee'bling)," he consoled her. "Wait and see."

When he had gone, she lifted her left hand and held it up in front of her. She moved her fingers and counted them. Even though the light was poor, she could see all five. She examined her fingernails. They shone faintly and they had little half-moons at the bottom. Then she leaned forward and stared at her red wool blanket. It was all hairy. She could see the hairs, hundreds of them.

Everything, everywhere she turned, looked new, looked different, looked miraculous. Anna smiled.

When Dr. Schumacher arrived to take Mama and her to the new school, Anna was ready with a bright bow on each of her thin braids.

"You look lovely, Anna." The doctor smiled.

Anna looked away. She knew better.

"It is so kind of you to take Anna to this school," Mama said, getting herself and Anna into their coats.

"Nonsense," Dr. Schumacher said. "I know Miss Williams. I can help with the English too. It won't take long."

The three of them found nothing to say to each other as they rode along. When they got out in front of the school, Anna marched along between her mother and the doctor. She tried to look as though this were something she did every day, as though her heart were not thudding so hard against her ribs it almost hurt. Franz Schumacher reached down his big warm hand and gathered up her cold little one. Anna tried to jerk away but he held on. She gulped and went on walking — one foot . . . the other foot.

Miss Williams was the first surprise in what was to be a day of surprises.

"It's lovely to have you with us, Anna," she said when Dr. Schumacher drew Anna forward and introduced her and Mama.

She doesn't know me yet, Anna reminded herself, not smiling in return. She hasn't heard me read.

"I've brought you a real challenge this time, Eileen," Dr. Schumacher said in an undertone.

Challenge? Dr. Schumacher had called her a challenge.

Anna did not know that word. Did it mean "stupid one"? But no, it couldn't. Franz Schumacher still had her hand in his and the kindness of his grasp had not changed as he said it. Anna kept the new word in her mind. When she got home, she would ask Papa.

Fifteen minutes later she sat at her new desk and watched her mother and Dr. Schumacher leave the classroom.

"Don't leave me!" Anna almost cried out after them, her courage deserting her.

Instead, she put one hand up to feel the crispness of her hair ribbon. One of the bows was gone. Anna pulled off the other one and shoved it out of sight into the desk. She must not cry. She must *not*!

Then the desk itself caught her attention and distracted her. She had never seen one like it before. It had hinges on the sides and you could tip it up so that your book was close to you. She looked around wonderingly. The desk was not the only thing that was different. The pencil in the trough was bigger around than her thumb. The blackboards weren't black at all — they were green. The chalk was fat too, and yellow instead of white.

Even the children were different. Most of them were older than Anna.

"We have Grades One to Seven in this room," Miss Williams had explained to Mama.

The desks were not set in straight rows nailed to the floor. They were pushed into separate groups. Miss Williams put Anna at one right beside her own desk near the front.

"You can sit next to Benjamin," she said.

Anna stared at the small boy with black tufty hair and an impish face. He was a good head shorter than she was, though his glasses were as big as hers. Behind them, his eyes sparkled.

Quickly, Miss Williams told Anna the names of all the other children in the class: Jane, Mavis, Kenneth, Bernard, Isobel, Jimmy, Veronica, Josie, Charles. The names flew around Anna's ears like birds, each escaping just as she thought she had it safely captured.

"You won't remember most of them now," the teacher said, seeing panic in the child's eyes. "You'll have to get to know us bit by bit. . . . Well, it's time we got some work done in this room."

Anna froze. What now? Would she have to read? She sat as still as a trapped animal while Miss Williams went to a corner cupboard. In a moment, she was back.

"Here are some crayons, Anna," she said. "I'd like you to draw a picture — anything you like. I'll get the others started and then I'll be free to find out where you are in your schoolwork."

Anna did not take the crayons. She did not know anything she could draw. She was nowhere in her schoolwork.

And what did *challenge* mean?

"Draw your family, Anna," Miss Williams said.

She spoke with great gentleness but firmly too, as though she knew, better than Anna did, what the girl could do. She picked up one of Anna's square, stubby hands and closed Anna's fingers around the crayon box.

"Draw your father and your mother, your brothers and your sisters — and yourself, too, Anna. I want to see all of you."

The feel of the box, solid and real, brought back Anna's courage. The crayons were big and bright. They looked inviting. The teacher put paper on the desk, rough, cream-colored paper. It was lovely paper for drawing — six pieces, at least!

"Take your time," Miss Williams said, moving away. "Use as much paper as you need."

Anna took a deep breath. Then slowly she picked out a crayon. She knew how to start, anyway. She would begin with Papa.

Miss Williams came and bent above her. "Who are they, Anna?" she asked.

Slowly Anna began to explain in German.

Miss Williams did not stop her and tell her to talk English instead. But when Anna pointed and said *"Mein Papa,"* the teacher said

"Your father. My, he is tall, isn't he?"

"Yes," Anna replied in English, only half aware she was switching. "They are gone on . . . to the sea."

"I thought they had," Miss Williams said.

It was not such a terrible day.

Not once did the teacher ask Anna to read from a book. She printed the story of Anna's picture on another piece of paper. The letters were large and black. Anna read each line as it appeared. She did not panic. She did not think of this as reading.

Here is Anna's father.
He is big. He is happy.
Anna's mother is here too.
She is small. She is happy too.
They are at the sea.
Gretchen is Anna's big sister.
Rudi is Anna's big brother.
Gretchen and Rudi
are happy at the sea.
Frieda is Anna's other sister.
Fritz is Anna's brother too.
Fritz and Frieda are twins.
The twins are happy here too.
Anna is in our class.
Our class is happy
Anna is here.

"You like drawing, don't you, Anna," Miss Williams said, picking up the picture and looking at it again, smiling at the bright colors. Anna did not answer. She was too startled, even if she had known what to say. She had always hated drawing in school. Her other teacher, Frau Schmidt, would put a picture of a tulip up on the board for them to draw. Once, as a special treat, she had brought real flowers in a vase. The others had been pleased with their pictures that day, but in Anna's, the flowers had looked like cabbages on sticks.

"Really, Anna!" Frau Schmidt had said.

Making this portrait of her family, Anna had forgotten that. This had not seemed the same thing at all.

She was still sitting with her mouth ajar when Miss Williams went on to say something else, something so much more surprising that Anna had to pinch herself to make sure she was not inventing the whole thing.

"You like reading, too. I can see that. And your English — I can hardly believe you've been in Canada such a short time. You are amazing, Anna."

Miss Williams was not nearly as amazed as Anna Elisabeth Solden. She, Anna, like reading!

She wanted to laugh but she did not. She still did not even smile openly.

All the same, Anna felt something happening deep inside herself, something warm and alive. She was happy.

She was also mixed up. She did not know how to behave. She had never felt this way before, not in school anyway. She sat perfectly still, her plain face as stern as usual. Only her eyes, blinking behind the big new glasses, showed her mixed feelings.

The teacher did not wait for an answer to what she had said. She took the picture and the story and tacked them up on the bulletin board where the whole class could see them. Then she got Benjamin to read the words aloud.

462

"Twins!" Ben said, his eyes sparkling with interest. "Wow!"

Anna sat and listened to other classes working. She learned about explorers with the boys and girls in Grade Five. Miss Williams did not seem to mind other children listening and learning.

After lunch the teacher wound up the gramophone and put on a record. Music, cool quiet music, flowed through the room.

"What did this make you think of?" Miss Williams asked when the record finished.

"Rain," Isobel said. She was in Grade Four and had fat, bouncy ringlets.

"I think water maybe," Ben tried.

"Rain's water," Isobel grinned at him.

"No, I mean water like a stream," Ben insisted, staying serious in spite of her.

"What do you think, Anna?" Miss Williams asked.

Anna blushed. She had not been going to say.

"I know that music from my home," she explained. "I know the name."

"Tell us." Miss Williams smiled.

"It is 'The Shine of the Moon,'" Anna said. "But ..."

She stopped short. Miss Williams waited. The others waited too. All the faces turned toward Anna were friendly faces. She took a deep breath and finished. "I think it is like rain too," she said.

"The record is 'The Moonlight Sonata' by Beethoven," Miss Williams said. "But Beethoven did not name it that. He could have been thinking of rain."

"Or a stream," Ben said stubbornly.

"Or a stream — or something else entirely," the teacher said. "Each of you, listening, will hear it differently. That's fine. That's what your imaginations are for — to use. Beethoven was a great composer. He was German — like Anna."

Anna held her head up at that. She and Beethoven!

Arithmetic was not hard. Numbers, in this classroom, were big and clear and they stayed still when you looked at them.

"Good work, Anna," Miss Williams said, looking over her shoulder.

When school was over, she walked past her own house and went on to the store where Papa was hard at work. She waited off to one side. When the customers were gone, she stepped up and leaned on the counter.

"How did it go in school, my little one?" he asked.

Anna knew what he hoped, but she didn't answer his question.

"Papa, what is a challenge?"

She had said the word over and over to herself all day long so she would be able to ask.

Papa scratched his head.

"A challenge," he repeated. "Well, it is ... something to be won, maybe. Something special that makes you try hard to win it."

Anna thought that over.

"Thank you, Papa," she said, turning away.

"But school," her father called after her. "Tell me about it."

"It was fine," Anna said over her shoulder. Then she whirled around and gave him one of her rare half-smiles.

"It was a challenge," she said.

"Something special," she repeated, as she started for home. "Dr. Schumacher thinks I am something special ... like Papa said ... but why something to be won?"

She gave a little hop all at once. She would not mind going back tomorrow.

"It is a challenge," she said over again, aloud, in English, to the empty street.

She liked that word.

AUTHOR

The popular Canadian author Jean Little was born on the island of Formosa, later known as Taiwan, where her parents were missionary doctors. She grew up in Guelph, Ontario. Blind at birth, she gained a bit of sight in one eye. From an early age, she loved books. She says, "I read, I daydreamed, and so I prepared myself for becoming a writer." Later, she was able to graduate from the University of Toronto even though she couldn't see the chalkboard. She points out that she didn't think of herself as blind but as a person like everyone else.

From Anna, part of which you have just read, is one of the many books Jean Little has written. Another, about a child who is disabled, is *Mine for Keeps,* her award-winning first book.

Flashlight

by JUDITH THURMAN

My flashlight tugs me
through the dark
like a hound
with a yellow eye,

sniffs
at the edges
of steep places,

paws
at moles'
and rabbits'
holes,

points its nose
where sharp things
lie asleep —

and then it bounds
ahead of me
on home ground.

466

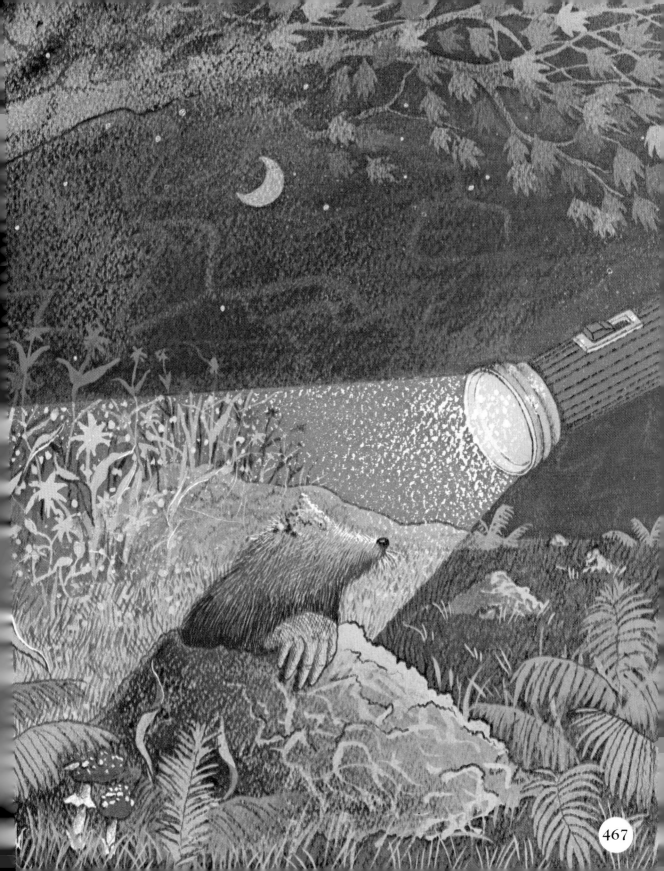

The Violin

by ROBERT THOMAS ALLEN

This story happened not very long ago on an island. It wasn't an island far out in the sea. It was an island in the harbor of a big city. Yet it was a real island, quiet and peaceful. In the winter, cottontail rabbits hopped across the frozen lagoons.

Chris and Danny lived on the island all winter. They were great friends. They played together in the snow and had a secret hiding place. It was the hollow of a big willow tree.

Chris, the older boy, was often quiet and thoughtful. He had been saving his money for a long time. He knew that now there should be enough to buy the wonderful thing that he had been longing to have.

On this special morning Chris reached into the tree and felt around.

"Is it there?" Danny asked.

Chris took a jar full of coins from the tree. He held it up and shook it and dropped a few more coins into the jar. There was enough! Anyway the boys thought there was enough.

The two boys began to shout. They danced in the snow and ran from the woods. They ran through an old garden of an empty cottage, down the path to the docks. They ran over the gangplank and onto the ferryboat that was ready to take people across the bay to the city.

Chris stood at the rail as the boat moved across the water. He looked serious now that his dream was soon to come true. Danny asked, "How do you know you can play it when you get it, Chris?"

"I know I can," Chris said.

The people on the busy streets hurried along looking straight ahead. For them there was nothing special in the store windows. But the window the boys finally reached and stared into was a magic world, like a stage. The winter sun shone on a patch of dull blue cloth. An orange cat was asleep in the corner. And there in the middle was the magic thing that Chris had wanted for such a long time, shiny as a new chestnut — a violin. It looked so beautiful that Chris just stood for a moment outside the door to the store. He was hardly able to believe that soon the violin would be his own.

When he opened the door, a man looked up from behind the counter. Chris handed him the jar of coins to pay for the violin — the one in the window.

"Oho! So you want to buy an expensive violin with a jar full of pennies and dimes?" The man looked at the jar of coins as if he didn't think very much of it. "By the time you save enough nickels for *that* violin, you'll have a long gray beard."

Chris just stared. But Danny thought he could help. He told the man that he could have other things besides the money. He began taking his prized possessions from his pockets — pictures of birds, a shiny alley, a hawk's foot. The man looked at them coldly.

"Chicken's feet I don't need," he said.

"It's a hawk's foot."

"I don't need hawks' feet either. With hawks' feet I can't pay the rent."

Sometimes, though, people aren't as mean as they first seem. When the boys started to leave, the man called to them, "Just a minute now. There was one — let me think." He moved some things around on a bottom shelf and held up another violin so Chris could see it. "Here. This one has everything the other one has — strings, a bow, a place to put your chin. It's a better one for a boy. I can let you have it for the money in the jar."

On the way home on the ferry, holding the violin, Chris felt somehow that the world had changed. He couldn't believe that the violin the man had sold him was as good as the one he had seen at first. Nothing would cheer him up, not even looking at Danny.

Chris had dreamed of owning and playing a violin ever since the day he went with his mother to a concert. He never forgot how he felt when a boy no older than he was came out and played a violin. Beautiful sounds seemed to fall from the air inside the concert hall.

When they were back home, Chris took the violin from the case and put it under his chin. He could almost hear the hush of a huge audience waiting for him to play. He drew the bow across the strings. But the sound that came from the violin was nothing like the music in Chris's head. It was like a squeaking door, or perhaps an angry pup.

Danny went outside and put his hands over his ears. Soon afterward, Chris came out of the cottage and sat down beside Danny on the step.

"This violin is no good," he said. He put the violin in its case and walked away from the cottage. Danny followed him.

When he came to a wire wastebasket, he dropped the violin in among the old newspapers. He felt better, but not much. It was snowing, and he began to make a snowball to throw at Danny. Then he noticed that Danny was watching something in the distance.

A man was coming along the path. He was a strange-looking man, wearing a black coat and a kind of high black hat Chris had never seen before. As he moved through the snow, his coat flapped, and he looked like a big crow that had decided to walk instead of fly. Chris and Danny watched him sit down on the park bench. Then the man looked into the basket and lifted out the violin.

He opened the case and took out the violin. You could tell he was used to violins. He tightened the bow and tuned the strings and put the violin under his chin, like something he was trying to warm up.

"But the man has not heard *that* violin!" Chris whispered to Danny. "I wonder what he'll do when he hears the awful sound it makes?"

But when the man began to play, with the snow falling around him, Chris knew that he had never heard such beautiful music. The boys came right up behind the bench where the man was playing, but he was so lost in his music that he didn't notice them. Chris knew now that it wasn't the fault of the violin when it made terrible sounds. It just needed someone who knew how to play it. He wanted his violin back.

"I didn't really throw it away," Chris whispered to Danny. "I just put it there for a while." (How easy it is to believe anything you want to believe, even when it isn't true!)

The man put the violin back in its case and started to walk away with it. Chris and Danny followed him. What would the man do, Chris wondered, when he asked for the violin back? Would the man turn around and yell or maybe even take a swing at them with the violin case?

Danny never seemed to worry about things like that, and when they caught up with the man, Danny just tugged his sleeve and said, "That's our violin."

Chris began to tell the man why the violin was in the wastebasket. The man looked at him over his glasses. Then he smiled and seemed so glad of their company that Chris knew he would give him not only the violin but almost anything. The man told them where his cottage was.

"I'll take the violin home with me," he said. "I'll polish it and tune it. If you tell your parents where you're going, you can come over and get it."

The old man's cottage was the most wonderful place. It had the same look that Chris liked about Danny — nice and friendly but falling apart. Magazines and books had fallen off shelves. There were piles of sheet music where there should have been cups and plates. There were cups and plates on top of sheet music. There was a pet rabbit on the table and a pigeon in a cage. Things fell from strange places if you touched anything. "Never mind picking them up," the man would say.

A pink umbrella fell off a bookcase. "Don't bother picking it up," the man said. "I found that. I use it as a sunshade when I go out in my rowboat."

You could have lost Danny among the things that hadn't been put away in their proper place. Chris asked the man if he'd play the violin for him again. This time the man played a different tune — light and fast and kind of funny.

He played to the pigeon. He played to the rabbit. He played to Chris and Danny. It looked so easy that Chris wanted to try again. But when he did, he made such a squawking sound that Danny put his hands over his ears and went outside.

Chris knew now that he *did* want to learn to play the violin after all.

The man showed him how the violin was made. And he told him something of its special place among instruments. A violinist can make almost as many sounds with a violin as a singer can with the human voice, playing notes that are very low and very high, making music sad or soft, light, gentle, bright, or strong.

Violins, the man said, were first made over four hundred years ago in the small town of Cremona in northern Italy. One maker was Antonius Stradivarius, who made the finest violins of his time.

The man showed Chris how to hold the violin and how to draw the bow across the strings. When he did it, he made a wonderful, sweet sound. When Chris tried, the sound he made was like wood cracking. Before he left, the man told him to come back and he would teach him how to play.

During the following months, when he gave Chris lessons, the man sometimes looked off into space, as if his thoughts were thousands of miles away. He'd say "I remember one time . . ." and tell of something that happened long ago. Gradually Chris formed pictures in his mind. He saw a mountain village and peaks that turned gold in the sun. He saw big cities and after-theater parties, and a bright far-off world where people loved music and talked music and lived for music. Then something had happened that sent the man wandering into strange lands with his violin.

The snow began to thaw, and by the time the lake had turned pale blue and the willows looked like green fountains, the man seemed pleased with his pupil. On warm days he and Chris played duets sitting on the rocks by the shore of the lake.

The man talked more and more often now of the mountains he had known as a boy. And sometimes, he was far away in his thoughts. Once when Chris told him he'd never want to be without his violin — the one he once threw away — the man looked at him a long time and then said, "We sometimes become too attached to things." He looked down at his own violin. "This is like an old friend to me, but if I had to part with it, I wouldn't stop loving music."

Chris thought it a strange thing to say. Then he forgot about it because he and Danny and the man were having so much fun together. They took rides on the ferryboat and went on picnics. Sometimes the man lay in the grass just looking up at the blue sky, listening to Chris play his violin.

Chris knew his violin like a friendly face. He knew there was a chip out of one of the pegs which tighten the strings. And a little dark swirl in the grain of the wood seemed to watch him like a friendly eye as he played.

Yet in a strange way, when he played down by the wooden bridge in the soft sunlight of late summer, he felt a bit sad. The lonely rustle of the cottonwood trees, or the way a leaf fell beside him, like a tear, seemed to tell him that a time comes when friends must part.

One day Chris and Danny were on the bridge. Chris had his violin. Danny was fishing — his kind of fishing. He was catching minnows in a net tied to the end of a line so that he could put them in a jar of water and look at them. Just as Chris started to play his favorite piece, Danny called out, "It's stuck!" He was tugging on his fishing line.

"Wait a minute," Chris said. "I'll help you." He put his violin down and went to help. But Danny didn't want help even from Chris. "Leave it alone!"

Chris caught hold of the pole. Danny butted him with his head.

"Stop it. Stop it!" Chris said. Grabbing Danny, he fell backward, laughing.

There was an awful cracking sound. Chris took the violin from the case. It was a terrible sight. It was crushed and splintered, its strings limp like the ties of an open package. For Chris it was as if a cloud had passed over the sun. Danny was talking anxiously beside him. "I'll fix it, Chris," he was saying. "I'll nail it together. I'll glue it together. I'll buy you a new one."

"I'll never play a violin again," Chris said. He wouldn't say any more.

Chris leaned against the railing of the bridge. His stomach felt sore with sadness. He didn't even look up when he heard Danny racing down the steps. He didn't know, or care, that Danny was racing off to find the man and tell him about the accident. Danny was sure the man would know what to do to help.

When Danny got to the man's cottage, he found a note on the door. He could read a few words. He read "Dear Boys," and he knew the man had written it for them and that he wasn't there. Where had he gone?

Danny knew the man often went for a walk along the shore of the lake. He pulled the note off the door and ran towards the lake as fast as he could.

When Danny found the man, he said all in one breath, "I broke the violin. I mean Chris broke it, but I pushed him. He's sitting on the bridge. He said he'll never play again."

At first the man looked at him sadly as if he didn't hear. He spoke as if to himself, "Chris must not say that." Then he said, "Wait here for a minute, Danny. I'd like to talk to Chris alone." He began to walk quickly toward the bridge.

Danny felt sure the man would know what to do. Sometimes, though, grown-ups aren't sure what to do. Walking toward the bridge, the man knew he had to make a difficult decision. He had owned his violin for a long, long time. But it wasn't because it was a very special violin that the decision was so hard to make. It was because he wasn't sure that his decision would help Chris. A gift for music is only a beginning. It takes years of hard work to become a musician. Still, he could think of nothing else to do. He went up the steps.

Chris looked up and saw the man standing in front of him in his strange coat and hat, his face looking sad and worried. "Danny told me what happened," he said. He held his own violin out to Chris. "This is yours now. I can get another — some day. But only you know if you will go on and practice and work hard to become a fine musician.

Chris just shook his head. His throat felt tight. He couldn't speak. He never wanted to play a violin again —any violin. The feeling of knowing that he could play had come to an end.

The man went down the steps and stood on the path for a long time, looking very thoughtful. Then he put his violin on the bottom step, picked up the pigeon cage and his other things, and walked slowly away.

Chris just sat there. The man had been gone a few minutes when Danny raced up the bridge calling, "Chris! Chris!" He handed the letter to Chris. "I found this nailed to his door. He's gone. The pigeon is gone. The rabbit is gone. We may never see him again."

Chris ran down off the bridge. Danny started after him, then turned and picked up the violin the man had left for Chris. He caught up with Chris as he ran through the woods.

"Where will he be?" Danny asked.

"I don't know."

They reached the old willow tree where they once hid their jar of coins, long ago last winter.

Chris climbed up into the branches and looked around.

"I see him! Over there. In his boat. He's rowing out from shore."

They raced down a path through the woods and gardens
and along a boardwalk. They reached the rocks on the shore
where Chris and the man had played their duets. The man
was out on the lake in his boat, rowing with the pink umbrella shading the pigeon and rabbit. He was too far out to
hear the boys' shouts, or perhaps too far away in his
thoughts.

Then Chris felt Danny touch him with the violin. Chris knew what Danny meant. Perhaps music would be the only thing the man could hear. He thought of his own old violin lying broken on the bridge. He had never played another violin. He was afraid he would make the same squawking sounds on this violin that he made when he first tried to play his own. Yet the violin felt just right under his chin. He began to play a tune the man had taught him.

As Chris played, he felt as though the man were beside him once again. The music went out over the blue water, as light as a seagull gliding on a summer breeze.

"He hears you!" shouted Danny. Danny was crying. "But we won't ever see him again," he said.

Chris pretended he didn't hear Danny. Later, he'd tell him that nobody ever says good-by who leaves the world beautiful music.

AUTHOR

Robert Thomas Allen is one of Canada's best-known authors. He wrote the story for the prize-winning Canadian film *The Violin* on which the text for the book of the same name was based. Maurice Solway, a well-known concert violinist, played the part of the violinist in the film.

In 1976 the book *The Violin* was the winner of the Ruth Schwartz Memorial Award, which is given each year to an outstanding children's book published in Canada.

MUSIC

To me music is
Like playing, jumping, hopping
And like running soft.

ARACELI JIMENEZ

Music makes me
Feel as if I am in the
Moon flying very fast.

ARACELI VEGA

483

SKILL

Graphs

Written material that contains many numbers is sometimes hard to understand. To help you understand written information that includes facts about numbers, a writer may use a special drawing called a **graph.** The information is given in a graph because the writer thought it was important and would give you a better understanding of what you are reading.

Graphs are often included in social studies and science books and in newspapers and magazines. Read the following paragraph that contains numbers and might appear in a school newspaper:

> The boys and girls in the fourth-grade classes at Jefferson School belong to a book club. They buy books once a month. Their last order was so large that the book club allowed each student to choose one free book. There are fifty students in the fourth-grade classes. The students chose nineteen mysteries, eighteen sports stories, nine animal stories, and four cartoon books.

Even though you may understand these facts about numbers, you will be able to compare them better when you see the information in a graph. The school newspaper might include a pictograph or a bar graph to help you picture the information in the paragraph.

What is a pictograph?

The information about the free books ordered can be shown by pictures. A graph that uses pictures to stand for numerical information is called a **pictograph.** A picture can be used to stand for each free book ordered. The information about the books can be seen quickly, and the pictures make the graph more interesting and clear to you.

Free Books Ordered by Jefferson School Fourth-Grade Classes

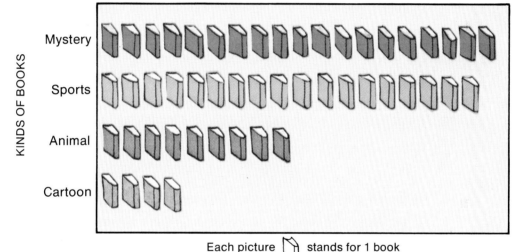

Each picture stands for 1 book

To read and understand the graph, first read the title above it. The title tells you what information the graph shows. Then read the key below the graph. A pictograph includes a key that tells what each picture stands for. In this pictograph, one picture stands for one book. Next read the labels at the side to find out what kinds of books were ordered. You can see that the kinds of books are Mystery, Sports, Animal, and Cartoon.

To find out how many books of one kind were chosen, you count the pictures in that row. Use the pictograph to find how many sports books were ordered. You can see that there were 18. You can quickly see that the students ordered one more mystery book than sports books. The pictograph helps you to see at a glance that those were the two largest groups of books ordered.

In some graphs, a picture stands for more than one thing. A key tells you how many things each picture stands for. For example, the key on this graph might say that one picture of a book stands for 10 books. If it did, 4 pictures in the row labeled *Cartoon* would show that 40 cartoon books were ordered. You would count the pictures and then add or multiply to find the total number of books.

What is a bar graph?

The graph on page 487 is a bar graph. The title tells you that this graph, too, shows information about books ordered at Jefferson School by the fourth-grade classes. Instead of using pictures, a **bar graph** uses bars to stand for numerical information.

Look at the left side of the bar graph to find a label and a scale. The label is NUMBER OF BOOKS. The **scale** is the numbers from 0 to 20 that stand for the numbers of books ordered. Lines across the graph help you to find the number of each kind of book ordered. On this graph, the space between the lines stands for two books.

The bars that run up and down are labeled at the bottom of the graph to show that they stand for the kinds of books ordered. Find those labels. You can see that there is a bar for

Free Books Ordered by Jefferson School Fourth-Grade Classes

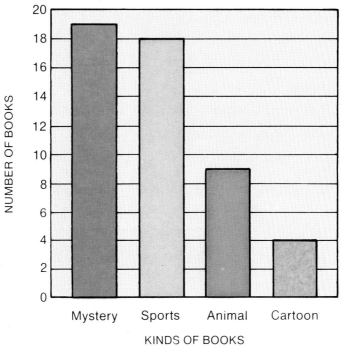

each of the four kinds of books, Mystery, Sports, Animal, and Cartoon. Look at the bar for the number of animal books. It ends halfway between two lines. If you read the scale, you can see that those lines are marked 8 and 10. You can judge that the bar for animal books stops at 9. Find how many free mystery books were ordered. The top of that bar is halfway between the lines that stand for 18 and 20. You can judge that the bar represents 19 books.

Like the pictograph, the bar graph helps you to picture the information written in the paragraph about the free books. You can see how the number of books ordered in one group is like or different from other groups. For example, you can quickly see that sports books were twice as popular as animal books. Animal books, however, were more popular than cartoon books.

Sometimes the bars on a graph go across the graph instead of up and down. The graph below has the labels for the kinds of books at the side and the number of books ordered at the bottom. It shows the same information as the pictograph and the first bar graph.

Free Books Ordered by Jefferson School Fourth-Grade Classes

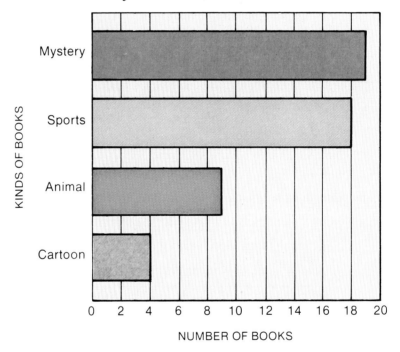

You may have noticed that if you drew a wide line, or bar, through each row of pictures in the pictograph, it would look somewhat like the bar graph on this page. That is because each graph shows the same numbers of books. The two kinds of graphs use different things to stand for those numbers.

Other kinds of graphs may also be drawn to show information about numbers. Line graphs and circle graphs are two other kinds of graphs that might be used.

REVIEW

Look over the heading questions in this lesson, and recite again the answers to them. You should be ready now to read some graphs on your own.

READING GRAPHS

On a sheet of paper, copy the number and letter of each question that follows, and then write your answer to it.

1. According to the pictograph on page 485,
   a. how many animal books were ordered?
   b. were more animal books or mystery books ordered?
   c. sports books were twice as popular as what other kind of book?
2. According to the bar graph on page 487,
   a. how many cartoon books were ordered?
   b. animal books were twice as popular as what other kind of book?
   c. were more animal books or sports books ordered?
3. According to the bar graph on page 488,
   a. how many sports books were ordered?
   b. how many more mystery books were ordered than sports books?
   c. which kind of book was the least popular?

The Strange Voyage
of Neptune's Car

by JOE LASKER

On July 1, 1856, Captain Joshua Patten and his wife, Mary, set sail from New York on their second journey around the world. They were sailing on *Neptune's Car*, a great clipper ship. It was Joshua's first command. As the captain, he was allowed to take his wife along on a sea voyage.

As they sailed out of the harbor, Mary thought of the beginning of their first journey almost two years before.

"What a homesick, seasick landlubber I was!" she thought. "How I missed my mother and my home! How bored and lonely I was!"

To pass away the time, Mary had decided to learn all about the ship, so Joshua had taught her navigation. She learned how to find where the ship was in the great ocean. She learned how to figure in which direction it should sail. And she discovered how to find the distance it had sailed from one point to another. The journey had lasted a year and a half. When it was over, Mary was in love with ships and the sea.

The sailors called Joshua "The Old Man," and Mary "The Old Woman," even though Joshua was only twenty-nine and Mary nineteen.

As they set sail, Joshua said, "We are in a race, Mary. Two other clippers left New York at the same time as *Neptune's Car,* all steering the same course. It's fifteen thousand miles to San Francisco, and I hope we can win."

Just then the lookout shouted, "Sail ho!" One of the other clippers had been sighted.

After several weeks at sea, the weather changed. Cold winds blew, and a heavy snow fell. Joshua shook his head. "If the weather is this bad up here, what is it like down there at Cape Horn?" he wondered.

He soon found out. His ship crossed paths with another ship that was limping north to Rio de Janeiro, Brazil, for repairs and a new crew. Its captain told Joshua, "We tried to fight our way around Cape Horn. After forty days, the first mate and nine sailors were lost overboard. It's the worst Cape winter in memory. If I were you, I'd turn back now."

But Joshua didn't turn back.

The harsh weather made for hard work and mean tempers. Mr. Keeler, the first mate, was bad-tempered most of the time anyway. Now he was even worse. He was mean to the crew, and they disliked him. Mr. Hare, the second mate, was the opposite of Mr. Keeler. He was always cheerful and helpful, but he, too, worried about what lay ahead.

Because Mary could see that Mr. Keeler disliked her and the captain, she felt troubled. Then when they were coming close to Cape Horn, something happened to make her even more afraid. One night when Mr. Keeler was supposed to be on watch, he fell asleep. A wind shift caused the sails to go loose and flap wildly, making a loud noise and changing the ship's direction. The noise, like the snapping of a whip, awoke Joshua and Mary.

Joshua dashed up on deck, and when he saw Keeler asleep, he was furious. The wind could have torn the sails. He awakened Keeler and ordered, "Call the crew to trim the sails! Then report to me in the cabin!"

Waiting in the dining saloon, Mary could hear Joshua's angry voice. "Mr. Keeler, you endangered the ship and everyone on board! You set a terrible example for the crew. I warn you, abandon your duty once more, and you will be kept under arrest all the way to San Francisco!"

The first mate said nothing.

Things got worse. Joshua discovered Keeler sleeping on watch again. This time, he ordered the first mate locked in his cabin, under arrest. Now Joshua had to add Mr. Keeler's duties to his own, and Cape Horn lay just ahead.

Howling winds and knife-edged sleet hit the ship, coating it with ice. Joshua was on deck day and night, doing his own and the first mate's work, while Mary stayed below. He caught what sleep he could, sitting in a chair lashed to the rail to keep from being washed overboard. Mary worried about him because he was always cold and wet. Even his food was icy and soaked by the time the steward could get it to him.

During a break in the storm, Joshua joined Mary in the cabin. He was coughing and shivering with fever. She begged him to rest and to put Mr. Hare, the second mate, in charge until he felt better. Joshua refused.

Then Mary told him, "Joshua, before *Neptune's Car* returns to New York, you will be a father. I can't rest easy with you so sick, staying up on deck day and night. Please, get some rest."

Joshua touched her hand gently and said, "How wonderful that we are going to have a baby! You will need your rest." He sighed. "All right, get Mr. Hare. He'll be in command."

Joshua explained to the second mate why he was being given command of the ship. Mr. Hare said, "Sir, I can handle the ship and the crew all right. The problem is I don't know how to read or write or reckon." He pointed to the navigating instruments, maps, and logbooks on the table. Joshua looked at Mary, and they felt each other's helplessness and fear.

"All right, Mr. Hare," said Joshua. "We'll do it together."

Driven by roaring winds, *Neptune's Car* reached Cape Horn. Mountainous waves thundered over the rail. Suddenly, Mr. Hare burst into Joshua and Mary's cabin carrying Joshua, who was unconscious. Mr. Hare had grabbed him just in time to save him from being swept overboard by a wave.

As they put Joshua to bed, Mr. Hare said, "You will have to take over, ma'am."

"What do you mean?" cried Mary.

"It's you or Keeler," answered Mr. Hare. "You two are the only ones left who can navigate, and nobody trusts Keeler."

"But I must stay by the captain's side now and look after him."

"You must take command!" Mr. Hare said. "The ship must be saved first! Make the captain comfortable.

I'll see to the ship and crew and then report back to you for orders."

Mary knew he was right. She must save the ship.

For the next two nights she did not sleep. While she nursed Joshua, she plotted the ship's course by "dead reckoning" through heavy fog. She avoided the rocky coast, but icebergs would appear suddenly through the fog like ghosts. Mr. Hare cheerfully followed Mary's

command. The ship groaned and shuddered from the pounding of the seas, but somehow it kept going.

Meanwhile, Joshua was shivering with fever. He could not see or hear. Mary studied the ship's medical books to learn how to treat his illness. She learned that Joshua had what was called "brain fever." "I feel so alone, so tired," she said to herself.

The next day, when Mary and Mr. Hare were on deck, they watched the sailors untie frozen knots and claw at the heavy ice-coated sails. Mary shouted at Mr. Hare in order to be heard over the roar of the sea and wind. "The crew is so brave!" she said. "Look how they risk

death, climbing up the icy rigging in this blinding wind. Their fingers are bleeding, cracked, and numbed from the cold!"

From that night on, Mary decided she would sleep in her clothing to be ready for any emergency.

Before daybreak, Mary was suddenly awakened and called up on deck. Three sailors, aloft on the wildly swaying topsail yard, had just been blown off into the sea.

Mary cried out. Already half the crew was helplessly sick. "The ship will be crippled if we lose more of the crew," she thought. "What will I do then?"

Again Mary got no sleep. There was too much to do.
Waves, like walls of water, crashed into the ship. *Neptune's Car* was soaked. The cook's fires were drenched,
so there was no hot food and no way to dry out their wet
clothing.

Mr. Keeler sent Mary a note begging to be returned to

duty. He promised that he would bring the ship safely to San Francisco. Mary tore the note up angrily. "Does he think I can forget how he put us all in danger?" she said. "He thinks I'm a fool! I know if he were ever in command, he would take revenge on Joshua, who is sick and helpless. Let him stay where he is."

"We did it!" shouted Mr. Hare, bursting into the cabin and awakening Mary, who had fallen asleep sitting at Joshua's bedside. "Cape Horn couldn't stop us. We have just sailed into the Pacific Ocean!"

Mary leaped to her feet. She looked at Joshua, who was still unconscious. How she wished she could tell him! Then she turned to Mr. Hare and said, "We brought this clipper around the Horn in eighteen days. I'm proud of the crew." They shook hands.

The weather cleared briefly as if to celebrate, and sunlight danced on the water. "How good to be alive," Mary thought to herself.

But there was still Mr. Keeler. He was always trying to stir up the crew against Mary. He would send them ugly messages. One message read, "Are you mad, letting a nineteen-year-old girl sail this clipper? She is bad luck! Three men died off Cape Horn. The captain is dying. Don't let her turn this ship into a coffin. Get rid of her!"

Mr. Hare told Mary to trust the crew. "They don't want Keeler to be their captain," he said. "They remember how cruel he was to them. They remember that he endangered the ship by sleeping when he was on watch."

Mary thought this advice was good, so she paid no attention to Mr. Keeler.

Trade winds and the warm southern sun favored *Neptune's Car*. It raced along almost on its own, allowing Mary more time to nurse Joshua. Sometimes his sight and hearing returned to him for a while.

Working over her charts and maps one day, Mary saw that the ship was nearing California. "Soon this strange journey will be over," Mary thought. "I'll miss this ship. I'm proud to be its commander and proud that I navigated safely for eight thousand miles."

When *Neptune's Car* sailed into San Francisco Bay, crowds along the docks watched it come in. Mary could see the other sea captains studying her closely through long telescopes. She smiled. Their puzzled faces showed surprise that a woman was at the captain's post.

Before noon the sails came down, and the clipper was snugged in at the dock.

Joshua was immediately rushed to the hospital. Two armed guards took Mr. Keeler to the city jail. Close friends met the ship to take Mary to their home. "What a brave thing you did, Mary," they said to her. Mary looked across the bay to the open sea.

"For the past fifty nights I have slept in my clothing," said Mary. "Tonight I hope to have a hot bath, and sleep in my comfortable nightgown, in a soft, dry bed. . . . I hope Joshua will be all right." Then she sighed. "I'm so tired," she said, and walked away with her friends.

Historical Note

In the race with the two other clippers, Neptune's Car finished second, reaching San Francisco on November 15, 1856, after a trip of four and a half months. Mary Patten is the only woman to have commanded a clipper and one of the very few women in history to command any large seagoing ship.

Captain Joshua Patten, blind and deaf, died in Massachusetts on July 15, 1857, only four months after the birth of his son, Joshua, Jr.

Mary Patten died on March 17, 1861, of an illness brought on by the hardships of the voyage.

The hospital at the United States Merchant Marine Academy, King's Point, New York, is named in memory of Mary Patten.

AUTHOR

Joe Lasker, the author of *The Strange Voyage of* Neptune's Car, also drew the pictures for it. He was born in Brooklyn, New York, where, as a boy, he liked to walk, read, and draw. When he was in the third grade, he won a prize for his drawing. Since then, he has won many art awards. These have made it possible for him to study and paint in Europe, Mexico, and the United States.

Mr. Lasker has been an art teacher as well as the author and illustrator of several children's books. The Laskers have three children and live in Norwalk, Connecticut, where Mr. Lasker has his studio.

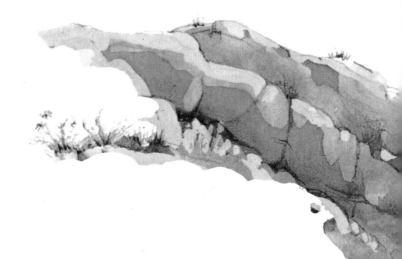

... and now Miguel

by JOSEPH KRUMGOLD

The trouble with Miguel Chavez (mee-gel′ chah′ves) was that he was too young to do an adult's job and too old to enjoy children's play. He longed for a chance to prove to his father that he was ready to do the work of an adult on their New Mexico sheep ranch. When an unexpected storm scattered part of the flock, Miguel thought his chance had come at last. But his father would not let him take part in the search for the missing sheep. Disappointed, Miguel headed for school. There his friend Juby told him that he thought he had seen the sheep across the river heading for Arroyo Hondo (uh-roy′oh ohn′doh). Now, Miguel felt that he just had to disobey his father. Surely if he found the sheep and brought them back home all by himself, his father would be pleased.

As the school bell rang, and the teacher called the children in, Miguel ran off to try to find the sheep. He ran down a steep hill in "big champion jumps," crossed the river, and climbed up the cliff on the other side. Carrying his books with him made the climb difficult, but Miguel was determined.

When I got up to the top and looked, I didn't see them. I guess I did expect a little bit they'd be up there waiting for me. But they weren't. I didn't mind too much. The kind of thing I was doing had to be hard. Such a big thing couldn't be too easy. It'd be like cheating. I set out, walking to the north.

Up on the mesa, it looked empty. Like one of those pictures that Pedro draws. One straight line across the middle of the page and big zigzags off to one side for the mountains. Then dark on top for the clouds, which he makes by smudging up all the pencil lines. And dark on the bottom for the mesa, which he makes with a special black crayon. That's all there is in the picture. And that's why it's a good picture. Because that's all there is. Except for some little bushes, juniper and chaparral and sagebrush. With nothing sticking up, only a high soapweed or a crooked-looking cactus. Nothing else.

Especially, no sheep.

I walked from one rise to the next. Every three or four steps turning all around as I walked. And when I got near to the top of each rise, I had to run. Because I thought in the next ten, fifteen steps up top there, sure, I'd see them. The first few times I saw nothing, which I didn't mind too much. And the next few times, I saw nothing too. Pretty soon I was getting ready to see them, because after an hour or so of walking and turning around and running, I figured it was hard enough. Even for something big.

Besides, I had a pebble in my left shoe. I felt it down there coming up the cliff. I didn't mind then, because it only made everything even harder. And that was all right with me. But now it was getting to hurt good. And I couldn't sit down and take it out. That would be like giving up.

Besides, I didn't have any time to waste. The mesa spread out, as far as you could see, with many breaks — everywhere little canyons and washes. And it was sure that on top of the next canyon, maybe, I was going to see them, those sheep. If I didn't waste time getting up there. Which I didn't. But all I saw was the same kind of nothing that I saw from the last high place, just this wide straight line stretching right across the middle.

Walking down was harder than walking up. For one thing, walking down on my left heel made the pebble bigger. It was getting to feel like a rock. And for another, walking down, you've already seen what there is to see all around, and there's nothing to look forward to until you start to walk up again. It got so I was running more than I was walking. Running downhill because I wanted to get that part over with, and running up because I couldn't wait to get to the top. And all the time, turning around. I got pretty good at being able to turn around and keep running at the same time.

Except what good was it, getting pretty good at anything? The only thing that counted was to get one look, one quick look at those sheep.

All the turning around did was to get me so mixed up I didn't know whether I was going north, south, east, or west. Not that it made any difference, I guess. The sheep weren't particular which direction you went to find them. They weren't in any direction. There were just no sheep. There was all the dark sky, and all this straight flat plain you'd ever want to see. But no sheep.

And after a couple of hours of seeing no sheep, I would've been glad to see any sheep, even if they weren't ours. I kept trying to see sheep so hard, it was as if my eyes got dry and thirsty just to see sheep. To see nothing for two, three hours, especially sheep, it gets hard on your eyes.

It was getting hard on my left foot, too, with that big rock pressing in.

And it wasn't so easy on my hands, either, on account of the books. The books weren't very heavy, but when you keep that rope wrapped around your hand, it can pinch. And even if you take it off

one hand and put it on the other, it isn't long before it's pinching that hand, too.

Another thing was, it got to be hard breathing. Because there was no time to stop and get a good breath. There was always somewhere to go take a look, and you couldn't stop because maybe that very second the sheep were moving away out of sight, and that very second if you were up on a top you'd see them.

After so many hours of it being so hard, I figured it was hard enough by then. It was getting long past the time I ought to find our sheep. Only it didn't make any difference how I figured. They weren't there to be found. Not anywhere.

And after a while, walking, walking, every place started to look as if you'd been there before. You'd see a piece of tumbleweed. And you were sure it was one you saw an hour before. It didn't help to think that maybe you were just walking

506

up and around the same hill all the time.

Then looking, looking, I thought I heard a bell. I listened hard in the wind. One of the ewes that was lost might have a bell. In the flock, there are ten or a dozen sheep with bells. Each one is like the leader of a bunch. I stood still, listening. Then I heard it again, and it was for sure a bell. But it was the school bell, far away, back in Los Cordovas. It must've already become noon, and that was the bell for noontime. Soon the ringing far away stopped. And there was nothing to listen to again, except the quiet wind.

It was never the same, after I heard that bell. It made me feel hungry. Because the bell meant going home to eat. And feeling hungry, I got to feel not so good in the other parts of me. Like lonely. At the beginning, being alone was the best part of it, going off by myself to bring home the sheep. But now it was getting to look as if I wouldn't be bringing home any sheep. And that made a lot of difference about being alone, while everybody else was back there going home to eat. The only way I could go home was to find them. It wasn't only so I could bring the sheep back. I had to find them so I could go back, too.

From then on, I got very busy. I didn't stop to walk anymore. I ran. Everywhere I went, I kept up running, and I did most of my breathing going downhill when I didn't have to try so hard to keep running. There was hardly any breath left over to keep looking with. And that was the hardest part of all, the looking. Because there was never anything to see.

And after a long while, I heard the bell again. School was out for the day.

It was hard to figure out what to do next.

I could leave home. That's about all that was left. I couldn't go back without the sheep. Not after what my father said at breakfast, and especially not after the way he looked. And it was clear enough that, in all this whole empty place, I was never going to find them, those sheep. I could just as well stop, that's all. I could take some time and do a lot of breathing. I could bury my books under a bush. I could sit down and take off my shoe and get rid of that rock with all the sharp edges on it. Then I could go somewhere until I saw a lot of sheep and sit down and look at them, till I got enough again of looking at sheep. And then I could decide where I was leaving home to go to.

Maybe even to the Sangre de Cristo Mountains. On my own, by myself.

But when I looked at the mountains, I knew that was no good. It was impossible. There was only one way to go up into the Mountains of the Sangre de Cristo. And that was to make everyone see you were ready, and then you would go.

Indeed, in order that I should go this way, that's why I was looking for the sheep right now. And if I gave up looking for the sheep, then the idea of going up into the mountains, I had to give that up, too. I

guess, if you are going to leave home, you just leave home, that's all, everything.

Except, it wasn't up to me anymore. It wasn't a question that I should give up looking for the sheep.

It was just no use.

I could keep running from the top of one rise up to the next, looking, looking with my eyes getting drier and drier, without any breath, and the bones in my hands like they were cracking, and the heel of my left foot like it was getting torn away, listening to nothing but the wind. I could keep on doing that forever. It wasn't a question of me giving up, it was a question that just everything had given up, me and everything.

So I sat down. I took a deep breath. And I started to untie the laces from my left shoe. And then — what do you think?

I smelled them.

It is not hard to know that what you're smelling is sheep. If only there are some sheep around to smell. They smell a little sweet and a little old, kind of like coffee that's been left over in a cup on the kitchen table for a very long time. That's sort of what they smell like.

So when there was this smell, I looked around. I found out from which direction was the wind. And in that direction I went to the top of the next rise, a dozen steps. And no farther away than you could throw a rock, there they were coming up the hill toward me, about fifteen ewes and their lambs, ambling along, having a good time eating, just taking a walk as if there were no trouble anywhere in all the world.

Wahoo! I took off. Around my head in a big circle, I swung my books like a rope. I was going to throw a loop on all fifteen at once.

Wahoo! I took off down that hill as if I were a whole herd of buffalo and the sheep were somebody's chuck wagon that was going to get stampeded. Wahoo!

The sheep looked up, a little like a bunch of people in church interested to see who was coming through the door.

I showed them who was coming through the door. Before they knew what was happening, they were moving *Whoosh* — I let my books swing out, and I hit one right in the rump. *Whish* — I kicked another one with my foot that had the rock, so that it hurt me more, I think, than the sheep. I picked up a stone and — *wango* — I let a third one have it in the rear. I got them running right in the opposite direction from the one they were going.

I kept them going at a gallop. Running first to the one side, then to the other, swinging the books around my head all the time. Yelling and hollering so they wouldn't even dare slow down. They looked scared, but I didn't care. I had waited too long for this. And now I wanted them to know that I was here. I ran them down the hill fast enough to be a stampede. And whichever one ran last was the unlucky one. There were a lot of rocks around, and I throw rocks good.

At the bottom of the hill, I quieted down. Why was I acting so mad? I had no reason to be mad at the sheep. It wasn't as if they started out to get me in trouble. Indeed, because of them, here I was doing a great thing. I was finding them and bringing them home. If they hadn't taken it into their heads to go out and get lost, I never would have this big chance.

I quieted down. I stopped and I breathed. The air was good. After the rain, it was clean and it smelled sweet, like a vanilla soda in Schaeffer's Drugstore in Taos (tah'ohs) before you start to drink it with the straw. I took in the air with deep breaths. I sat down and took off my shoe. I found the rock down near the heel. But my goodness, it wasn't any kind of rock at all. Just a little bit of a chip off a stone. In my foot it felt like a boulder. But in my hand it didn't look like anything at all.

I was quieted down. We started off. It was going to be a long drive home. I didn't mind. There were so many good things to think about. What my father would say to me, and my grandfather.

It is no great trouble to drive a small bunch of sheep. You just walk behind them, and if one begins to separate, you start in the same direction that it starts and that makes it turn back and bunch up again. It was very little work. So there was much time to think what my uncles would say, and my big brothers. And how Pedro would watch me.

There was much time to look around. At the mountains, not so dark now and not so mad. There was much to see, walking along thinking, breathing, and looking around. How the clouds now were taking on new shapes, the dark ones separating and new big white ones coming up. And on the mesa everything looked fine. I saw flow-ers. Before, when I was looking, there were no flowers. Now, there they were. The little pink ones of the peyote plants. And there were flowers on the hedgehog cactus, too, kind of pinkish purple some, and others a real red.

After a little while, I had something else to do. One of the lambs lay down. Whether it was tired or why, I don't know. I picked it up, the lamb under my arm, and in the other hand the rope with my books. It was not so bad. Even the rope didn't pinch anymore. And when the lamb got heavy under one arm, I put it under the other.

I felt better, now, than in a long time.

Even when I had to pick up this second lamb, which was straggling behind, I still felt good. It was harder this way because now I couldn't use one arm after the other when the lambs got heavy, and there were the books I had to carry in addition. By now, though, we were coming down the dry wash that led to the river. There was not much farther to go.

They were a good bunch of sheep, all of them. When I brought them to the place in the river that was not so deep, they went right across without any trouble. As for me myself, I almost fell in, but all the way this time. I was balancing myself all right on the rocks going across when one of the lambs started to wriggle as if it wanted to shake itself apart. But I held on, and I kept my balance and didn't fall in. I wouldn't have minded, anyway, if I had. If I came to the house with all my clothes wet, that would make what I did look as if it was even harder than it was.

Blasito was the first one to see me.

He was walking across the top of the hill near the corral when I came around the bend from the river.

"Hey, Mickey," he yelled, "where you been? What's those sheep you got?"

"Yours," I shouted back.

"Mine? What do you mean mine? The lost ones?"

"That's what," I yelled. "The lost ones!"

"No! No fooling?" He turned away from me. "*Ai,* Grandpa. *Padre de Chavez. Mira!* Miguel's here, with the bunch of sheep that

was lost!" He looked back to where I was coming up the hill. "Bravo, Miguelito (mee-guh-lee'toh)! Where'd you find them? How did it happen?"

"I'll tell you." I needed my breath to get up the hill with those two lambs under my arms. "Wait'll I get there."

The two of them were waiting for me, Blasito and my grandfather.

Grandpa took one of the lambs from my arms. I let the other one down. Blasito shooed the bunch into the corral. And all three of us talked at once.

"Where did you find them?" asked Blasito.

"How did this happen?" said Grandfather.

"I'll tell it to you all," I said, "from the beginning. On the way to school this morning, I started to think."

Blasito interrupted. "Can't you tell us where you found them?"

"But that's what I'm trying to do. It started on the way to school."

"Miguel!" Grandfather wouldn't let me talk. "That part, you can tell us later. Where were they, the sheep?"

"Well, I'll tell you that first, then. I found them on the way to Arroyo Hondo, about twenty or thirty miles from here. But the way it started —"

"How many miles?" My grandfather looked at me with a smile.

"Oh, many miles. Many, many. What happened was —"

"How come you went north?" asked Blas. "All morning we've been riding toward the Arroyo del Alamo. In just the other way."

"First comes the way I went down the hill." I tried to explain. "With world-record jumps."

"Why is it that you don't want to answer your big brother Blas?" asked Grandpa. "How did you know where to look?"

"But why can't I tell it the way it happened? There was much trouble and it's very interesting."

"Later," said Grandpa. "Now, how did you know?"

"Well, I figured it out, and then I kept my ears open to hear things."

"What things?" said Blasito.

"Things people say."

"Like who?"

"Like Juby."

"He told you?"

"Look," I said to Blasito. "If I can't tell you in my own way, then what's the use? The kind of questions you ask, it makes it all sound like nothing. If I have to tell it this way, just to answer a few little questions, then what's the use my going out and finding the sheep anyway?"

"Use?" Blasito started to laugh. He banged me on the back. "It's a great thing, finding those sheep. I mean it, Miguel. You did fine!"

"What did you say?"

"I said great, fine!"

Grandfather took me by the hand and shook it like two men shaking hands.

"It's the truth," he said. "This that you have done, it was good."

"What?" I asked Grandpa.

"It was good."

"Better than the rest of us could do," said Blasito.

"What?" I asked Blasito.

"Better than the rest of us!" Blasito shouted so I would hear.

Grandpa still held my hand, and he shook it again. "You brought them in all right, Miguel. Like a real pastor."

"What?" I asked my grandfather. I wanted to hear everything twice.

"A real pastor," Grandpa said again, and we all looked at each other and smiled.

"Anything else?" I asked.

Before anyone could answer, there was a great shout from the house. "Miguel!" It was my father. It was a shout that sounded like thunder. "Miguel, get over here!"

He stood, he and my mother both, they stood in front of the house. And with them was Mrs. Mertian, my schoolteacher. They stood with Mrs. Mertian, who had come from the school in Los Cordovas, and they talked together.

My father looked around at us once again. "Miguel!"

Grandpa nodded to me that I should go to my father. "Take off," said Blasito. "You'd better get going."

I went. What else? It was too bad, real bad, my teacher should talk to my father before I even got a chance. I knew now that the things I was thinking about on the way home, of what my father would say to me, I knew that these were most likely not the things he was going to say to me now. I walked to the house, where they stood, and Mrs. Mertian smiled at my mother, and they shook hands. Then she smiled at my father and shook hands with him. Then everybody smiled at each other and she left. But when they turned to watch me coming up the path, my father and mother, nobody smiled.

"Where'd you go?" said my father.

"Up there to the Arroyo Hondo. Many miles."

"What's in Arroyo Hondo?"

I knew my father didn't want to know what's in Arroyo Hondo. He knew as well as I. Just a grocery store and some houses. If I told him that, then everything would get all mixed up.

"It was not for what's in Arroyo Hondo. It's that I went after the sheep that were lost."

"This morning at breakfast, didn't we talk about the lost sheep?"

"Yes." I knew what he meant. "And you told me to go to school. And I did, I went to school."

"That is true. But it is only one small piece of what is true. The rest is, you didn't go in."

"Because of Juby. He is my oldest friend."

"And why is it, Miguel, that you will obey your oldest friend? But your parents, who are friends to you even older than your oldest friend, what they say means nothing."

"But Juby told me where the missing sheep were. So I went. I got them. I brought them home."

This is not the way I wanted to tell it at all. It was worse than with Blasito and Grandpa. It didn't sound hard this way, or like a big thing. It was like going down to the spring for a pail of water, no more. But what else was there to do? If things kept up like they were, it could get bad.

"You brought what home?"

"The missing sheep. They are in the corral."

My father and mother looked. Blasito and my grandfather, who were watching us, they pointed out the bunch in the corral.

"Well!" My father, at least, he didn't sound so mad anymore when he looked back to me.

"That's why I didn't go in."

"Well." My father put his hands in his back pockets and looked down at me. "That's different. But not so different to make too much difference, Miguel. The sheep are important. Sure! But you, too, that you go to school is important. Even more important. Always there has to be something done with the sheep. And if every time something had to be done, you stayed away from school, my goodness, you'd grow up to be a burro. And you tell me, do we need a burro around this place?"

"No. Only mules and horses."

"And even more, what we need is young people who are educated, who have learned to know what is the difference between what is right and what is wrong. Do you understand?"

"I understand. And I promise. I will never miss my school again."

"Good. Now get into the house. Mrs. Mertian brought the lessons from today. So go in and do them and write your homework for tomorrow."

My mother took me by the back of the head to go into the house with me. And then my father did a wonderful thing. He gave me one good spank. And when I looked around up at him, he was smiling.

"It would not be true," he told me, "if I didn't say also I am glad to have the sheep back. How you did it was wrong. But for what you did, I want to thank you."

And then he went off to go to Blas and Grandpa where they were working on the tractor. My mother took me with her into the house.

"Come, Miquito (mee-kee'toh). That's enough for today. Good and bad, you've done enough."

*How will Miguel Chavez finally prove that he can do an adult's job? You can find out by reading the rest of Joseph Krumgold's book . . . **and now Miguel.***

AUTHOR

Joseph Krumgold was born and grew up near New York City. His father owned and ran several movie theaters, and in their home there was always a great deal of talk about movies. It is no wonder, then, that Joseph, at the age of twelve, decided that he wanted to make movies. When he graduated from college, he went to work as a writer at one of the movie studios in Hollywood, California. Later he began to make his own films — documentaries, or films that tell about real people and places. Then he left Hollywood and traveled and lived in many places, such as France, Israel, and Italy, making more films. These films won a number of prizes in America and abroad.

One of the films that Mr. Krumgold wrote and directed was made in New Mexico. It, too, was about real people — the Chavez family — and it was filmed while the story was really happening. Mr. Krumgold felt that he had more to say about Miguel Chavez than he could say in the movie, so he wrote the book . . . *and now Miguel.*

In 1954 . . . *and now Miguel* won the Newbery Medal. This award led Mr. Krumgold to write two more books, set in other parts of the United States, about how a child grows up. The titles of those books are *Onion John* and *Henry 3*. When Mr. Krumgold won the Newbery Medal for *Onion John,* he became the first author to win this award twice.

...Not What They Seem

In the story about the ship *Neptune's Car*, Mary Patten said of her first journey, "What a *homesick, seasick* landlubber I was!" *Homesick* is a compound word made up of *home* and *sick*. You know what each word means on its own, of course. But think about what the words mean when they are used together. *Homesick* means "longing for home; unhappy away from home." In other words, it means "sick *for* home."

Now think for a minute about the word *seasick*. If you changed the word *home* in the definition to the word *sea*, would the definition fit *seasick*? Does *seasick* mean "longing for sea; unhappy away from sea"? It means something quite different. *Seasick* means "made sick by the movement of a boat on the sea." It means "sick *because of* the sea." When you are *homesick*, the only place you want to be is at home. When you are *seasick*, the last place you want to be is at sea!

Have you ever heard of a person being *heartsick? Heart-sick* doesn't mean that something is wrong with a person's heart. It means "terribly disappointed and sad." People are *heartsick* when they hurt way down deep inside, when they feel as if their hearts are broken. They are "sick *at* heart."

Some people get confused about "sick" words. Read the following conversation between Froop and Boop.

Froop: Mary can't take her dog Speck in their old car anymore. Speck always gets carsick.

Boop: Oh, so that's why Speck was looking at new cars — sick for a car, eh?

Froop: Boop! *Carsick* doesn't mean sick for a car!

Boop: It doesn't? Oh, will I ever learn about those "sick" words?

Boop will learn someday, we think. *Carsick* is like *seasick.* When you are *carsick,* you are "made sick by the movement of a car on the road." You are sick *because of* the car, not sick *for* it.

You can see, then, that not all compound words are what they seem at first glance. Think about the words *handshake, handstand,* and *handbag.* You may want to write definitions for them.

Books to Enjoy

Doodlebug by Irene Brady
Jennifer uses her life savings — fourteen dollars — to save the shaggy pony with the lame foot from the horsemeat butcher.

Greedy Mariana by Dorothy Sharp Carter
These twenty tales from Puerto Rico, Cuba, Haiti, Jamaica, and other nearby islands are full of magic, nonsense and humor.

Arthur the Kid by Alan Coren
Pint-sized but quick-witted Arthur joins some outlaws and makes them change their ways in this funny Western adventure.

A January Fog Will Freeze a Hog
compiled by Hubert Davis
Here are thirty American folk sayings about the weather —some useful, some nonsense, all fun.

The Rocking Horse Secret by Rumer Godden
In the attic of the English country house where her mother works, Tibby finds an antique rocking horse and learns that it holds the key to a mystery.

Something on My Mind by Nikki Grimes
Verses by a new young poet match sketches of children drawn by the noted artist Tom Feelings.

Glossary

Glossary

Some of the words in this book may have pronunciations or meanings you do not know. This glossary can help you by telling you how to pronounce those words and by telling you the meanings with which those words are used in this book.

You can find out the correct pronunciation of any glossary word by using the special spelling after the word and the pronunciation key at the bottom of each left-hand page.

The full pronunciation key below shows how to pronounce each consonant and vowel in a special spelling. The pronunciation key at the bottom of each left-hand page is a shortened form of the full key.

FULL PRONUNCIATION KEY

Consonant Sounds

b	bib	k	cat, kick, pique	t	tight
ch	church	l	lid, needle	th	path, thin
d	deed	m	am, man, mum	_th_	bathe, this
f	fast, fife, off, phase, rough	n	no, sudden	v	cave, valve, vine
		ng	thing	w	with
g	gag	p	pop	y	yes
h	hat	r	roar	z	rose, size, xylophone, zebra
hw	which	s	miss, sauce, see		
j	judge	sh	dish, ship	zh	garage, pleasure, vision

Vowel Sounds

ă	pat	ī	by, guy, pie	ōō	boot, fruit
ā	aid, they, pay	î	dear, deer, fierce, mere	ou	cow, out
â	air, care, wear			ŭ	cut, rough
ä	father	ŏ	pot, horrible	û	firm, heard, term, turn, word
ĕ	pet, pleasure	ō	go, row, toe		
ē	be, bee, easy, leisure	ô	alter, caught, for, paw	yōō	abuse, use
				ə	about, silent, pencil, lemon, circus
ĭ	pit	oi	boy, noise, oil		
		ŏŏ	book	ər	butter

Stress Marks

Primary Stress ′
bi·ol′o·gy (bī ŏl′ə jē)

Secondary Stress ′
bi′o·log′i·cal (bī′ə lŏj′ĭ kəl)

Pronunciation key and word meanings adapted from *The American Heritage School Dictionary,* © 1972, 1977, by Houghton Mifflin Company.

a•broad (ə brôd′) *adv. & adj.* **1.** In or to foreign places: *going abroad.* **2.** Outdoors and about: *There were people abroad in spite of the rain.*

ad•ver•tise (ăd′vər tīz′) *v.* **ad•ver•tised, ad•ver•tis•ing. 1.** To call public attention to (a product), as by announcing on the radio, placing a notice in a newspaper, etc.: *Manufacturers advertise their products.* **2.** To give public notice of something, as of something wanted or offered for sale: *We advertised in the lost and found section of the paper.*

af•fec•tion•ate•ly (ə fěk′shə nǐt lē) *adv.* In a tender and loving manner.

a•gue (ā′gyo͞o) *n.* A fever in which there are periods of chills, fever, and sweating.

aim (ām) *v.* **1.** To direct (a weapon, blow, remark, etc.) at someone or something: *She aimed at the target.* **2.** To have as a goal: *We aim to please.*

aisle (īl) *n.* **1.** A passageway between rows of seats, as in a church or theater. **2.** Any passageway, as between counters in a department store.

a•jar (ə jär′) *adj. & adv.* Partly open: *leave the door ajar.*

al•ley[1] (ăl′ē) *n., pl.* **al•leys. 1.** A narrow street or passageway between or behind buildings. **2.** A bowling alley.

al•ley[2] (ăl′ē) *n., pl.* **al•leys.** A large playing marble, often used as a shooter.

a•loft (ə lôft′) *or* (ə lŏft′) *adv.* **1.** In or into a high place. **2.** In or toward a ship's upper rigging.

al•um (ăl′əm) *n.* A powdered mixture of aluminum, chromium, or iron and potassium or sodium.

am•ble (ăm′bəl) *v.* **am•bled, am•bling.** To walk or move along at a slow, easy pace: *We ambled down the street.*

an•ces•tor (ăn′sĕs′tər) *n.* Any person from whom one is descended, especially if of a generation earlier than a grandparent.

an•ten•na (ăn tĕn′ə) *n., pl.* **an•ten•nae** (ăn tĕn′ē). One of the pair of long, slender feelers growing on the head of an insect or a shellfish such as a lobster or shrimp.

ant•ler (ănt′lər) *n.* One of a pair of bony, often branched growths on the head of a deer or related animal. Antlers are usually found only on males.

anx•ious•ly (ăngk′shəs lē) *or* (ăng′-) *adv.* In an uneasy or worried manner: *The father waited anxiously for his child.*

ap•pre•ci•a•tion (ə prē′shē ā′shən) *n.* Thankfulness; gratefulness: *They showed their appreciation with a gift.*

ap•pro•pri•ate (ə prō′prē ĭt) *adj.* Suitable for a particular person, condition, occasion, or place; proper: *appropriate clothes.*

as•ton•ish (ə stŏn′ĭsh) *v.* To fill with wonder; amaze; surprise: *The size of the apple astonished the king, and he called everyone over to see it.*

bach•e•lor (băch′ə lər) *or* (băch′lər) *n.* A man who has not married.

ă pat / ā pay / â care / ä father / ĕ pet / ē be / ĭ pit / ī pie / î fierce / ŏ pot / ō go / ô paw, for / oi oil / o͝o book / o͞o boot / ou out / ŭ cut / û fur / th the / th thin / hw which / zh vision / ə ago, item, pencil, atom, circus

bank (băngk) *n.* **1.** Ground, often sloping, along the edge of a river, creek, pond, etc. **2.** A hillside or slope. **3.** Earth or other material piled into a sloping mass or surface: *a bank of earth against the cabin wall; a snow bank.*

beak•er (bē'kər) *n.* A large drinking cup with a wide mouth.

bear (bâr) *v.* **bore** (bôr) *or* (bōr), **borne** (bôrn) *or* (bōrn), **bear•ing. 1.** To hold up; support: *a vine strong enough to bear the weight of a grown person; a president bearing the burden of national leadership.* **2.** To produce; yield: *Some trees bear fruit early in the spring.*

bed (bĕd) *n.* **1.** A piece of furniture for resting. **2.** A small piece of ground for growing things: *a bed of flowers.* **3.** Anything that forms a bottom or supporting part: *the bed of a stream.* **4.** A mass of rock, clay, etc. that reaches under a large area and is surrounded by different material. —*v.* **1.** To provide with a bed or sleeping quarters. **2.** To make a bed for (an animal): *She bedded down her horse at night.*

bel•low (bĕl'ō) *n.* **1.** The loud, roaring sound made by a bull or certain other large animals. **2.** A loud, deep shout or cry. —*v.* **1.** To roar as a bull does. **2.** To shout in a deep, loud voice.

bin (bĭn) *n.* An enclosed space for storing food, coal, etc.

bit[1] (bĭt) *n.* **1.** A small piece or amount. **2.** A brief amount of time.

bit[2] (bĭt) *n.* **1.** A tool for drilling that fits into a brace or electric drill. **2.** The metal mouthpiece of a bridle, used to control one's horse.

bit•ter (bĭt'ər) *adj.* **bit•ter•er, bit•ter•est. 1.** Having or being a taste that is sharp or unpleasant: *a bitter drink.* **2.** Causing sharp pain to the body or discomfort to the mind; harsh: *a bitter wind: bitter memories.*

bluff (blŭf) *n.* A steep headland, cliff, river bank, etc.

blun•der (blŭn'dər) *n.* A foolish or stupid mistake. —*v.* **1.** To make a stupid mistake. **2.** To move clumsily or blindly; stumble: *A small fly blundered into the spider's web.*

blunt (blŭnt) *adj.* **1.** Having a thick, dull edge or end; not pointed. **2.** Abrupt and frank in manner.

blush (blŭsh) *v.* **1.** To become suddenly red in the face from modesty, embarrassment, or shame. **2.** To feel ashamed.

board (bôrd) *or* (bōrd) *v.* To get on a ship, train, or plane.

book•plate (boŏk'plāt') *n.* A label pasted inside a book and showing the owner's name.

breech•es (brĭch'ĭz) *pl.n.* **1.** Short, fitted trousers ending at or just below the knees. **2.** *Informal.* Any trousers.

brisk (brĭsk) *adj.* **1.** Moving or acting quickly; lively; energetic: *a brisk walk.* **2.** Very active; not sluggish: *a brisk demand for books.* **3.** Fresh and invigorating: *a brisk morning.* —**brisk'ly** *adv.* —**brisk'ness** *n.*

britch•es (brĭch'ĭz) *pl.n. Informal.* Breeches.

brow (brou) *n.* **1.** The forehead. **2.** Either of the lines of hair growing above the eyes; an eyebrow. **3.** An expression of the face: *a puzzled brow.*

browse (brouz) *v.* **1.** To inspect in a leisurely and casual way: *browse* *through a book.* **2.** To look over goods in a store casually without seriously intending to buy them: *browse around in a department store.*

bru•tal (brōōt′l) *adj.* Cruel; harsh.

budge (bŭj) *v.* To move or cause to move slightly: *The boulder did not budge.*

buff (bŭf) *n.* **1.** A soft, thick, yellowish leather made from the skins of buffalo, elk, or oxen. **2.** The color of this leather; a yellowish tan. —*v.* To polish or shine with a buff or cloth.

bulge (bŭlj) *n.* An outward curve or a swelling. —*v.* To swell or cause to swell beyond the usual size: *His eyes bulged with surprise.*

cab (kăb) *n.* **1.** A taxicab. **2.** A one-horse carriage for public hire. **3.** A place for the operator or driver of a train, locomotive, etc.

ca•nal (kə năl′) *n.* **1.** A waterway that is wholly or partly artificial, used for any of several purposes—to supply farmland with water; for shipping; for drainage; for travel. **2.** A tube or duct, as in the body.

cap•tiv•i•ty (kăp tĭv′ĭ tē) *n., pl.* **cap•tiv•i•ties.** The condition of being held under control; not free: *Few aardvarks have lived long in captivity.*

car•go (kär′gō) *n., pl.* **car•goes** or **car•gos.** The goods carried by a ship, airplane, etc.

cel•lar (sĕl′ər) *n.* **1.** A storage room beneath a house. **2.** A dark, cool room

for storing some kinds of food and drink.

chal•lenge (chăl′ənj) *n.* **1.** A call to take part in a contest or fight to see who is better, stronger, etc.: *a challenge to a race.* **2.** A goal that makes a person work very hard to achieve it: *Learning to walk again was a great challenge to Jim after the accident.* **3.** A special quality naturally belonging to something and requiring full use of one's abilities, energy, or resources: *The French girl loved the challenge of English.*

chan•de•lier (shăn′də lîr′) *n.* A fixture that holds a number of light bulbs or candles and is hung from a ceiling.

chan•nel (chăn′əl) *n.* **1.** The cut in the earth through which a river or stream passes. **2.** A part of a river or harbor deep enough to form a passage for ships.

chant (chănt) *or* **(chänt)** *n.* A melody, often with many words or syllables sung on the same note. —*v.* To call out in a repeating, rhythmic way.

Chi•ca•no (shĭ kä′nō) *or* **(chĭ-)** *adj.* Of or pertaining to Mexican-Americans.

chip (chĭp) *n.* A small piece cut or broken off: *a chip of wood.*

chop (chŏp) *n.* **1.** The jaw. **2.** A small cut of meat, usually having a bone.

cho•re•og•ra•pher (kôr′ē ŏg′rə fər) *or* **(kōr-)** *n.* Someone who creates, arranges, and directs ballets or other dances.

chry•san•the•mum (krĭ săn′thə•məm) *n.* **1.** A plant with showy, vari-

---

ă pat / ā pay / â care / ä father / ĕ pet / ē be / ĭ pit / ī pie / î fierce / ŏ pot / ō go / ô paw, for / oi oil / ŏŏ book /
ōō boot / ou out / ŭ cut / û fur / *th* the / th thin / hw which / zh vision / ə ago, item, pencil, atom, circus

ously colored flowers. **2.** The flower of such a plant.

chuck wag•on (chŭk′ wăg′ən) *n.* A wagon equipped with food and cooking utensils for a team of workers on the move, as on a cattle drive.

chute (sho͞ot) *n.* An up-and-down or slanting passage down which things can be dropped or slid.

cin•der (sĭn′dər) *n.* **1.** A piece of partly burned wood or coal. **2. cinders.** Pieces of ash, sometimes packed hard and used to surface racetracks.

cleft (klĕft). *n.* A separation, split, or hollow: *a cleft in a rock.*

clump (klŭmp) *n.* A thick group or cluster of trees, bushes, etc.

coach (kōch) *n.* **1.** A large, closed four-wheeled carriage pulled by horses. **2.** A railroad passenger car.

cob•ble•stone (kŏb′əl stōn′) *n.* A naturally rounded stone once much used for paving streets.

co•coon (kə ko͞on′) *n.* A covering of silky strands spun by the wormlike form of a moth or other insect as protection during that stage of its life.

coil (koil) *n.* Connected rings made by winding something long and bendable around a center a number of times: *a coil of rope.* —*v.* To wind into a coil or a shape like that of a coil.

com•mu•ni•ty (kə myo͞o′nĭ tē) *n., pl.* **com•mu•ni•ties. 1. a.** A group of people living in the same area and under the same government. **b.** The district or area in which they live. **2.** A group of people who have close ties, as through common nationality or interests: *New York's Puerto Rican community; the college community.*

com•pa•ny (kŭm′pə nē) *n., pl.* **com•pa•nies. 1.** A group of people; a gathering. **2.** A guest or guests: *soup good enough for company.* **3.** A body of performers organized to present stage works such as plays, operas, and ballets, or to produce motion pictures. **4.** A unit of soldiers, especially one consisting of two or more platoons. **5.** The officers and crew of a ship: *the ship's company.*

con•ceal (kən sēl′) *v.* To keep from being seen, noticed, or known; hide: *A bank of clouds concealed the setting sun. Jill smiled and joked to conceal her hurt feelings.*

con•ceit•ed (kən sē′tĭd) *adj.* Too proud of oneself.

con•fi•den•tial•ly (kŏn′fĭ dĕn′shə lē) *adv.* Doing in a trusting manner: *I knew I could speak confidentially to my brother.*

con•sid•er•a•tion (kən sĭd′ə rā′shən) *n.* Careful thought.

con•sole[1] (kən sōl′) *v.* **con•soled, con•sol•ing.** To comfort in time of disappointment or sorrow: *He consoled his sister when she did not get picked for the team.*

con•sole[2] (kŏn′sōl′) *n.* A cabinet for a radio or television set, made to stand on the floor.

con•tent•ed (kən tĕn′tĭd) *adj.* **1.** Satisfied with things as they are. **2.** Showing contentment: *a contented look on one's face.* —**con•tent′ed•ly** *adv.*

cor•al (kôr′əl) *or* (kŏr′-) *n.* **1.** A hard, stony substance formed by the skeletons of tiny sea animals massed together in great numbers. It is often white, pink, or reddish, and some kinds are used for making jewelry.

2. A mass of this substance, often branched or rounded in shape.

county seat (koun′tē sēt) *n.* A town or city that is the center of government in its county.

court (kôrt) *or* (kōrt) *n.* **1.** A short street enclosed by buildings on three sides. **2.** An area marked and fitted for a sport. **3.** A royal mansion or palace. **4.** The people who assist a king or royal ruler. —*v.* To woo and seek to marry.

craft•y (krăf′tē) *or* (kräf′-) *adj.* Skilled in sneaky dealing and dishonesty.

crave (krāv) *v.* **1.** To ask. **2.** To have a strong desire for.

creek (krēk) *or* (krĭk) *n.* **1.** A small stream, often a shallow body of water connected to a river. **2.** *British.* A small inlet in a shoreline.

cud (kŭd) *n.* Food that has been swallowed and brought up to the mouth again for further chewing by animals such as cattle, sheep, etc.

dart (därt) *v.* **1.** To move suddenly and fast: *A squirrel darted across the path.* **2.** To send forth with a quick, sudden movement: *They darted angry glances behind them.*

de•gree (dĭ grē′) *n.* A title awarded by a college or university after completion of a required course of study.

de•ject•ed (dĭ jĕk′tĭd) *adj.* Low in spirits; depressed.

del•i•cate (dĕl′ĭ kĭt) *adj.* **1.** Very finely made: *delicate lace.* **2.** Easily broken or damaged: *a delicate eggshell.*

de•scend•ant (dĭ sĕn′dənt) *n.* A person, plant, or animal coming from a particular family line of people, plants, or animals: *Is Judy Boone a descendant of Daniel Boone? Those roses are descendants of the famous Cherokee rose.*

de•sert (dĭ zûrt′) *v.* To leave or abandon: *She deserted her pets.*

de•test (dĭ tĕst′) *v.* To dislike strongly. *My dog Max detests dry dog food.*

de•vice (dĭ vīs′) *n.* Something that is designed to be used for a particular purpose.

dig•ni•ty (dĭg′nĭ tē) *n., pl.* **dig•ni•ties. 1.** The condition of being worthy or honorable: *a certain dignity in every human being.* **2.** A manner that is worthy of respect: *She spoke to the crowd with dignity.*

dis•cour•age (dĭ skûr′ĭj) *or* (-skŭr′-) *v.* **dis•cour•aged, dis•cour•ag•ing. 1.** To make less hopeful or enthusiastic; depress: *The size of the problem discouraged me.* **2.** To try to prevent. *They lit a fire to discourage the mosquitoes.*

dis•gust (dĭs gŭst′) *n.* A feeling of sickness, extreme annoyance, etc.

dis•mal•ly (dĭz′məl ē) *adv.* In a way that shows gloom or discouragement.

dog•ged•ly (dôg′ĭd lē) *adv.* In an untiring manner; persistently: *Although he had failed the test twice, he went on doggedly to take it once more.*

doo•dle (dōōd′l) *v.* **doo•dled, doo•dling.** To scribble (a design or figure) while thinking about something else.

ă pat / ā pay / â care / ä father / ĕ pet / ē be / ĭ pit / ī pie / î fierce / ŏ pot / ō go / ô paw, for / oi oil / ŏŏ book / ōō boot / ou out / ŭ cut / û fur / th the / th thin / hw which / zh vision / ə ago, item, pencil, atom, circus

dou•ble back (dŭb′əl băk′) *v.* To go back over the same ground, usually to check something.

doze (dōz) *v.* **dozed, doz•ing.** To sleep or appear to sleep lightly; nap. —*n.* A short, light sleep; a nap.

drape (drāp) *v.* **draped, drap•ing. 1.** To cover or hang with cloth in loose folds: *He draped the unfinished painting.* **2.** To arrange or hang in loose, graceful folds: *She draped the veil over her head. Silk drapes easily.* **3.** To hang loosely: *He draped his legs over the chair.*

draw (drô) *v.* **drew, drawn, draw•ing.** To pull or move so as to cover or uncover: *drew the blanket up to her neck.* —*n.* **1.** A small natural ditch with a shallow bed. **2.** A contest ending in a tie.

drear•y (drîr′ē) *adj.* **drear•i•er, drear•i•est. 1.** Gloomy: *a dreary January rain.* **2.** Boring; dull.

drift (drĭft) *v.* To be or cause to be carried along by or as if by a current of water or air: *The boat drifted toward shore. The fishermen drifted their nets. The smoke drifted out through the window.*

dug•out (dŭg′out′) *n.* A rough shelter dug into the ground or on a hillside.

dune (dōōn) *or* (dyōōn) *n.* A mass of sand blown by the wind into the form of a hill or ridge.

eaves (ēvz) *n. (used with a plural verb).* The part of a roof that forms the lower edge and stands out beyond the walls.

em•i•grate (ĕm′ĭ grāt′) *v.* **em•i•grat•ed, em•i•grat•ing.** To leave a na-tive country or area to settle in an-other: *In 1908 she emigrated from Italy.* —**em′i•gra′tion** *n.*

en•chant (ĕn chănt′) *or* (-chänt′) *v.* **1.** To put under a spell; bewitch. **2.** To delight; charm.

en•dure (ĕn dŏŏr′) *or* (-dyŏŏr′) *v.* **en•dured, en•dur•ing. 1.** To undergo; bear up under. **2.** To put up with.

en•gi•neer (ĕn′jə nîr′) *n.* **1.** A person who is trained in the field of planning and building things, such as roads and bridges. **2.** A person who runs a locomotive. **3.** A person who is skilled in the planning, building, and use of engines or machines.

en•grave (ĕn grāv′) *v.* **en•graved, en•grav•ing.** To carve or cut a design or letters into a surface: *engrave a name on a plate.*

e•nor•mous (ĭ nôr′məs) *adj.* Of very great size. —**e•nor′mous•ly** *adv.*

en•thu•si•as•tic (ĕn thōō′zē ăs′tĭk) *adj.* Showing or having great interest, excitement, or admiration: *She was enthusiastic about her team's chances.* —**en•thu′si•as′ti•cal•ly** *adv.*

ewe (yōō) *n.* A female sheep.

ex•haust (ĭg zôst′) *v.* To wear out completely; tire: *She exhausts herself with work.*

express rider (ĕk sprĕs′ rī′dər) *n.* A person on horseback who rides between two points without making stops in between.

ex•te•ri•or (ĭk stîr′ē ər) *n.* **1.** The outside, as of a car. **2.** Outward appear-ance: *a friendly exterior.*

fair•ly (fâr′lē) *adv.* Actually: *The walls fairly shook with his screaming.*

fan·ci·ful (făn′sĭ fəl) *adj.* Created in the mind; imaginary; unreal: *fanciful tales.* —**fan′ci·ful·ly** *adv.* —**fan′ci·ful·ness** *n.*

fan·cy (făn′sē) *v.* To imagine; picture: *As she looked at herself in the mirror, she tried to fancy herself as an adult.* —*interj.* Used to express surprise. Often used with *that: Fancy that! He's awake!*

fas·ci·nate (făs′ə nāt′) *v.* **fas·ci·nat·ed, fas·ci·nat·ing.** To capture and hold the interest of someone.

fash·ion (făsh′ən) *v.* To make into a particular shape or form: *fashion figures from clay.*

fa·vor (fā′vər) *n.* A kind or helpful act: *He agreed to do it for me as a special favor.* —*v.* **1.** To resemble in appearance: *She seems to favor her father more than her mother.* **2.** To treat with care: *Johnny favored his hurt ankle when he walked.*

fee·ble (fē′bəl) *adj.* **fee·bler, fee·blest.** Without strength; weak.

felt (fĕlt) *n.* A smooth, firm cloth made by pressing wool, fur, or other fibers together.

fer·ry (fĕr′ē) *n., pl.* **fer·ries. 1.** A boat used to carry people, cars, goods, etc.; a ferryboat. **2.** The place where a ferryboat docks.

field (fēld) *n.* **1.** A broad area of land without forests, mountains, or towns. **2.** A meadow: *a field of tall grass.* **3.** A range or category of interest, particular activity, or specialization: *the field of medicine.*

fife (fīf) *n.* A small, high-pitched musical instrument similar to a flute, often used with drums in playing military music.

fleet·ing (flē′tĭng) *adj.* Passing quickly; very brief: *a fleeting glimpse.*

fluke (flo͞ok) *n.* One of the two flattened divisions of the tail of a whale or related animal.

flush (flŭsh) *v.* To turn red in the face.

fold¹ (fōld) *v.* To bend together, double up, or crease so that one part lies over another: *Fold your paper in half.* —*n.* A crease formed by folding.

fold² (fōld) *n.* A pen for sheep or other tame animals.

for·eign (fôr′ĭn) *or* (fŏr′-) *adj.* **1.** Being different from one's own: *a foreign country.* **2.** Of or from another country or other countries: *a foreign person; a foreign custom.*

for·ger·y (fôr′jə rē) *or* (fŏr-) *n.* **1.** The act or crime of imitating a signature, painting, etc., with the intention of passing off the copy as the real thing. **2.** The thing imitated.

frame (frām) *n.* **1.** Something built to shape or support: *a car frame.* **2.** An open rim used to hold or go around something: *a door frame; a picture frame.*

frisk (frĭsk) *v.* To move about briskly and playfully: *Baby squirrels frisked in the trees.*

fu·ri·ous (fyo͝or′ē əs) *adj.* **1.** Full of or marked by great anger. **2.** Fierce; violent: *a furious speed; a furious battle.* —**fu′ri·ous·ly** *adv.* —**fu′ri·ous·ness** *n.*

ă pat / ā pay / â care / ä father / ĕ pet / ē be / ĭ pit / ī pie / î fierce / ŏ pot / ō go / ô paw, for / oi oil / o͝o book /
o͞o boot / ou out / ŭ cut / û fur / *th* the / th thin / hw which / zh vision / ə ago, item, pencil, atom, circus

fur•row (fûr′ō) *or* (fŭr′ō) *n.* **1.** A long, narrow, shallow ditch made in the ground by a plow or other tool. **2.** Any track, groove, or sunken area similar to this: *furrows cut in the dirt road by water.*

fur•ther•more (fûr′thər môr′) *or* (-mōr′) *adv.* Moreover; also.

game (gām) *n.* **1.** Animals, birds, or fish hunted for food or sport: *big game.* **2.** The flesh of such animals, used as food.

gang•plank (găng′plăngk′) *n.* A board or ramp used as a bridge between a ship and a pier.

gauge (gāj) *n.* A device used in making and showing measurements: *The gas gauge shows that the tank is full.*

gen•er•al store (jĕn′ər əl stôr) *n.* A small store that sells many different items—general things such as food, firewood, sewing supplies, toothpaste, etc.

gen•er•os•i•ty (jĕn′ə rŏs′ĭ tē) *n.* Willingness in giving or sharing.

ge•ra•ni•um (jĭ rā′nē əm) *n.* A plant with rounded leaves and red, pink, or white flowers, often grown in a flower pot.

glass•y (glăs′ē) *or* (glä′sē) *adj.* **glass•i•er, glass•i•est. 1.** Like glass: *glassy rocks.* **2.** Without expression; lifeless; blank: *a glassy stare.*

glit•ter (glĭt′ər) *v.* To sparkle brightly: *The stars glittered and winked.*

gloom•i•ly (glōōm′ĭ lē) *adv.* **1.** In a dark, dreary way: *The old house stood gloomily in the uncut grass.* **2.** Hopelessly: *She looked gloomily at her broken doll.*

glow•er (glou′ər) *v.* To look or stare angrily. —*n.* An angry or threatening stare.

glut•ton (glŭt′n) *n.* A person or animal that overeats.

gnaw (nô) *v.* **gnawed, gnawed** *or* **gnawn** (nôn), **gnaw•ing.** To bite or eat away little by little with the teeth.

gos•ling (gŏz′lĭng) *n.* A young goose.

grade (grād) *n.* **1. a.** A slope or incline, as of a road. **b.** The degree to which something, such as a road or railroad track, slopes. **2.** A class or year in a school: *the fourth grade.* **3.** A mark showing the quality of a student's work: *He got a good grade in science.*

graft (grăft) *or* (gräft) *v.* To join (a plant shoot or bud) to another living plant so that the two grow together as a single plant.

grain•ing (grān′ĭng) *n.* **1.** The markings, pattern, or texture in wood, fabric, meat, etc. **2.** The direction of such markings.

gram•o•phone (grăm′ə fōn′) *n.* A record player; phonograph.

grand•stand (grănd′stănd′) *or* (grăn′-) *n.* A stand for spectators, as at a stadium.

green (grēn) *n.* **1.** The color of most plant leaves and growing grass. **2.** A grassy lawn or park in the center of a village or town: *the village green.*

grim (grĭm) *adj.* **grim•mer, grim•mest. 1.** Harsh; stern: *a grim look.* **2.** Worried; gloomy: *a grim mood.* —**grim′ly** *adv.* —**grim′ness** *n.*

grub (grŭb) *n.* The thick, wormlike larva of certain beetles and other insects.

guar•an•tee (găr′ən tē′) *n.* **1.** Anything that makes certain that a particular

533

condition will come about: *Money is not a guarantee of happiness.* **2.** A personal promise: *You have my guarantee that I'll finish the job on time.* **3.** A promise, such as one given by a manufacturer as to the quality of a product. —*v.* **guar•an•teed, guar•an•tee•ing.** To make certain; to assume responsibility for: *guarantee a loan.*

gul•ly (gŭl′ē) *n., pl.* **gul•lies.** A ditch cut in the earth by running water, especially after a rain.

gust (gŭst) *n.* A sudden, strong wind.

hail (hāl) *n.* Water that falls to earth as small pieces of ice or snow, usually during thunderstorms.

hail•stone (hāl′stōn′) *n.* Any of the small pieces of snow or ice that form hail.

haunch (hônch) *or* (hänch) *n.* The hip, buttock, and upper thigh of a person or animal: *The dog settled back on its haunches.*

haz•ard (hăz′ərd) *n.* **1.** A chance of being injured, lost, etc.; danger; risk: *Space travel is full of hazards.* **2.** Something or someone that is likely to cause harm; a possible source of danger: *a fire hazard.*

head (hĕd) *n.* A single animal or person: *seven head of cattle.*

heat (hēt) *n.* A single course in a race or contest, which one runs to qualify for the final race.

hired hand (hīrd′ hănd) *n.* A person paid for doing day-to-day work, usually on a farm, in a shop, or in a household.

hoe (hō) *n.* A tool with a flat blade on a long handle, used for breaking up soil, weeding, growing plants, etc. —*v.* **hoed, hoe•ing.** To dig, weed, etc., with a hoe.

hol•low (hŏl′ō) *adj.* **hol•low•er, hol•low•est.** Having a space or opening inside: *a hollow log; a hollow rubber ball.* —*n.* A small valley.

home•sick (hōm′sĭk′) *adj.* Unhappy because one is away from one's home and family; longing for home. —**home′sick′ness** *n.*

hom•i•ny (hŏm′ə nē) *n.* A food made from grains of corn that have had the outer hulls removed.

ho•ri•zon (hə rī′zən) *n.* **1.** The line along which the earth and sky appear to meet. **2.** The range of one's experience, knowledge, interests, etc.: *people with narrow horizons.*

im•i•ta•tion (ĭm′ĭ tā′shən) *n.* **1.** The act or process of copying: *learning a song through imitation.* **2.** An act of mimicking; copying the actions of someone else: *The comedian does imitations of television actors.*

im•pa•tient (ĭm pā′shənt) *adj.* Not able or willing to put up with trouble, hardship, or delay without complaining or becoming angry.

imp•ish (ĭm′pĭsh) *adj.* Of or like an imp; playful; mischievous: *her impish humor; an impish grin.*

ă pat / ā pay / â care / ä father / ĕ pet / ē be / ĭ pit / ī pie / î fierce / ŏ pot / ō go / ô paw, for / oi oil / ŏŏ book /
ōō boot / ou out / ŭ cut / û fur / *th* the / th thin / hw which / zh vision / ə ago, item, pencil, atom, circus

in•cline (ĭn klīn') v. **in•clined, in•clin•ing.** To lean, slant, or slope: *a road that inclines steeply.* —*n.* (ĭn'klīn'). A surface that inclines; a slope.

in•cred•i•ble (ĭn krĕd'ə bəl) *adj.* **1.** Unbelievable: *an incredible excuse.* **2.** Amazing.

in•di•rect (ĭn'də rĕkt') *or* (-dī-) *adj.* **1.** Not straight to the point, as in talking. **2.** Not directly planned for; secondary: *indirect benefits.* —**in•di•rect'ly** *adv.* —**in•di•rect'ness** *n.*

in•fin•i•ty (ĭn fĭn'ĭ tē) *n., pl.* **in•fin•i•ties.** A space, distance, period of time, or quantity that is or appears to be without limit or end.

in•her•i•tance (ĭn hĕr'ĭ təns) *n.* **1.** Property, money, etc. received from someone, as a parent, after he or she dies. **2.** Something passed down from previous generations; heritage: *Many American place names, foods, and legends are part of our inheritance from Native Americans and the first European settlers in America.*

in•sane (ĭn sān') *adj.* Very foolish; not making sense; wild. —**in•sane'ly** *adv.*

in•ter•rupt (ĭn'tə rŭpt') *v.* **1.** To break in upon: *interrupt a speech.* **2.** To break the continuity of: *His father's illness interrupted his schooling.*

junc•tion (jŭngk'shən) *n.* The place at which railway tracks or roads cross and the settlement built there: *We pulled into the junction and headed straight for the station.*

ju•ni•per (jōo'nə pər) *n.* An evergreen tree or shrub related to the pines, having small or prickly leaves and bluish berries.

keen (kēn) *adj.* Sharp; excellent; bright.

kro•ne (krō'nə) *n., pl.* **kro'ner** (krō'nər). The basic unit of money of Denmark and Norway.

la•goon (lə gōon') *n.* A body of water, separated from the sea by sandbars or coral reefs.

land•ing (lăn'dĭng) *n.* A level area at the top or bottom of a set of stairs.

land•lord (lănd'lôrd') *n.* A person who owns a house or apartment building, from whom others rent living space.

land•lub•ber (lănd'lŭb'ər) *n.* A person unfamiliar with sailing or with life aboard a ship or boat.

lash¹ (lăsh) *v.* **1.** To strike with or as if with a whip: *I lashed my horse's flank with all the strength of my arm.* **2.** To wave, move, or strike with a thrashing, whiplike motion: *The cat crouched low and lashed its tail from side to side.* **3.** To use angry words to attack or criticize: *The senator lashed back at the reporters.*

lash² (lăsh) *v.* To hold tightly in place with rope, cord, straps, etc.: *The boys lashed the weak tree to a strong post to help the tree grow straight.*

las•so (lăs'ō) *or* (lă sōo') *n., pl.* **las•sos** or **las•soes.** A long rope with a loop that can be pulled tight at one end, used especially to catch horses and cattle. —*v.* **las•soed, las•so•ing, las•soes.** To catch with a lasso: *lasso a runaway calf.*

launch (lônch) *or* (länch) *v.* **1.** To move or set in motion with force: *launch a rocket into space.* **2.** To move (a boat or ship) into the water.

lest (lĕst) *conj.* For fear that; so as to prevent the possibility that: *Take care lest the flowers become crushed.*

life•boat (līf′bōt) *n.* **1.** A boat carried on a ship for use if the ship has to be abandoned. **2.** A boat used for rescue service.

lim•ber (lĭm′bər) *adj.* **1.** Bending easily: *limber muscles.* **2.** Moving easily, lightly, and quickly: *a limber athlete.*

link (lĭngk) *v.* To connect or join with or as if with rings or loops forming a chain.

li•no•le•um (lĭ nō′lē əm) *n.* A sturdy, washable material made in sheets, used for covering floors and counters.

lit•ter (lĭt′ər) *n.* Young animals borne at one time by a single mother: *a litter of puppies.*

loaf¹ (lōf) *n.* A shaped mass of bread, meat, cake, etc., baked in one piece.

loaf² (lōf) *v.* To spend time lazily or aimlessly: *We loafed all morning.*

log•book (lôg′bŏŏk) **1.** An official record of speed, progress, and important events, kept on a ship or aircraft. **2.** Any journal or record.

lone (lōn) *adj.* **1.** Single, one: *a lone rider.* **2.** Far away; not often traveled on or to: *the lone prairie.*

lope (lōp) *v.* **loped, lop•ing.** To run or ride in a steady, easy way.

lot (lŏt) *n.* **1.** An object used to determine or choose something by chance: *They drew lots to see who would go first.* **2.** Fortune in life; fate; luck: *the lot of the common people.*

lurch (lûrch) *n.* An unsteady or sudden swaying movement. —*v.* To move unsteadily; stagger.

mag•ni•fy (măg′nə fī) *v.* **mag•ni•fied, mag•ni•fy•ing, mag•ni•fies. 1.** To cause to appear greater or seem more important: *Don't magnify small problems into large ones.* **2.** To make (an object) appear larger than it really is, especially by the use of one or more lenses.

mam•mal (măm′əl) *n.* Any of a group of animals that have hair or fur on their bodies and, in the females, special glands that produce milk for feeding their young. Cats, dogs, cows, elephants, mice, bats, whales, etc. are all mammals.

man•gy (mān′jē) *adj.* **man•gi•er, man•gi•est. 1.** Having many bare spots; shabby: *a mangy old fur coat.* **2.** Having a dirty appearance.

mar•ma•lade (mär′mə lād) *n.* A preserve made from the pulp and tough skin of fruits.

mar•vel (mär′vəl) *n.* Someone or something that causes surprise or wonder: *The space capsules are a modern marvel.* —*v.* **mar•veled** or **mar•velled, mar•vel•ing** or **mar•vel•ling.** To be filled with surprise or wonder: *marvel at seeing the snowy peaks of the Rocky Mountains.*

mean (mēn) *adj.* Lacking kindness and good will; cruel; spiteful: *a mean remark.*

ă pat / ā pay / â care / ä father / ĕ pet / ē be / ĭ pit / ī pie / î fierce / ŏ pot / ō go / ô paw, for / oi oil / ŏŏ book /
ŏŏ boot / ou out / ŭ cut / û fur / *th* the / th thin / hw which / zh vision / ə ago, item, pencil, atom, circus

meek·ly (mēk′lē) *adv.* In a gentle or peaceful manner. —**meek** *adj.*

meet (mēt) *n.* A gathering of two or more teams for athletic contests or games.

meg·a·phone (mĕg′ə fōn′) *n.* A funnel-shaped object that makes louder the voice of someone who speaks or shouts into its smaller end.

me·sa (mā′sə) *n.* A flat-topped hill with steep sides, common in the southwestern United States.

mid·dlings (mĭd′lĭngz) *n.* The coarse part of ground grain.

midge (mĭj) *n.* A very small, gnatlike fly.

mill (mĭl) *n.* **1.** A machine that grinds or crushes something into powder or fine grains: *a coffee mill.* **2.** A building for grinding corn, wheat, etc., into flour or meal. —*v.* To move around in a confused or disorderly manner: *an angry crowd milling about in front of the theater.*

mint (mĭnt) *n.* A large amount, especially of money.

mi·rac·u·lous (mĭ răk′yə ləs) *adj.* Being or seeming impossible to explain by the laws of nature.

mi·rage (mĭ räzh′) *n.* An imagined sight in which water that is not really there and upside-down reflections of distant objects are seen.

mod·est (mŏd′ĭst) *adj.* **1.** Tending to play down one's own talents or abilities. **2.** Quiet in manner; shy.

muf·fle (mŭf′əl) *v.* **muf·fled, muf·fling. 1.** To wrap up in order to keep warm, protect, etc.: *Mother muffled him up in a heavy coat and wool cap.* **2.** To make less loud or less distinct; deaden. —**muffled** *adj.*

muk·luk (mŭk′lŭk′) *n.* **1.** A soft boot made of reindeer skin or sealskin. **2.** A slipper made like this boot.

mush (mŭsh) *n.* Corn meal, or other meal, boiled in water or milk until thick.

nav·i·ga·tion (năv′ĭ gā′shən) *n.* The science of charting, or planning, a course for a ship or aircraft.

neck (nĕk) *n.* Any narrow part connecting a larger, wider part: *a neck of land; the neck of a bottle.*

no·ble (nō′bəl) *adj.* **no·bler, no·blest.** Of, in, or belonging to a class of people called the nobility: *a noble family; a person of noble birth.*

nour·ish·ment (nûr′ĭsh mənt) *or* (nŭr′-) *n.* Anything that a living thing uses to grow; food.

nudge (nŭj) *v.* **nudged, nudg·ing.** To push or poke gently: *He nudged her with his elbow.* —*n.* A gentle push.

ob·jec·tion·a·ble (əb jĕk′shə nə bəl) *adj.* Causing or apt to cause offense; unpleasant: *objectionable odors.*

old country (ōld kŭn′trē) *n.* The country where one used to live.

or·na·ment (ôr′nə mənt) *n.* Something that decorates or makes more attractive or beautiful. —*v.* (ôr′nə mĕnt′). To supply with ornaments: *ornament with gold.*

own (ōn) *v.* **1.** To have or possess: *own a car.* **2.** To acknowledge or admit: *I own that I've made a mistake.*

ox·y·gen (ŏk′sĭ jən) *n.* One of the elements of the earth, a colorless, odorless, tasteless gas: *About one-fifth of air is oxygen.*

pace (pās) *n.* **1.** A step made in walking. **2.** The rate of speed at which a person, animal, or group walks or runs. **3.** A gait of a horse in which both feet on one side leave and return to the ground together. —*v.* **paced, pac•ing.** To walk up and down or back and forth across: *The tiger paced nervously in its cage.*

pan•ic (păn′ĭk) *n.* A sudden, terrible fear. —*v.* To be suddenly and terribly frightened. **pan•icked, pan•ick•ing, pan•ics.**

pant (pănt) *v.* To breathe in short, quick gasps. —*n.* A short, quick gasp.

pa•pier-mâ•ché (pā′pər mə shā′) *n.* A material made from paper pulp mixed with glue or paste that can be molded into various shapes when wet.—**pa•pier mâ•ché** *adj.*

par•cel (pär′səl) *n.* Something wrapped up in a bundle; a package.

par•ings (pâr′ĭngz) *n.* The outer covering or skin that has been removed from something by peeling with a knife or similar tool: *apple parings.*

par•tic•u•lar (pər tĭk′yə lər) *adj.* Giving or demanding close attention to details; fussy: *She's very particular about how her meat is cooked.*

pas•tor (păs′tər) *n.* **1.** A minister who is the leader of a church. **2.** A person who cares for a flock of sheep; a shepherd.

pas•ture (păs′chər) *or* (päs′-) *n.* A piece of land covered with grass and other plants where grazing animals such as cattle, horses, or sheep feed.

peer (pîr) *v.* **1.** To look searchingly, or with difficulty. **2.** To be partially visible; show: *The moon peered from behind a cloud.*

pen•in•su•la (pə nĭn′syə lə) *or* (sə lə) *n.* A portion of land nearly surrounded by water and connected with a larger body of land.

picket line (pĭk′ĭt līn) *n.* A rope tied to a pointed stake that has been driven into the ground and used to keep a horse or other animal from wandering or running away.

pil•lar (pĭl′ər) *n.* A column used to support or decorate a building.

pitch (pĭch) *n.* **1.** A line of talk which tries to talk a customer into buying something without thinking. **2.** A throw or toss.

plas•ter (plăs′tər) *or* (plä′stər) *n.* A mixture of sand, lime, and water that hardens to form a smooth solid surface, used for covering walls and ceilings. —*v.* To cover, coat, or repair something with plaster.

pla•za (plăz′ə) *or* (plä′zə) *n.* A public square or similar open area in a town or city.

plumb (plŭm) *adv.* **1.** Straight up and down: *a post that stands plumb.* **2.** *Informal.* Completely; utterly: *plumb wrong.*

por•rin•ger (pôr′ĭn jər) *or* (pŏr′-) *n.* A shallow cup or bowl with a handle.

por•trait (pôr′trĭt′) *or* (-trāt′) *or* (pōr′-) *n.* A painting, photograph, or other likeness of a person, especially one showing the face.

ă pat / ā pay / â care / ä father / ĕ pet / ē be / ĭ pit / ī pie / î fierce / ŏ pot / ō go / ô paw, for / oi oil / ŏŏ book /
ōō boot / ou out / ŭ cut / û fur / *th* the / th thin / hw which / zh vision / ə ago, item, pencil, atom, circus

pos•ses•sion (pə zĕsh′ən) *n.* Something that is owned; *leaving most of their possessions behind.*

post rid•er (pōst ri′dər) *n.* A person who delivers mail on horseback to stations, called posts, along a fixed route; a mail carrier.

pot•ter•y (pŏt′ə rē) *n., pl.* **pot•ter•ies.** Objects, such as pots, vases, or dishes, shaped from moist clay and hardened by heat.

prance (prăns) *v.* **pranced, pranc•ing.** **1.** To rise on the hind legs and spring forward, as a lively horse does. **2.** To run, leap, or dance about playfully. —**pranc′ing** *adj.*

pray (prā) *v.* Please. Used to introduce a request or invitation: *Pray excuse me. Pray be seated.*

pre•serve (prĭ zûrv′) *v.* **pre•served, pre•serv•ing.** To protect (food) from spoiling and prepare it for future use, as by freezing, canning, etc. —*n.* Often **preserves.** Fruit cooked with sugar to protect against decay.

press (prĕs) *v.* **1.** To urge on or push forward: *pressing the driver to go faster.* **2.** To crowd or push together or in a certain direction: *The police pressed the crowds back. Shouting crowds pressed against the walls.*

pro•hib•it (prō hĭb′ĭt) *v.* To prevent from doing something by law or authority: *Laws prohibit people from riding bicycles on highways.*

prov•en•der (prŏv′ən dər) *n.* Dry food, such as hay, for livestock; feed.

pul•ley (pŏol′ē) *n., pl.* **pul•leys.** A device having a freely turning wheel with a groove around its edge through which a rope, chain, cable, etc., runs.

pum•per•nick•el (pŭm′pər nĭk′əl) *n.* A dark bread made from coarsely ground rye.

pu•ny (pyōo′nē) *adj.* **pu•ni•er, pu•ni•est.** Small or inferior in size, strength, or worth; weak. —**pu′ni•ly** *adv.* —**pu′ni•ness** *n.*

quar•ry[1] (kwôr′ē) *or* (kwŏr-) *n., pl.* **quar•ries.** An open hole in the earth from which stone is obtained by digging, cutting, or blasting. —**quar•ried, quar•ry•ing, quar•ries** *v.*

quar•ry[2] (kwôr′ē) *or* (kwŏr′-) *n., pl.* **quar•ries.** **1.** An animal hunted or chased. **2.** Anything hunted for in a similar manner.

qua•ver (kwā′vər) *v.* To shake, as from fear.

rag•tag (răg′tăg′) *n.* Someone thought to be worthless. —*adj.* Having a careless, haphazard appearance.

range (rānj) *n.* **1.** The distance to an object being viewed or aimed at; the reach. **2.** The area in which a kind of animal or plant normally lives or grows. **3.** The limits within which something (such as a feeling or emotion) may be expressed.

rare (râr) *adj.* **rar•er, rar•est.** **1.** Not happening or found often: *a rare disease.* **2.** Highly valued; special: *a rare gift for carving.*

rat•tan (ră tăn′) *n.* The stems of a climbing tropical palm tree, used for furniture, canes, etc.

raw•hide (rô′hīd′) *n.* **1.** The hide of cattle before it has been tanned. **2.** A whip or rope made of such hide.

re•as•sure (rē′ə shŏŏr′) v. **re•as•sured,
re•as•sur•ing** To cause to feel sure
again. *Just hearing Jan's voice reas-
sured me.* —**re′as•sur′ance** n.

re•bel (rĭ bĕl′) v. **re•belled, re•bel•ling.**
To refuse loyalty to a government or
ruling authority. —n. **reb•el** (rĕb′əl). A
person who refuses loyalty to a government or ruling authority.

reck•on (rĕk′ən) v. **1.** To count or cal-
culate; figure: *reckon time; a child
who learned to reckon before he
could talk.* **2.** *Informal.* To think or assume: *Do you reckon we'll be through
in time?*

rec•re•a•tion (rĕk′rē ā′shən) n., Relax-
ing one's mind or body after work
through some activity, such as sports
and games. —*modifier: a recreation
center.*

red•coat (rĕd′kōt′) n. A British soldier
during the American Revolution and
the War of 1812.

re•gion (rē′jən) n. **1.** An area of the
earth's surface, especially a large
area: *the polar regions.* **2.** Any area:
the uncharted regions of outer space.

re•im•burse (rē′ĭm bûrs′) v. **re•im•
bursed, re•im•burs•ing.** To pay back.
*Paul reimbursed everyone who had
lent him money.*

rein (rān) n. Often **reins.** A long, narrow leather strap attached to the bit
in a horse's mouth and held by the
rider or driver to control the horse.

re•pel (rĭ pĕl′) v. **re•pelled, re•pel•ling.**
To drive off, force back, or keep
away: *repel an enemy attack.*

re•pel•lent (rĭ pĕl′ənt) n. Something
that acts or tends to repel: *Mom
sprayed a cat repellent on the couch.*

re•sult (rĭ zŭlt′) n. What happens because of a particular action, oper-
ation, or course; outcome: *The book
is the result of years of hard work.* —v.
To come about because of something: *Good things resulted from her
efforts.*

re•tire•ment (rĭ tīr′mənt) n. The giving up of one's work, business, or career, usually because of advancing
age: *His retirement from baseball
gave him time to do other things.*

re•venge (rĭ vĕnj′) v. **re•venged, re•
veng•ing.** To punish in return for (an
injury or insult).

rheu•ma•tism (rōō′mə tĭz′əm) n. Any
of several diseased conditions that
affect the muscles, tendons, bones,
joints, or nerves, causing pain and
disability.

rose•wood (rōz′wŏŏd′) n. **1.** The hard,
often sweet-smelling wood of any of
several tropical trees. It has dark or
reddish markings and is used for furniture and other fine woodwork. **2.** A
tree having such wood.

ruf•fle (rŭf′əl) v. **ruf•fled, ruf•fling. 1.**
To disturb the smoothness: *ruffled
the boy's hair affectionately.* **2.** To upset: *ruffled his dignity.*

ru•in (rōō′ĭn) n. Often **ruins.** The remains of a structure or group of
structures that has been destroyed or
has fallen into pieces from age: *Aztec
ruins.* —v. To harm beyond repair.

ă pat / ā **pay** / â **care** / ä **father** / ĕ **pet** / ē **be** / ĭ **pit** / ī **pie** / î **fierce** / ŏ **pot** / ō **go** / ô **paw, for** / oi **oil** / ŏŏ **book** /
ōō **boot** / ou **out** / ŭ **cut** / û **fur** / *th* **the** / th **thin** / hw **which** / zh **vision** / ə **ago, item, pencil, atom, circus**

rum•ple (rŭm′pəl) *v.* **rum•pled, rum•pling. 1.** To wrinkle or crease: *Don't rumple the suit. Pack the clothes so that they won't rumple.* **2.** To muss up: *He rumpled the boy's hair.* —*n.* A wrinkle or untidy crease.

sage[1] (sāj) *n.* A very wise person, usually old and highly respected.

sage[2] (sāj) *n.* **1.** A plant with grayish-green, spicy-smelling leaves used as flavoring in cooking. **2.** Sagebrush.

salt lick (sôlt lĭk) *n.* A natural deposit of salt that animals lick.

sa•vour *or* **sa•vor** (sā′vər) *n.* **1.** The taste or pleasant smell of something. **2.** A pleasing quality, especially one that arouses interest; zest. —*v.* To taste or enjoy very much; relish. (*Savour* is the British spelling.)

scamp (skămp) *n.* **1.** A scheming person; a rascal. **2.** A playful, mischievous person.

scan (skăn) *v.* **scanned, scan•ning. 1.** To examine (something) closely: *scan his pockets for change.* **2.** To look (something) over quickly: *scan the page for answers.*

sched•ule (skĕj′ool) *or* (-oo əl) *or* (skĕj′əl) *n.* Any plan showing something to be done within a certain time. —*v.* To plan for a certain time or date. —**sched′uled** *adj.: a scheduled flight.*

scheme (skēm) *n.* **1.** A plan for doing something. **2.** A secret plan. —*v.* **1.** To make up a plan or scheme for. **2.** To plan in a sneaky or secret way. —**schem′ing** *adj.: a scheming person.*

scrawl (skrôl) *n.* Irregular or hard-to-read handwriting.

scringe (skrĭnj) *v.* To shrink down in fear; crouch; move away from.

scrub (skrŭb) *n.* A growth of small, straggly trees or shrubs. —*adj.* Small and straggly: *a scrub oak.*

shab•by (shăb′ē) *adj.* **1.** Worn-out, frayed, and faded; threadbare: *shabby clothes.* **2.** Old and in need of repair: *shabby houses.*

shoot (shoot) *n.* A plant or plant part, such as a stem, leaf, or bud, that has just begun to grow, sprout, or develop.

shrill (shrĭl) *adj.* **shrill•er, shrill•est.** High-pitched and piercing: *a shrill whistle; a shrill voice.* —*v.* To make a high-pitched sound or cry: *The wind shrilled outside.* —**shril′ly** *adv.* —**shrill′ness** *n.*

shy (shī) *adj.* **1.** Easily startled; timid: *a shy animal.* **2.** Bashful; reserved: *a shy person.* —*v.* **shied, shy•ing, shies.** To draw back, as from fear or caution: *The cat shied at the sound of barking dogs.*

sight (sīt) *n.* A device used to help in aiming a firearm, telescope, etc. —*v.* To take aim or observe with the help of a sight: *She sighted the telescope and looked at the biggest star.*

sil•ver•smith (sĭl′vər smĭth′) *n.* A person who makes and repairs articles of silver.

site (sīt) *n.* **1.** The place where something was, is, or is to be located. **2.** The place or setting of an event.

skim (skĭm) *v.* **skimmed, skim•ming. 1.** To move, pass, or glide lightly and swiftly over (a surface): *The sailboat skimmed the lake.* **2.** To read, glance at, or consider hurriedly: *skim the chapter; skimming through a book.*

slab (slăb) *n.* A broad, flat, thick piece of something, as of cake, stone, or cheese.

sloop (slo͞op) *n.* A single-masted fore-and-aft-rigged sailing vessel.

slop (slŏp) *n.* **1.** Watery mud or a similar substance. **2.** Spilled liquid or food. **3.** Unappetizing, watery food. **4.** Often **slops.** Waste food fed to animals; swill.

smart (smärt) *v.* To cause to feel a stinging pain: *My leg began to smart from the hornet's sting.* —*n.* A stinging pain. —**smart'ly** *adv.* —**smart'ness** *n.*

snout (snout) *n.* The long, pointed or projecting nose, jaws, or front part of the head of an animal: *The snout of a pig; the snout of an alligator; the snout of a boll weevil.*

snug (snŭg) *v.* To put in a condition so as to be safe from a storm.

sor•ry (sŏr'ē) *adj.* Worthless or inferior; poor: *a sorry excuse; a sorry collection of junk.*

spec•ta•cles (spĕk'tə kəlz) *pl. n.* A pair of eyeglasses: *His spectacles sat impishly on his nose.*

spi•der (spī'dər) *n.* A frying pan having a long handle and short legs.

sprain (sprān) *n.* An injury to a joint or muscle, usually caused by stretching or twisting in the wrong way.

sprawl (sprôl) *v.* **1.** To sit or lie with the body and limbs spread out awkwardly. **2.** To spread out or cause to spread out in a straggling or disordered fashion. —*n.* A sprawling posture or condition.

spunk•y (spŭng'kē) *adj.* **spunk•i•er, spunk•i•est.** *Informal.* Having spirit and courage. —**spunk'i•ly** *adv.*

spur (spûr) *n.* A U-shaped device with a point or sharp-toothed wheel behind, worn on the heel of a rider's boot and used to make a horse go faster.

squash (skwŏsh) *or* (skwôsh) *n.* **1.** Any of several types of fleshy fruit related to the pumpkins and the gourds, eaten as a vegetable. **2.** A vine that bears such fruit.

squint (skwĭnt) *v.* To look with the eyes partly open.

stage•craft (stāj'krăft') *n.* The practice of or skill in theatrical techniques: *Good actors know about stagecraft.*

starting block (stär'tĭng blŏk) *n.* A device that gives a runner a firm surface against which to place his or her feet at the start of a race.

stealth•i•ly (stĕl'thə lē) *adv.* In a quiet manner, so as to avoid notice.

stew (sto͞o) *n.* A dish cooked by boiling slowly; especially a mixture of meat or fish and vegetables.

stew•ard (sto͞o'ərd, styo͞o') *n.* **1.** A person who manages another's property, money, etc. **2.** An attendant on a ship or airplane who waits on the passengers.

stir•rup (stûr'əp) *n.* A loop or ring with a flat base, hung by a strap from either side of a horse's saddle to support the rider's foot.

stoke (stōk) *v.* **stoked, stok•ing.** To tend (a fire or furnace).

ă pat / ā pay / â care / ä father / ĕ pet / ē be / ĭ pit / ī pie / î fierce / ŏ pot / ō go / ô paw, for / oi oil / o͝o book / o͞o boot / ou out / ŭ cut / û fur / *th* the / th thin / hw which / zh vision / ə ago, item, pencil, atom, circus

stow•a•way (stō′ə wā′) *n.* A person who hides aboard a ship, plane, train, etc., to travel without paying.

strand (strănd) *n.* **1.** A single fiber, filament, thread, or wire, especially one of those twisted together to form a rope, cord, or cable. **2.** Something made up of fibers or filaments twisted or bunched together, as a piece of yarn or a lock of hair. **3.** A string of beads, pearls, etc.

stride (strīd) *v.* **strode** (strōd), **strid•den** (strĭd′n), **strid•ing.** To walk with long steps and with energy. —*n.* **1.** A long step. **2.** A step forward: *new strides in the field of medicine.*

strut (strŭt) *v.* To walk in a stiff, self-important manner.

stub (stŭb) *n.* **1.** The short blunt end remaining after something has been cut or broken off or worn down: *the stub of a pencil.* **2. a.** The part of a check or receipt retained as a record. **b.** The part of a ticket returned as a voucher of payment. —*v.* **stubbed, stub•bing.** To strike (one's toe or foot) against something.

sub•ject (sŭb′jĭkt) *n.* **1.** A person or th■■■■■t which something is said ■■■■■■bject of discussion; the ■■■■■ painting. **2.** An area of ■■■■favorite subject in school.

■■■■ (sŭl′fər) *n.* Also **sulfur.** A ■■■-yellow powder used in some medicines.

su•perb (soo pûrb′) *or* (sə-) *adj.* Excellent: *a superb meal.*

sus•pi•cious•ly (sə spĭsh′əs lē) *adv.* Distrustfully: *Mary looked suspiciously at the cat when she saw the overturned carton of milk.*

swirl (swûrl) *v.* To rotate or spin as if in a whirlpool: *The wind swirled the snow. The dancers swirled about the room.* —*n.* **1.** The motion of whirling or spinning. **2.** Something that swirls; a whirlpool or eddy.

sym•pa•thize (sĭm′pə thīz′) *v.* To share or understand another's feelings or ideas.

tav•ern (tăv′ərn) *n.* A public place where people who are traveling can stop for food and lodging; a hotel.

tem•per (tĕm′pər) *n.* **1.** A condition of the mind or emotions; mood; disposition. **2.** A tendency to become angry or irritable: *a bad temper.*

ten•ant (tĕn′ənt) *n.* A person who pays rent to use or occupy land, a building, or other property owned by another.

tend (tĕnd) *v.* To look after.

thaw (thô) *v.* **1.** To change from a solid to a liquid by gradual warming; melt. **2.** To become warm enough for snow and ice to melt: *It often thaws in January.* —*n.* **1.** The process of thawing. **2.** A period of warm weather during which snow and ice melt.

throt•tle (thrŏt′l) *n.* In a steam engine or similar engine, a valve that controls the flow of hot fluid to the various parts of the engine.

tier (tîr) *n.* Any of a series of rows placed one above another: *The layered cake had five tiers.*

to•ken (tō′kən) *n.* **1.** Something that serves as a sign: *A white flag is a token of surrender.* **2.** A keepsake; a souvenir: *This ring is a token of our wedding anniversary.*

top•sail (tŏp′sāl′) *or* (-səl) *n.* A square sail set above the lowest sail on the mast of a square-rigged ship.

topsail yard (tŏp′sāl′ yärd) *n.* The pole that is attached crosswise to the mast and that supports the topsail.

tot•ter (tŏt′ər) *v.* **1.** To sway as if about to fall: *A pile of books tottered at the edge of the table.* **2.** To walk unsteadily: *The baby tottered and fell down.*

tour•ni•quet (tŏŏr′nĭ kĭt) *or* (tûr′-) *n.* Any device, such as a tight band with a pad under it, used to stop temporarily the flow of blood in a large artery in a leg or an arm.

trans•port (trăns pôrt′) *v.* To carry from one place to another.

trough (trôf) *or* (trŏf) *n.* A long, narrow container for holding water or feed for animals.

tuf•ty (tŭf′tē) *adj.* Having a cluster of hair, feathers, grass, yarn, etc., growing or held close together at the base.

tum•ble•weed (tŭm′bəl wēd′) *n.* A weedy plant that when withered breaks off from its roots and is tumbled about by the wind.

tun•dra (tŭn′drə) *n.* A cold area of arctic regions, having only low-growing trees and stunted shrubs as plant life.

tusk (tŭsk) *n.* A long, pointed tooth, usually one of a pair, projecting outside of the mouth of certain animals, such as the elephant or walrus.

twi•light (twī′līt′) *n.* The space of time between sunset and nightfall.

ty•phoon (tī fŏŏn′) *n.* A severe tropical hurricane.

un•con•scious (ŭn kŏn′shəs) *adj.* Being unaware of one's surroundings, as in deep sleep or a coma.

un•der•tone (ŭn′dər tōn′) *n.* **1.** A speech tone of low pitch. **2.** A partly hidden feeling: *There were undertones of fear in his voice as he spoke to the crowd.*

valve (vălv) *n.* A device that controls the flow of liquid or gas through a pipe.

vast (văst) *or* (väst) *adj.* **vast•er, vast•est. 1.** Very great in area: *the vast expanse of the Pacific Ocean.* **2.** Very great in size, amount, etc.: *There is a vast difference between a village house and a castle.*

wash (wŏsh) *or* (wôsh) *n.* The dry bed of a stream.

whick•er (hwĭk′ər) *v.* To whinny or neigh, as a horse. —*n.* A whinnying or neighing sound, as made by a horse.

wit (wĭt) *n.* Often **wits.** Understanding; intelligence: *using one's wits.*

year•ling (yîr′lĭng) *n.* A one year old or between years old. —*modifier: a ye*

yuc•ca (yŭk′ə) *n.* Any of seve of dry regions of southern and ern North America, having stiff, pointed leaves and a large cluster of whitish flowers.

ă pat / ā pay / â care / ä father / ĕ pet / ē be / ĭ pit / ī pie / î fierce / ŏ pot / ō go / ô paw, for / oi oil / ŏŏ book / ōō boot / ou out / ŭ cut / û fur / *th* the / th thin / hw which / zh vision / ə ago, item, pencil, atom, circus

...ing abou
or done: *a s*
subject of *a*
study: *her*

sul•phur
pal